DISCARD

Y0-CAA-220

MONSON
Free Library and Reading Room
ASSOCIATION

NO.

53036

RULES AND REGULATIONS

Assessed fines shall be paid by every person keeping Library materials beyond the specified time.

Every person who borrows Library materials shall be responsible for all loss or damage to same while they are out in his name.

All library materials shall be returned to the Library on the call of the Librarian or Directors.

General Laws of Mass., Chap. 266, Sec. 99

Whoever willfully and maliciously or wantonly and without cause writes upon, injures, defaces, tears or destroys a book, plate, picture, engraving or statute belonging to a law, town, city or other public library shall be punished by a fine of not less than five nor more than fifty dollars, or by imprisonment in the jail not exceeding six months.

A Bird Watcher's Adventures
in Tropical America

NUMBER THREE

The Corrie Herring Hooks Series

A Bird Watcher's Adventures in Tropical America

By Alexander F. Skutch

Illustrations by Dana Gardner

University of Texas Press Austin & London

53056

Grateful acknowledgment is made for permission to reprint the
following material:

Chapter 5, "The Cotingas: A Study in Contrasts." Reprinted with
permission from ANIMAL KINGDOM. Copyright © 1968 by the
New York Zoological Society.

Chapter 8, "The Woodcreepers of Tropical America." Reprinted
with permission from ANIMAL KINGDOM. Copyright © 1962 by
the New York Zoological Society.

Chapter 10, "The Most Hospitable Tree," Skutch, A. F., *Scientific
Monthly*, Vol. 60, pp. 5–17, January 1945. Reprinted by permission
of *Science*.

Library of Congress Cataloging in Publication Data

Skutch, Alexander Frank, 1904–
    A bird watcher's adventures in tropical America.

    (The Corrie Herring Hooks series; no. 3)
    Bibliography: p.
    Includes index.
    √ 1. Birds—Latin America. 2. Birdwatching—Latin
America. I. Title.
QL680.S58 598.2/98   77-3478
ISBN 0-292-70722-3

Copyright © 1977 by the University of Texas Press

All rights reserved

Printed in the United States of America

TO PAUL SCHWARTZ,

devoted student of tropical American birds

Contents

MAPS

Preface

Earth's richest, most varied bird life is found in the Neotropical region, which includes South America, Central America, southern Mexico, and the West Indies. Here well over one-third of the planet's estimated 8,600 species of birds are concentrated in about one-seventh of its land area. Rodolphe Meyer de Schauensee's *A Guide to the Birds of South America* (1970) includes no fewer than 2,926 species belonging to 865 genera in 93 families. About one-third of these families are peculiar to the Neotropical region.

This richest of the earth's avifaunas is also the least known. I refer not to the description and classification of its multitudinous species, which are far advanced, but to knowledge of how they live and build their nests and raise their young, of their relations with one another. African birds that build their nests in savannas and other open country, where they are relatively easy to find and can often be approached by car, have been more widely studied than Neotropical birds, many of which inhabit dense rain forests and rugged mountains, where travel is laborious and nests hidden amid heavy vegetation are exceedingly difficult to detect. Even the seabirds that breed on remote islands, often in frigid Antarctic seas, have recently been receiving more detailed attention than the birds of tropical American woodlands. Thanks to the devoted efforts of a few indefatigable field workers, we now know much more than we did when I began to study them nearly half a century ago, but the gaps in our knowledge are still immense. The nests of hundreds of these birds are still unknown.

Today, ease of travel by air and road and an increasing number of comfortable hotels outside the big cities encourage many bird watchers to visit tropical America, alone, with a few friends, or on guided nature tours. Nearly all of these people come to see and list the birds rather than to study them in detail. More or less adequate field guides covering all parts of the region make identification relatively easy; on the tours, an experienced leader names the birds as they are seen. In two weeks tourists may list two or three hundred species, including many to add to each birder's "life list."

Three or four decades ago, when I made some of the journeys of which I tell in this book, the only field guides to any parts of the Neotropical region were Bertha Bement Sturgis's *Field Book of Birds of the Panama Canal Zone*, which was published in 1928 and has long been out of print, and James Bond's *Birds of the West Indies*, which appeared a few years later and has been followed by successive editions. Guided birding tours were still in the future; travel was more difficult to arrange and tolerable accommodations in the wilder areas harder to find; but, in compensation for these inconveniences, a great deal more wild, unspoiled country remained. Many of the more serious birders who visited the tropics collected their birds for identification, often depositing their specimens in some museum.

Since I did not wish to shoot birds, their identification became more difficult the farther I went from the Canal Zone and Sturgis's guide. My method was to write in my notebook the most detailed description that I could make of any bird new to me, at the same time recording all I learned about its habits and voice. Instead of the scores of species that one on a guided tour, or on his own with a good field guide, can list in a day, I considered myself fortunate if I could somewhat adequately describe five or six, after watching each unfamiliar kind as long as I could keep it in view. Then, months or perhaps years later, when I could refer to the detailed descriptions (without pictures) in the eight bulky volumes of Robert Ridgway's *The Birds of North and Middle America* (1901–1919) or, for South America, the *Catalogue of the Birds in the British Museum* (1874–1895), the colored plates in Emilio Goeldi's *Album de Aves Amazonicas* (1900–1906), or the specimens in some distant museum, I would try to identify the birds I had described. Usually I succeeded, although sometimes a species in a large and difficult genus defeated me. By this method I proceeded slowly, but the reward for my patience was intimate familiarity with the birds that I identified, especially those that I was able to study for many hours at their nests.

In this book I tell of some of my more memorable experiences on journeys that I made to study tropical American birds or, as on my travels in Peru and Ecuador as botanist of an expedition sent by the United States Department of Agriculture, when birds claimed most of the attention that I could spare from my duties. One chapter deals with my efforts to watch birds during one of the harassing "revolutions" or political upheavals from which even the more stable of the Latin American republics have not been free. Included also are chapters on more general topics, such as the relations of birds to the swarming ants of warm countries, and the so various dawn songs of tropical birds. Chronologically, the chapters in this book fall within the periods covered by two other books, *A Naturalist in Costa Rica* (1971) and *The Imperative Call* (forthcoming), but they treat of different countries or subjects and tell of different birds.

Acknowledgments

Professor Oakes Ames, when supervisor of the Arnold Arboretum of Harvard University, arranged for my collecting tour in western Guatemala in 1934 and 1935, en route to which I made the railroad journey through southern Mexico described in Chapter 1. While studying birds on the Sierra de Tecpán, as told in Chapter 2, I enjoyed the fine hospitality of Axel Pira, Sr., and Leonor de Pira. The Venezuelan farm of Chapter 11 was the property of Walter and Elena Arp, who generously permitted us to occupy their house and helped in many ways. Paul Schwartz arranged for us to stay there. Chapter 5, on the cotingas, and the greater part of Chapter 8, on the woodcreepers, first appeared in *Animal Kingdom*, and I am indebted to the New York Zoological Society for permission to include them in this book. Chapter 10, on the Cecropia tree, first appeared, in slightly different form, in the long-extinct *Scientific Monthly* and is reproduced here with the permission of the American Association for the Advancement of Science. George Miksch Sutton painstakingly read the manuscript and suggested improvements. To the careful editing of Carolyn Cates Wylie of the University of Texas Press this book owes much. To all these institutions and individuals (some of whom are no longer with us) I am most grateful.

A.F.S.

A Bird Watcher's Adventures
in Tropical America

CHAPTER I

Through Mexico by Train

White-Throated Magpie-Jay

I know of no better way to see a country, its people and vegetation, even its birds, than through the open window of a railroad train that runs at moderate speed, making leisurely stops at all the towns and villages. When highway systems were less extensive than today and few cars and buses bumped over the usually unpaved roads, such trains were the chief means of long-distance travel in much of tropical America. From the airplanes that now whisk us from point to point we survey, if clouds permit, wider expanses of territory but enjoy no intimate glimpses of a country and its life. Even if we do not sit behind the steering wheel of a motorcar, traffic along a dangerously busy highway often distracts our attention from the landscape.

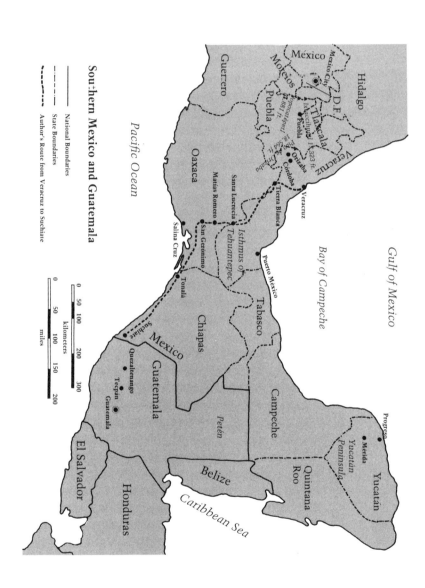

Southern Mexico and Guatemala

National Boundaries
State Boundaries
Author's Route from Veracruz to Suchiate

From Veracruz to Mexico City

No other part of continental tropical America is so easily accessible from the United States and Canada as that which lies in Mexico. With about one thousand species of resident and migratory birds in habitats ranging from rain forests to arid deserts, from coastal mangrove swamps to peaks capped with perpetual snow, from palm-studded savannas to highland woods of oak and pine, it offers a rich experience to visiting naturalists. Probably most North Americans who watch tropical birds begin in Mexico.

My acquaintance with tropical American birds started farther south, when botanical research took me to Panama in 1928. During the next few years I studied them in Honduras and Guatemala, countries that share many species with their neighbor to the north. But I never saw Mexico until 1934, when I went to western Guatemala to collect plants for the Arnold Arboretum of Harvard University. By landing at Veracruz and taking trains, I could travel through a large part of tropical Mexico en route to my work. This opportunity to visit a fascinating land was too good to miss.

On June 27, my bulky collecting equipment and I sailed from New York on the *Orizaba*, a large steamship crowded with tourists in a holiday mood. At noon on the fifth day of our voyage, as we were approaching Progreso at the tip of the Yucatán Peninsula but still far out in the Gulf of Mexico, a Common Gallinule,[1] flying low, overtook the ship from astern, rounded the bow, and vanished in the direction of the distant land, leaving me to wonder what took it so far out to sea.

On the following afternoon we docked at Veracruz. Although I had not planned to visit the Mexican plateau, when I learned how far my dollars would stretch when I converted some of them into pesos, I decided to take the train up to Mexico City the next morning. I would be sorry to have missed that spectacular and revealing journey.

Leaving the port, we rode over a gently rolling terrain where low, acacialike trees and scattered cacti indicated a dry climate. Isolated farmhouses, usually with thatched roofs, stood amid

1. When the common name of an organism is capitalized, its scientific name will be found in the Index.

fields of maize and wide pastures. Beyond all this, far ahead, like a whiter and more substantial cloud, rose my first peak crowned with eternal snow beneath a tropical sky, the extinct volcano Citlaltépetl, the Mountain of the Star, commonly known as the Pico de Orizaba. Peer of Cotopaxi and Sangay in the distant Andes, this highest of Mexico's mountains loomed pure and serene above the torrid plain of Veracruz. I was already glad that I had changed my plans and included this side excursion.

At the foot of the mountains an electric locomotive replaced the oil-burner that had already hauled us almost imperceptibly to an altitude of 1,500 feet. Now we wound upward through picturesque valleys to a wide, fertile, mountain-rimmed plain where, amid coffee groves and fields of sugar cane, stood the city of Córdoba. As soon as the train stopped, it was surrounded by Indians selling flowers. These were of considerable variety, but none was so abundant, or so commanded attention by its exquisite fragrance, as the gardenias, offered to us in simple bouquets, or arranged with other blossoms in more or less elaborate floral designs, or—what most excited my admiration—hidden in boxes of living vegetable tissue. These were made from the trunks of banana plants, which are not true stems but composed of the bases of the gigantic leaves, each of which is crescent-shaped in cross section and tightly embraces those within it. By removing the inner leaf bases but replacing the ends, one made a cylindrical box, which could be closed by a tightly fitting lid, cut from the outermost leaf base. When one of these boxes filled with gardenia flowers was opened, a delicious odor emanated from a container that was impervious to moisture and kept the blossoms fresh. It was hard to resist these little chests, which cost a peso—or less if one bargained.

Along with flowers, cut or with roots for planting, a variety of fruits was offered at the Córdoba station, but not so many as at Maltrata, situated in a pretty, sheltered valley at the foot of the railroad incline of the same name. Cherries, strawberries, figs, plums, avocados, and others less familiar were sold beside the waiting train. Surely, I thought, a place that yields such abundance should be named "Bientrata" instead of Maltrata—a corruption of Maltlatl, an Indian word that signifies "Burning Town."

At the industrial city of Orizaba, a second electric locomotive had been attached to our train to help draw it up to the edge of the Mexican plateau by way of the Maltrata incline, which, passing through long tunnels and crossing deep ravines on slender trestles, rises from 4,000 to 8,050 feet in only thirty miles of magnificent scenery. After this transition from sheltered, fruitful subtropical valleys to the vast emptiness of the cool Mexican plateau, passengers were given an opportunity to eat at the station restaurant at Esperanza, while the electric locomotives were exchanged for one driven by steam. Since I had already sampled many of the good things offered by the vendors at the stations, and, moreover, station restaurants often served far too much food to be comfortably eaten in the time allowed—as though the management conspired to give the passengers indigestion!—I decided to forego this meal and bought a large roll from a woman on the platform. I was more amused than angry when, on biting into it, I found a hollow large enough to contain a roll of ordinary size.

Leaving Esperanza, we sped across a vast, nearly level, almost treeless plain, rimmed in the distance by moderately high, sparsely wooded ridges. Passengers who had dressed lightly in warm Veracruz now reached for heavier garments in the thin, cool mountain air. At first, maize was the chief crop on the intensively cultivated plain, but as we continued westward more maguey was grown in vast plantations. These thick-leafed plants, source of fibers and the heady pulque, were set in straight rows that continued unbroken for miles, never deviating from their course even when they passed over a ridge or hill. Arranged in quincunxes, the maguey plants formed straight diagonal as well as longitudinal rows, producing a striking effect as the lines suddenly changed direction in the eyes of the speeding traveler. Elsewhere on the plateau were vast, level pastures, sometimes stretching for miles back to the enclosing mountain ridges, with never a fence and hardly a tree. The low houses on these empty plains were gathered into little villages or towns, or clustered around some large ranch house, often at a considerable distance from the railroad, so that the stations stood lonely and isolated amid the fields. From some of them tramlines, with mule-drawn cars, led to the ranch or village. In the evening we reached Mexico

City, after a twelve-hour ride that covered 264 miles and took us from the tropics to the temperate zone.

Early next morning I visited Xochimilco, the "Field of Flowers," less than an hour by electric car from the center of Mexico City. When I stepped down from the car, an Indian with a straggly beard, immediately recognizing me as a sight-seer, led me through several streets to a canal where an imposing array of flat-bottomed boats, with no difference between bow and stern, were moored. The central part of each was covered by a rounded canopy with an arch in front, where a feminine name was spelled out with flowers against a floral background. After we had haggled over the fee, which seemed to be the customary procedure in all transactions between private individuals in Mexico, a chair for me was set on the flat bottom of the *Cecilia*. A lad named Tomás stepped into the stern with a long paddle, with which he poled me on a leisurely voyage through the still waters of this floral and horticultural Venice.

Xochimilco was unlike anything I had ever seen. Originally, it was one of the shallow lakes that once covered large areas of the now much drier Valley of Mexico. On this lake, I was told, Indians built rafts and covered them with soil in which they planted crops. As the rafts became waterlogged and sank lower, more soil was added to raise the surface, until they rested on the bottom, a process possibly accelerated by a fall in the water level of the lake. I found Xochimilco a crowded archipelago of islands, separated by narrow canals that formed a complex network.

These islands were intensively cultivated with maize and a wide variety of temperate-zone garden vegetables, including beans, spinach, celery, and cabbage. Among the vegetables blossomed sweet peas, daisies of various kinds, asters, carnations, larkspurs, violets, nasturtiums, gladioli, pansies, and the shrubby Floripondio with great, dangling, bell-like corollas. These flowers did not make the exuberant display that written descriptions had led me to expect; for that I must come in March or April, I was told. Nevertheless, the many blossoms nodding over the waterways made delightful scenes. Most abundant were the carnations, which in great, fragrant white, pink, or red bunches filled dugout canoes. What a cargo to paddle along the quiet waterways of this rural Elysium! For a pittance I might have bought a bouquet of carnations almost too bulky to carry; but what was a wanderer, who knew no single soul in all Mexico, to do with such a floral gift?

This land of canals was naturally perfectly flat and would have lacked character but for the presence of a single kind of tree, a variety of willow, called *huijote* (we-hu-tay) by the Indians, that grew on the islands and along the waterways in great numbers. It had the Lombardy poplar's habit of growth to an exaggerated degree. The small branches ascended close to the main trunk instead of spreading outward, giving the whole tree the form of a tall, slender, perfectly erect pillar of green. It is doubtless because this compact, parsimonious habit of the willow tree made it cast little shade that the Indians permitted it to grow so abundantly amid their gardens. These thin green columns, bordering all the waterways, gave a unique character to the landscape, converting an otherwise flat and featureless expanse of land and water into a parkland of peculiarly light and graceful aspect. Contrasting with these erect willows, their very antithesis in arboreal form, grew a much smaller number of weeping willows with long, pendent branchlets. An acacialike tree with small heads of yellow florets was the only other tree that I noticed.

As my small boatman conveyed me along the flowery waterways, Song Sparrows sang sweetly on every side, flew across the narrow canals, or descended to the muddy banks to search for food. Never elsewhere have I found Song Sparrows so abundant as here at the southern limit of their vast range. I was sorry, but not surprised to detect Tomás shooting pebbles at them from his catapult, while I was looking elsewhere. I tried, doubtless with no lasting effect, to make him understand how wrong this was. Oh, those miserable catapults, cheap and easily made—being no more than a band of rubber attached to a forked stick—which, in the hands of small boys and even men, play such havoc with the birds of Latin America! They, along with vendors of caged birds, cats, and other enemies are responsible for the fact that, in the more populated districts, migrant birds from the north often seem more abundant than the resident species during the winter months. The migrant passerines, protected in the United States and Canada where they nest, confront these hazards during only part of the year. The resident birds, protected by no laws or laxly enforced ones, are exposed to catapults, bird-catchers, and other outrages throughout the year.

Loggerhead Shrikes were also exceedingly numerous at Xochimilco and called loudly on every side. With their contrasting areas of white, gray, and black, they made a pretty display as they hovered low over the gardens snatching up insects. Yellow Warblers sang their familiar song from the willows along the canals. In early July, all were doubtless residents rather than migrants; and later in the day, at Chapultepec, I watched one feed a fledgling. We floated beneath a Common Yellowthroat singing in a tree above the water. Just as our gondola docked at the end of our inland voyage, I noticed a flock of black-faced Bushtits foraging amid the foliage above the landing place. They carried my thoughts southward to the highlands of Guatemala, where I knew them well. The other four species that I noticed at Xochimilco range into temperate North America, but south of Mexico only the two warblers are found, these only as migrants.

In the afternoon I visited Chapultepec and the palace that recalled the tragic history of the Emperor Maximilian and Empress Carlota. In the park grew huge cypresses of two kinds, *Cupressus lusitanica* and *Taxodium mucronatum*. The latter had trunks four or five yards in diameter, but they failed to equal in girth the famous big cypress of Tule. Chipping Sparrows were abundant; Dark-backed Goldfinches sang; and American Robins hopped over the lawn. In the garden in front of the palace, a White-eared Hummingbird hovered before bright blossoms.

After the single day in the city that my excursion ticket permitted, I returned to Veracruz by the morning train. At the stations on the plateau, red-faced House Finches delivered their full, rich songs from the telegraph wires and trees within hearing of the train. As we sped across the level plain, the snowy summits of the great volcanoes Popocatépetl and Ixtaccíhuatl stood out plainly in the clear morning air; but Orizaba was veiled by clouds when we came within view of it.

Across the Isthmus of Tehuantepec

After a night in Veracruz, I bought a ticket for Santa Lucrecia and, toward the middle of the morning, set forth on the first stage of the 571-mile railroad journey to the Guatemalan border. I planned to travel only by day, in order not to miss seeing any of the country. Leaving the city, the train passed through grassy fields, with the blue water of the Gulf of Mexico sparkling in the morning sunshine on our left, and the mountain rampart, dominated by the majestic Pico de Orizaba, rising into the sky far in the west. For many miles we rode through flat or gently rolling country, where scattered palms with feathery or fan-shaped fronds stood amid fields of maize and pastures grazed by sleek horses, donkeys, and horned cattle. The palms supplied the materials for most of the dwellings, which were neatly walled with slabs cut from the hard outer layer of the trunks and thatched with palm leaves. Even the large village of Tierra Blança consisted chiefly of palm-built cabins, pleasantly situated amid gardens and fruit trees.

Southward from Tierra Blanca the greater lushness of the vegetation revealed that we were entering a region of higher rainfall. After crossing the broad, muddy Río Papaloapam, we passed the first large banana plantation, another indication of a wetter area. When we stopped at Monte Carlo, school was in session in an open shed near the railroad tracks, and all the pupils were reciting together in loud voices, raising an extraordinary din, whether to impress the passengers or as part of the school's daily routine, I did not learn. The train fell so far behind its schedule that it was dark long before we reached Santa Lucrecia.

In the morning, I found myself in a large village, again consisting mainly of palm-built cabins, but less neatly constructed and less attractively situated than in the villages of the central part of the state of Veracruz. The surrounding vegetation was almost wholly the exuberant, vine-tangled second growth that one expects in wet tropical lowlands where the rain forest has been destroyed. Nearly all the birds I saw were old friends that I knew well in the Caribbean lowlands of Central America—Rufous-breasted Castlebuilders, Vermilion-crowned Flycatchers, Gray's Thrushes, Rufous-browed Peppershrikes, Melodious Blackbirds, Yellow-tailed Orioles, Spotted-breasted Wrens, Crimson-collared Tanagers, Banded-backed Wrens, and three kinds of saltators: Buff-throated, Black-headed, and Grayish. It was surprising to find several Red Cardinals, resident and singing, among these Central American birds—the only northern note in a tropical setting.

A few hours afield at Santa Lucrecia convinced me that I was not likely to find many birds that I did not already know well. Moreover, I did not relish the prospect of another night in a dirty hotel. I decided to continue onward by the train that traversed the Isthmus of Tehuantepec. Leaving the village late in the morning, we crossed a fairly large, muddy river, then continued for miles through low hills mostly covered by the same riotous second growth, with scattered milpas and habitations.

When the train stopped at the small village of Mogoñe, it was, as usual, approached by vendors of fruits and other comestibles, but these women were of a race I had not met before—Zapotec Indians, of whom I would see many more as I crossed the isthmus and turned eastward toward Chiapas. They were mostly tall, well-built, comely people, but some were unfortunately afflicted by a disease known as *pinta*, which caused large purple blotches to mar otherwise attractive faces. Although they preserved their distinctive dress and ancestral tongue, all that I accosted could answer me in Spanish.

Winding by steep grades up the narrow valley of a small, rushing river, then through low, arid hills, the train reached Matías Romero, headquarters of the railroad that crossed the isthmus. For its altitude of only 650 feet, the town enjoyed a surprisingly pleasant climate, thanks largely to the northeast trade winds that blew persistently across the isthmus, carrying away air heated by an ardent sun. When the wind blew briskly, the weather was delightful. As long as the smoke issuing from the chimney of the railroad shops trailed southward, the temperature was moderate; when the wind died away and the smoke rose almost straight upward, the day became oppressive. Not only the weather but also the buildings were hardly typical of southern Mexico at a low altitude. Many were made of kiln-hardened red bricks, the kind common enough in northern lands but rare in this part of the world, the product of a neighboring factory operated by a North American. Posted conspicuously about the railroad station were signs that read *Por educación y cultura, no pinta los paredes*. This appeal to education and culture evidently had the desired effect, for the walls were pleasantly free of the illiterate scribblings and crude drawings that disfigure many public places in Mexico and elsewhere.

I passed four days wandering through the low, rounded hills about Matías Romero. Those near the town were covered with gravelly soil that supported scattered small trees and scrubby growth not difficult to penetrate. To the west, beyond the Río Malatenco, were steeper hills and deeper valleys that reminded me of the serpentine barrens of Maryland, where I had often botanized during my student days, although the topography was on a larger scale. Here the disintegrating rock left the surface covered by loose fragments, with scarcely any soil. Stunted oaks, rarely more than thirty feet high, grew scattered amid low herbs that failed to cover considerable areas of crumbling, brownish stones. On certain ridges pine, rather than oak, was the dominant tree. The broader valleys supported a richer vegetation, which along the streams attained a luxuriance hardly inferior to that of humid lowlands. Farther west stood fairly high, wooded mountains, outliers of the highlands of Oaxaca, while to the east, at a greater distance, rose the foothills of mountainous Chiapas.

Here, two-thirds of the way across the Isthmus of Tehuantepec from the Gulf of Mexico, the bird life was predominantly that of the arid tropics, with an admixture of species from the wetter Caribbean regions that sought the moister habitats. A clear, familiar *bobwhite* issued from thickets where Common Bobwhites lurked in coveys difficult to see; but one obligingly perched for many minutes on a low branch while I wrote a description of him, noting that his chest was extensively black below his white throat. Inca Doves were very abundant, White-fronted Doves almost as numerous. In the lusher vegetation along a river, I found Violaceous and Citreoline trogons, the latter feeding a fledgling. Russet-crowned Motmots perched quietly in the thickets, swinging their racket-shaped tails slowly from side to side. Groove-billed Anis were numerous, Squirrel Cuckoos rather rare. The loud, foghorn call of the Lesser Roadrunner resounded over the arid hills; but I saw only one of these birds, and only two of the Lesser Ground-Cuckoos that skulked in dense thickets. The parrot family was represented by noisy flocks of Green Parakeets and less abundant White-fronted Parrots. The common woodpecker was a race of the Golden-fronted. Of the much larger Lineated Woodpecker, I saw only one.

Here, for the first time, I met the Banded Wren, which was abundant in the scrubby thickets on the hillsides as well as in the ravines. A delightful songster, it delivered a variety of phrases in a full, clear, mellow voice, and it often included a beautiful trill in its repertoire. Equally lovely were the songs that a Gray-crowned Yellowthroat, one of the finest vocalists among the wood warblers, repeated at sunset on a nearly barren hillside. Tropical Mockingbirds and Melodious Blackbirds were both abundant and songful.

One of the most curious of the new acquaintances that I made here was the Yellow-winged Cacique, a foot-long, black icterid with yellow wing patches, rump, under tail coverts, and outer feathers of its long tail. Its light-colored, slender bill was very sharp. The male had long, thin, erectile crown feathers, conspicuous when lifted by the wind. These birds appeared to be confined to the taller trees along the streams, where they traveled in straggling flocks, uttering a loud, harsh, jaylike *roar roar*. They had also a short, mellow whistled note. A male, perching in a treetop, bowed forward with half-spread wings while he emitted a screech not unlike one of the Great-tailed Grackle's utterances. A cacique was weaving a long, swinging pouch, like that of the Black-throated or Altamira Oriole, at the tip of a slender twig of a fig tree, fifty feet above a river bank.

Here the Brown Jay of the rainy Caribbean side of Middle America mingled with the White-throated Magpie-Jay of the drier Pacific side. The latter, a large, long-tailed, elegant bird, blue above and white below, with a waving crest of forwardly curved black feathers and a narrow black band across its chest, was the more abundant. Some were feeding fledglings, but belated pairs were still nesting. I regretted that I could not learn the contents of a nest of coarse sticks fifty feet up in a streamside tree, where a jay sat as though incubating. Brown Jays preferred the heavier growth on the lower lands. In a single flock I noticed a bird with a white belly and white tips on the outer tail feathers, another that had a brownish abdomen and no white tips, and still another with the abdomen tinged with brown but conspicuously whiter than its chest. Here the northern and southern forms of this noisy, aggressive jay met and interbred.

In an open grove of stunted oak trees I found a single pair of beautiful Green Jays, who scolded me so loudly and persistently (giving me a splendid opportunity to admire their green, yellow, violet, and black plumage) that I was sure they had a nest. Looking upward, I found it almost directly above me. Fifteen feet above the ground, the shallow, open cup of fine sticks was far out on a limb of an oak tree too slender to sustain me; but I climbed above it and, looking down, saw a Bronzed Cowbird, well feathered and almost ready to fly, sitting, awake and alert, between two young jays, bigger than it was but naked and slumbering. Cowbirds seem rarely to parasitize jays' nests, and this may well have been the first record of a jay raising a cowbird almost to the point of fledging.

After four memorable days at Matías Romero, I took the afternoon train for San Gerónimo, thirty-two miles nearer the Pacific. Beyond the sterile hills that surrounded Matías Romero, the railroad entered a range of moderately high, wooded mountains, reaching eventually an elevation of about 800 feet before beginning its descent to the Pacific. Beyond the broad plain where the Indian village of Chivela was situated, we entered another region of low, abrupt mountains and deep valleys, through which we twisted for miles, seeing few houses or signs of cultivation amid the low but fairly dense woods that covered the slopes. Many outcrops of whitish rocks, which in places formed long lines of cliffs, contrasted with the green of the woods.

Emerging from the hills near La Mata, we entered a wide, mountain-rimmed plain, covered chiefly with cacti and low, acacialike scrub—an arid land that offered scant sustenance to the cattle pastured upon it. In the midst of this plain lay San Gerónimo Ixtepec, a long, narrow village strung out for about a mile between the railroad station and the plaza, around which stood the church and municipal buildings. Its population consisted largely of Zapotec Indians, whose maize fields covered the more fertile lands along the river. Now in July this was a shrunken stream that one could wade without wetting one's legs much above the ankles, flowing along one side of a wide, shingly bed that could accommodate a current a hundred times greater. Most of the farmers lived in the village and went out soon after daybreak to cultivate their farms, carrying their equipment in oxcarts. Their plows or cultivators, primitive wooden affairs, were drawn by yokes of oxen whose mouths were tied shut to prevent their eating the young corn plants. The fields were fenced with thorny brush harder to penetrate than a five-strand barbed-wire fence. Beyond the cultivated fields stretched thorny scrub, amid which grew a few large opuntias and other cacti.

The two days that I remained at San Gerónimo were so intensely hot, with little relief even at night, that my plans for climbing some of the nearer hills melted away. In such a climate, even one's most cherished pursuits demand a burdensome effort. I restricted my walks to the plain, where I found the birds much the same as at Matías Romero; although those that prefer a more humid habitat, such as the Black-headed Saltator, Melodious Blackbird, and Brown Jay, were understandably absent. It was surprising to find the Common Bobwhites here very different from those at Matías Romero, only thirty miles away. The males had the head, neck, and most of the chest wholly black, without the white head stripe and throat so conspicuous on individuals I had seen at Matías Romero. The females of the two forms were quite similar, and both forms had the same crisp call, from which I inferred that they were races of a single species.

The Golden-fronted Woodpeckers had also changed in this short distance. Males at San Gerónimo had upper parts more broadly barred with black and white, and a band of gray between the red crown and yellow hindhead. Over much of northern tropical America, from Mexico to Venezuela and Tobago, *Centurus* woodpeckers of similar aspect, although belonging to different species, are among the most successful and abundant of birds, especially in the more open woodlands and areas with scattered trees.

Altamira Orioles with orange-yellow bodies and black throats were very common. Without searching for them, I noticed dozens of their long, woven pouches, old and new, hanging from the ends of slender branches, one so low that I could reach it without climbing. Peering in through the opening at the top of the long sleeve, I discerned one newly hatched nestling and one pipped egg. Equally abundant were the big Rufous-naped Wrens, which I had not found at Matías Romero. They seemed to replace the melodious Banded Wrens, so numerous there but neither heard nor seen here. Their nests were almost as easy to find as those of the Altamira Orioles. Two were only five feet up in bull's-horn acacias, one at the same height in a spiny shrub, and the fourth twenty-five feet up in a thorny tree. Three of these nests were still unfinished, and both birds were building. The completed nest was a roofed structure with a side entrance, made of straws and weed stems and lined with soft white down. It held three recently hatched nestlings and one egg, curiously mottled with tan and brown.

Just after I had waded the river, I heard cawing and, looking downstream, watched two Common Ravens circle around and descend to the margin, where they drank, then strutted about, apparently finding something to eat among the shingle. A number of Great-tailed Grackles bathed in the shallow water nearby, appearing to be on good terms with the ravens. As the latter flew, a pair of Tropical Kingbirds darted angrily at them, trying to drive them away. When one of the ravens alighted on top of a small, vine-draped tree, a Groove-billed Ani, which evidently had a nest there, attacked it so vigorously that it soon retreated. Ravens appear to have few friends, even among birds of their own color. In tropical America, where they range as far south as Nicaragua, they avoid the wetter, rain-forested districts and live in more arid, open regions, including the hottest and driest. Yet these adaptable birds nest in the Arctic Archipelago and Greenland, and have been found on the snowfields near the summit of the Pico de Orizaba!

Through Chiapas to Guatemala

After two rewarding days in the heat of San Gerónimo, I took the morning train for Tonalá in the state of Chiapas, 110 miles distant. The single passenger coach, trailing at the end of a long string of freight cars, was divided into two compartments. In the second-class compartment, which occupied two-thirds of the coach, passengers sat on hard wooden benches. First-class passengers, who paid almost twice as much, not only enjoyed more space and greater cleanliness but sat on padded cane seats, which made a great difference in comfort on a seven-hour ride.

The railroad kept near the inner edge of the coastal plain. As we traveled eastward, mountain after mountain rose up on our left, in a long, irregular range that became higher and more precipitous as we advanced. After we left the mountain-rimmed plain of San Gerónimo, only an occasional outlying hill stood between us and the Pacific, which once I seemed to glimpse beyond several miles of level, bushy land. The farther eastward we went, the less arid the country became. The maize was more flourishing, pastures lusher, flowing streams more frequent, the natural vegetation heavier and more luxuriant, although still lighter than along the Caribbean coast.

As we were leaving San Gerónimo, I watched from the train window two male Great-tailed Grackles fighting tenaciously. They clinched together and rolled over on the ground, continuing the combat as long as I could keep them in view. This conflict surprised me, for in Guatemala I had lived for months in the midst of a large nesting colony of these birds without ever seeing them fight. Farther along, I noticed a pair of Crested Caracaras following a plow, as gulls do in northern lands. When the train stopped beside a wide plain covered with short grass at Sidar, I heard unmistakably the clear, familiar song of the Eastern Meadowlark.

Beyond Las Anonas, the first free Double-striped Thick-knee I had ever seen stood in a bushy pasture near the track, seeming unperturbed by the noise and rush of the passing cars. The thick-knees' preference for open ground makes them easy to see from moving vehicles. Many years later, I spied three of these long-legged birds with big yellow eyes sitting on as many "nests" while I sped by in motorcars. Two were in northwestern Costa Rica, the third on the llanos of Venezuela. Each thick-knee covered a single large gray egg, blotched all over with dark brown and pale lilac, that lay on bare ground in a spot with scant shade. Usually the mate stood close by the incubating partner, and neither retreated until I descended from the car and advanced close to them. Others have found Double-striped Thick-knees incubating two eggs.

I found Tonalá a small, rather dirty town situated at the foot of high and very steep mountains, above the crests of which I glimpsed still loftier summits. One of the nearer mountains, known as Tres Picos from its three peaks, was locally reputed to be the highest in Chiapas, its summit untrodden by human feet. On the other sides of the town unpaved roads, well shaded by double rows of densely foliaged trees, led between bushy pastures where bull's-horn acacias grew amid lush grass. It was delightful to walk along these shady lanes while many birds sang as they foraged in the leafy boughs.

Amid the pastures I met a bird new to me, the Giant Wren, known also as the Chiapas Wren because it is found only in the south of this state. With a black cap, rich chestnut-brown upper plumage, and immaculate white under parts, these wrens are as remarkable for the elegant simplicity of their attire as for their exceptional size. They live in pairs which, like those of related species, sing in unison, repeating a single mellow note in strong, deep voices. Their covered nests, bulky and conspicuous, were easy to find in the acacia trees but difficult to reach.

On my second evening at Tonalá, I watched two Giant Wrens, evidently a pair, retire for the night in separate nests, each ten or twelve feet up in acacia trees growing about a hundred feet apart. The following afternoon, I borrowed a ladder from the farmer on whose land these nests were situated and with his help set about to inspect them. The first, composed of straws, weed stems, bits of vines, and the like, was about fourteen inches high by eleven inches in diameter. Most of its height was in the part above the brood chamber, which seemed to serve as a thatch to shed rain. This nest, unlike any other wren's nest that I have examined, had two doorways, one facing north and the other east. Inserting a hand through one of them, I found two fat nestlings with eyes just opening and a single infertile egg, which was heavily mottled with brown on a light buffy ground.

This acacia tree was swarming with ants that lived in the paired hollow thorns and had been thoroughly aroused by shaking when we pruned away some branches to make a place for the ladder. Running in all directions over the tree, they seemed to be angrily searching for whatever had disturbed their peace. Nevertheless, not a single one had attacked the nestlings, and none crawled over the hand that I stuck into the nest. Yet, if I had touched the tree itself only briefly, I would have paid for my temerity with painful stings, as I learned while examining the second nest. This smaller structure, with only a single doorway, was the male's dormitory, where he slept while his mate brooded the nestlings.

While the ants rushed wildly about, ready to defend their tree, the big parent wrens stayed at a safe distance, showing little concern beyond uttering a few harsh vocal protests. In similar circumstances, smaller birds, including a Slaty Antshrike and a Gray Catbird, have bitten my hand or buffeted the back of my head.

The farmer who helped me to examine the wrens' nests, a Texan by birth, told me about some Indian ruins, known locally as "La Iglesia Vieja" ("The Old Church") situated in the mountains above Tonalá. Next morning I set out alone to visit them, as they were said to be easy to find. However, I should most probably have gone astray if an Indian, of whom I asked directions, had not volunteered to guide me for a peso. The indistinct pathway wound up a mountain beside the town, through light woods and across many pretty rivulets of clear water that trickled down the steep slope.

Not far above the plain, I noticed a large, black termites' nest eighteen feet up in a small tree near the trail. As I approached to examine it, a male trogon darted out and away, to repeat his dry *kec, kec, kec, kec* out of sight amid the trees. Climbing to the termitary, I found the round opening in its side too small to admit my hand. On this archaeological expedition I had foolishly failed to bring the mirrors and light that I use for looking into such structures. Although I was reluctant to alter a bird's nest, to learn the contents of this, my first nest of the Citreoline Trogon, seemed of sufficient scientific importance to warrant slightly enlarging the doorway. The black material of the termitary was so hard that I had great difficulty scraping it away with the blunt point of my guide's machete, while I lay prone along the supporting branch and termites swarmed over my hands and forearm, sometimes reaching my neck and face and administering bites that were slightly painful on tender skin. When the aperture had become just wide enough to squeeze in a hand, I removed two pure white eggs, very recently laid, as I could see through the thin, translucent shells. They rested on some loose debris, mostly fragments of the termitary, on the bottom of the rounded chamber.

Carefully I replaced the eggs, hoping that the trogons would not abandon a nest chamber that they had hollowed out with so much hard work. When we returned down the trail in the evening, I was relieved to find one member of the pair of trogons perching near it, apparently having flown out when it heard our footfalls. This made the third kind of trogon that I had found nesting in black arboreal termitaries. The other two were the closely related Black-headed Trogon and the Massena or Slaty-tailed Trogon.

I descended from the trogons' nest with my clothes as wet with perspiration as though I had come through a shower. Climbing was now intensely hot work that necessitated frequent pauses, not so much to rest as to cool off slightly. Halfway up the mountain, we reached a fairly level area with a small platform of earth, walled with large blocks of cut stone. One stone bore a crude circle in low relief; another, what looked like a fat human leg; while on a third was an object that I failed to recognize. Nearby were the ruins of other large mounds, so overgrown with vegetation that it was hard to see of what they were made.

Leaving these mounds, my guide led me to a little wooded ravine, where a rivulet flowed from beneath a huge rock. Never have I drunk so deeply of water so delightfully refreshing! A mango tree beside the stream supplied delicious fruits that we ate while we rested. After I filled my canteen, we resumed our climb and soon reached the cleared upper slopes, where cattle grazed and a cooling breeze blew away the heat and sweat, which were soon forgotten in the delight of being in the fresh upper atmosphere, with all the broad coastal plain spread out at our feet. At the mountain's base clustered the red tile roofs of Tonalá. Close by the town the Río San Francisco rushed between boulders and wastes of sand that it had spread far beyond its banks when in flood. Beyond, the plain was a pattern of green pastures separated by lines of trees of a slightly darker shade of green. Nearer the coast, broad lagoons and narrower belts of water intersected the land. To the west, an expanse of water many miles long and broad

Black-headed Trogon

was separated from the ocean by only a long line of white surf that revealed the position of a low, impassable bar. Beyond this belt of sea foam the Pacific spread on and on until lost in the haze of distance.

Near the mountaintop, amid green pastures, spread the remains of what was evidently, centuries ago, a large and complex ritual center of a vanished people. At different levels on the steep slope were many flat, rectangular, or nearly square courts, the largest about six hundred feet long by two hundred feet wide, all now overgrown with grass and weeds. Some of these quadrangles were walled with rough stones or with huge blocks of very different sizes, all squared and carefully fitted together, but now becoming displaced by the roots of the trees and shrubs that grew upon them. On the courts rose a number of earthen mounds, many of them enclosed in stone walls. The tallest that I saw, about twenty-five feet high, was surrounded by a terrace halfway up, in the style of many Aztec and Mayan structures. Quadrangles at different levels were connected by stone-paved ramps that were often steep, while less inclined roadways were of earth, with retaining walls of stone at the sides. Some of these unpaved ways were densely overgrown with sensitive plants which, folding their delicate leaves as we walked through them, made conspicuous trails.

The only carved stone that I noticed here was a nearly round, flat-topped zoomorph, about six feet in diameter, with a crudely executed animal face at one end. The monolith's shape suggested a tortoise, although its face was hardly chelonian. A human head, well carved, decorated each of the sides and the rear of this zoomorph. All three heads had excessively large, projecting ears with heavy pendants. The center of the rock's nearly level upper surface was bare, but around the edges various curved lines formed figures whose significance I could not divine.

Near the southern end of the largest quadrangle, shaded by a clump of small trees, stood a huge boulder of dark-colored rock, with a sort of handle or ring cut into one end. My guide explained that this ring was for tethering horses; but I was certain that it had been chiseled from the rock, with stone tools, long before horses, save the long-extinct precursors of our modern types, ever trod the soil of the Western Hemisphere. The innumerable outcrops and huge boulders of blackish rock strewn in immense profusion all over the upper slopes and level summit must have supplied the builders of this elaborate complex with an abundance of material.

Although I noticed no sign of digging by archaeologists, doubtless, since the date of my visit, they have described the site far more thoroughly and expertly than I did, with charts and explanations sounder than I could give. Although undoubtedly of great ethnological importance, the archaeologists' discoveries are often far from reassuring to our wavering faith in the soundness of mankind. Sweeping aside the mantle of green that hides the traces of an often tragic past, they restore to the light of day grim evidence of all the asperities of a barbarous age. They reveal the prevalence of human sacrifice and slavery, of war and torture, or priestcraft and debasing superstition and phallic orgy. Although human curiosity must be satisfied, I cannot avoid a suspicion that it might be better to let such things remain buried beneath the kindly soil and its tapestry of green. The human story is already full enough of distressing records!

As I roamed about the ruins, enjoying the refreshing mountain breezes and the glorious panorama of plain, lagoons, and ocean on one side, of towering, forbidding peaks on the other, it pleased me to muse upon the forgotten people who dwelt in so exhilarating a site. Without pushing aside a single creeper or turning up one spadeful of earth, I tried to imagine the kind of people who *should* have dwelt upon this fair mountaintop, in such peace and happiness as Hellenic poets were wont to ascribe to men of the Golden Age. They should have been gentle, truthful, and simple, neither coveting great wealth nor feeling the pinch of poverty, living in harmony with nature and one another, loving the flowers that brightened their mountain home, protecting the songful birds that nested in their fruit trees or beneath their eaves, never avoidably harming the smallest creature. They should have had minds so clear and chaste that they fell into no savage superstitions, nor peopled heaven and earth with jealous gods and malicious devils, to appease whom they devised hideous rites. Here might have flourished, all unchronicled, the perfect society that utopian dreamers try with doubtful success to plan.

While I indulged in these pleasant fancies, I could not dispel the nagging suspicion that the bar in that huge black boulder was for tying, not horses, but captives destined to be sacrificed; that the flat top of the big zoomorph was an altar where human victims were immolated in the cruel Aztec manner.

Growing profusely in the thickets on the mountaintop and amid the ruins was a shrub of the melastome family, evidently a species of *Conostegia*, with large, sweet black berries that I sampled freely. Those superb songsters, the Banded Wrens, were as abundant at "La Iglesia Vieja" as they were around Matías Romero and Tonalá and throughout the light woods and thickets through which we climbed from the town to the ruins. Theirs were almost the only songs that we heard along the way. I noticed many of their nests, all in their preferred sites, the bull's-horn acacias; but the only one I could reach was a yard above the ground in an acacia shrub at the foot of a great cyclopean wall. It was impossible to see what was inside this structure that had roughly the shape of a tube bent into the form of an open, inverted U, with one end closed and the opposite end opening downward. Since the nest looked old and weathered, and no wren was in sight to claim it, I carefully removed it for closer examination. To my surprise, it contained one fresh egg, probably laid that same morning. As a penance for my meddling, I replaced the firmly made, elbow-shaped structure as best I could, while the ants punished me severely. Probably the egg in this weathered nest was for a second brood.

Another bird that nested amid the ruins was the Striped-headed Sparrow. An open cup a foot above the ground in a low bush cradled three nestlings. A similar nest that I had found, at the same height in a thorny shrub near San Gerónimo, also held three nestlings. Although the latter were barely feathered, when I tried to examine them two jumped out and hopped rapidly away over the ground. When replaced in their nest, they refused to stay. These attractive sparrows, whose heads are boldly striped with black and white, range along the Pacific side of the continent from Mexico to northwestern Costa Rica. Sociable at all seasons, they forage near the ground, in bushy growths and weedy fields, in family groups that usually contain from four to seven individuals. Once, at the height of the dry season, I counted eighteen in a flock that probably had been formed by the temporary association of several families. It has been reported that more than two birds attend the same nest, and they would well repay a careful study.

Late in the afternoon, I reluctantly decided that it was time to descend from this cool, fascinating mountaintop to the hot plain. On our way down, we refreshed ourselves again at the spring that issued from beneath the rock and feasted upon the mangos scattered around it. Arriving hot and tired at the little hotel near the railroad, I bathed in what was to me a novel fashion that in later years I frequently used—by pouring water over myself from a large earthen jar, or *tinaja*, that stood in a corner of the bathroom. Although this was the cheapest hotel in which I had lodged, I found it satisfactory. For the equivalent of forty-two cents a day, I had three meals, of which black beans were the mainstay, a well-swept room, and a bed with springs covered by a mat and a clean bedspread, upon which I lay. A sheet to cover me would have been unendurable on a stifling July night in Tonalá.

After four days at Tonalá, I took the morning train for the Guatemalan border. Although scheduled to depart at 7:10 A.M., it did not leave until 10:00. The abrupt mountain rampart before which we had already ridden for many miles continued to rise on our left. Soon lagoons and mangrove swamps appeared on our right, some so near that I had good views of stately, pure white Great Egrets wading in shallow water, scarcely disturbed by the sound and sight of the long train. With them were a few Snowy Egrets, now without nuptial plumes. I could not recall having seen so many egrets in a single day as I did on this journey. The station at Mojarras was beside a small fishing village right on the edge of a lagoon, where I might have stopped for a day or two and explored the waterways in a cayuca, had I known about the place in advance.

Beyond Tres Picos, we passed over a well-watered plain, covered with tracts of fairly heavy forest. As we continued eastward the forest became more extensive, the openings in it more widely separated. Between Echagaray and Mapastepec we rode for twenty miles through forest that appeared primeval, which pressed up to the tracks on both sides and was interrupted only at long intervals by tiny villages of palm-thatched cabins surrounded by small clearings. Tall trees laden with lianas and epiphytes, a profusion of great-leafed heliconias and shellflowers in the undergrowth, gave a truly tropical aspect to this woodland, which apparently owed its preservation to the poorly drained or swampy land on which it grew. To ride by train through so much unspoiled tropical forest was a rare, exciting experience, for the woods along railroads and highways seldom escape exploitation. I wonder whether these have remained intact through the four decades since I saw them.

Beyond Mapastepec the mountains receded and agriculture became more prominent, with large, irrigated banana plantations scattered over the broad plain. On the railroad sidings leaf-padded cars waited to be filled with bunches of green bananas, which they would carry nearly four hundred miles, across the Isthmus of Tehuantepec to Puerto México (now Coatzacoalcos) on the Gulf, for shipment to New Orleans. These plantations extended as far as Huixtla, where the plain stretched so far inland that, for the first time since we left San Gerónimo, we lost sight of the mountains. Night was now falling, and, since the batteries for lighting the first-class coach had failed, we rode by starlight, with Scorpio shining splendidly to our right. Several hours late, we reached the straggling, unkempt village of Suchiate, terminus of the railroad. Next morning, July 19, I engaged a skiff to ferry me and my baggage across the broad, shallow Río Suchiate to Guatemala.

CHAPTER 2

Birds on a Guatemalan Mountain

Banded-backed Wren

An abrupt introduction to the profuse life of the lowland tropics can be a bewildering experience for an earnest naturalist. Amid humid heat and strange surroundings, it may even discourage or depress him. In his temperate-zone homeland, he was familiar with a wide variety of the more common and conspicuous organisms and perhaps could name all that he saw in his special field of trees, wildflowers, birds, or whatever it was. Now, unless he has painstakingly prepared himself beforehand or accompanies a competent mentor, nearly everything he meets is nameless to him. It is as though he had suddenly been demoted from college to kindergarten.

Ideally, one who grew up in the North Temperate Zone should enter the tropics by easy stages, working southward in one's own hemisphere at a leisurely pace, observing how, as the latitude decreases, certain northern plants and animals drop out of the landscape, to be replaced by southern or tropical forms. Those who from Canada or the United States gradually extend their knowledge of nature southward into Mexico enjoy this enlightening experience. Or, if one prefers a longer initial leap, one might choose for the first visit to the tropics the highlands of southern Mexico or Guatemala, where, in a bracing climate, many familiar plants and animals of northern types will prevent discouraging bewilderment while one slowly becomes acquainted with the tropical forms that will also be found there.

I did not begin to study tropical nature in this ideal fashion that I would choose if I were to start over again with adequate time and means. My first visit to the tropics came at the end of my first year of graduate study, when the botany department of Johns Hopkins University made one of its periodic pilgrimages to Jamaica, which as a British colony inspired a sense of security that was not then felt with regard to the Spanish-speaking countries of the tropical American mainland. My summer on the island, divided between the Blue Mountains and a banana plantation in the lowlands, gave me only a slight foretaste of what I would find when, two years later, I plunged into the more exuberant life of the humid continental tropics in the Almirante Bay region of western Panama. An overwhelming profusion of strange plants and animals, for which I lacked field guides, induced a state of pleasant excitement not unmixed with despair. Had anyone challenged my right to hold the doctorate in botany that I had recently earned, I might have relinquished it without protest.

Half a year in Panama was followed by an equal interval on the northern coast of Honduras, before I made more than a fleeting visit to tropical highlands. After a month's sojourn on the Sierra de Tecpán, in the Guatemalan department of Chimaltenango, late in 1930, I passed the whole of the year 1933 there, on estates owned by Axel Pira, Sr., the Swedish father of a friend I had made in Honduras. His land stretched from the plateau at about seven thousand feet up to the summit of the range at ten thousand feet.

At mid-levels of the mountain, where I spent most time, the

alternation of wooded slopes and level or gently inclined fields and pastures sometimes made me feel that I was back in the Piedmont region of Maryland, where I learned to love nature—an illusion that vanished whenever, from a point of vantage, I gazed across a wide plateau to distant volcanic cones rising majestically into the blue. The woods were composed largely of oaks, pines, and alders that grew to be tall trees, with an admixture of maples, wild cherries, arbutus, and species of the tropical American laurel family. The epiphytic growth of ferns, orchids, bromeliads, and other plants on these trees was such as would never be found in temperate-zone woods, although not as profuse as on lower, more constantly wet tropical mountains. In the undergrowth were blueberries, blackberries, viburnum, and evonymus, along with fuchsias, dahlias, and other less familiar tropical shrubs. Meadows were adorned with violets, buttercups, chickweeds, cinquefoils, and other familiar northern herbs, including many widespread weeds. It was pleasant to meet so many plants that I could identify at sight, as to genus and sometimes even species, along with a greater number strange to me. The upper slopes of the range supported forests of majestic cypress trees, with an admixture of broad-leafed species that supplied more food for birds.

Among the birds, as among the plants, familiar northern species mingled in the most surprising manner with unfamiliar members of tropical families. Sometimes, in the woods on the upper levels of the Sierra de Tecpán, I watched a Brown Creeper and a Spotted-crowned Woodcreeper climbing up the same trunk. Superficially, these two birds resembled each other rather closely, in habits as well as appearance. Both were shades of brown, which made them inconspicuous againt a background of bark; both had slender, sharp bills that they used to probe into crevices and beneath the scales of bark, in search of insects and spiders; both clung upright and always crept upward, using their sharp-pointed tail feathers for support, then flew from high on one tree to a point near the base of the next. Even their weak, rather plaintive voices were rather similar. The most conspicuous difference between them was in size, the woodcreeper being considerably the larger.

Much as they resembled each other, these two creepers seemed not to belong in the same woodland. Seeing them together seemed to flout the laws of geographic distribution, as though one were to meet a lemming and a sloth in the same patch of woods. The Brown Creeper represents the northern woodlands, where it ranges over much of Eurasia as well as North America. The Spotted-crowned Woodcreeper belongs to a family of about fifty species confined to the Neotropical region. Their presence in the same trees was symbolic of the mingling of boreal and tropical elements on this high mountain fifteen degrees from the equator.

Among the permanently resident, breeding species of the Sierra de Tecpán were several that I knew as a boy in the eastern United States, including the Eastern Bluebird, Eastern Meadowlark, Golden-crowned Kinglet, Hairy Woodpecker, Whip-poor-will, and Turkey Vulture. A larger number of the breeding residents range into the mountainous west of temperate North America, including the Band-tailed Pigeon, Red-shafted Flicker, Acorn Woodpecker, Broad-tailed Hummingbird, Black Phoebe, Steller's Jay, Bushtit, American Dipper, Hutton's Vireo, Dark-backed or Lesser Goldfinch, and Yellow-eyed Junco. The Guatemalan representatives of some of these species closely resemble those that breed much farther north; in others, such as the Bushtit and the junco, geographical differences are so pronounced that the southern and northern forms are sometimes classified as separate species.

Among the birds of tropical families that mingled with these species well known in temperate North America, or even more widely, were the vanishing Horned Guan; the lovely, red-bellied Mountain Trogon; the shy Blue-throated Green Motmot; the Emerald Toucanet; the elusive Scaled Antpitta; and the Cinnamon-bellied Flower-piercer, which steals nectar from flowers that it fails to pollinate. The Slate-throated Redstart and Golden-browed Warbler are members of large genera confined to tropical America, where they occur chiefly in the highlands.

As I roamed widely over the Sierra, watching the 123 species of birds, including 34 long-distance migrants from the north, that I identified there, many questions occurred to me. How did the biology or pattern of life of these inhabitants of cool tropical heights differ from that of North-Temperate birds which had been far more thoroughly studied, or from that of birds of the warm tropical lowlands that I had already watched for three seasons?

Did they migrate altitudinally? Did they lay more or fewer eggs? Did they seek shelter in nests or holes on chilly mountain nights?

One of the first things that I noticed was that females tended to resemble males, even when the latter were so colorful that in the North Temperate Zone they would probably have duller mates. This was especially evident in the wood warbler family, in which the males of the migratory northern species, when brilliant, are nearly always more handsome than the plainly attired females. But here in tropical highlands the sexes were often indistinguishable by plumage, even in such colorful species as the Pink-headed Warbler, Golden-browed Warbler, Slate-throated Redstart, and Painted Redstart. Among the orioles, the sexes of the resident Yellow-backed and Black-vented are equally brilliant in their yellow and black attire, although the females of the migratory Baltimore and Orchard orioles are much duller than the males. Even in the most handsome of the resident finches, including the Chestnut-capped Brush-Finch and the Yellow-throated Brush-Finch, the sexes are alike, while in northern species of the family the females are usually duller than the more colorful males.

In tropical American lowlands, I had already noticed this tendency for the sexes of passerine birds, including some of the most brilliant, to be alike much more often than in northern members of the order. This difference appears to be related to the fact that many tropical birds remain paired and on their territories throughout the year, instead of migrating for long distances or joining in wandering flocks, as many birds do in lands where a snowy winter makes food scarce. Except when they were accompanied by dependent young, I almost invariably found Pink-headed Warblers and the brush-finches in pairs. On the Sierra, Painted Redstarts and Slate-throated Redstarts did not remain in pairs after the breeding season, but I have found more southerly races of the latter in pairs throughout the year. The tendency for birds that are constantly paired to be alike in plumage is well illustrated in the tanager family, in which many beautiful species of the genus *Tangara* maintain pair bonds throughout the year and show little sexual difference in coloration, whereas in *Ramphocelus* flocking is associated with pronounced differences between the sexes.

In species in which males and females, alike in plumage, re-

Chestnut-capped Brush-Finch

main constantly mated, the young of both sexes often acquire the handsome adult attire, and may even join in pairs, in the fall when they are only a few months old, as I found in Pink-headed Warblers and Chestnut-capped Brush-Finches and, in Costa Rica, Slate-throated and Collared redstarts. This contrasts with the situation in migratory wood warblers and finches, in many of which the young travel southward and pass the winter in undistinguished plumage that makes them difficult to identify, not acquiring adult coloration until the following spring, when they prepare to return to their distant nesting grounds, as happens in the Chestnut-sided Warbler, the Indigo Bunting, and numerous others. Even the colorful adult males may don a more sober attire for the winter months.

Seasonal changes in coloration are rare among the resident birds of tropical America. As far as I know, they occur only in species in which the sexes differ strikingly and which flock without evident pair bonds, such as the Blue Honeycreeper and the Blue-black Grassquit. The degree of plumage change often appears to be connected with the extent of the migration. The adult male Summer Tanager comes to the tropics in his bright red summer dress, which he preserves throughout the winter. The Scarlet Tanager, which travels farther, never sojourning in Central America where Summer Tanagers are abundant during the winter months, changes into an olive-green and yellow dress much like the female's. Is it only a coincidence that the greatest traveler among the icterids, the Bobolink, exhibits the most striking seasonal changes in plumage to be found in its family?

When the male bird is much brighter than the female, his presence on the nest, especially if it is open, is more likely to attract the attention of such predators as find their prey by sight rather than by scent. But when the sexes are nearly identical in plumage and remain closely attached throughout the year, we might expect them to participate more equally in all domestic chores. To learn whether they do so, I have watched many nests, especially of wood warblers, tanagers, finches, icterids, and certain other families that contain species in which the sexes are alike along with species in which they differ in coloration, without ever seeing a male sit on the eggs. Coloration has little effect upon the participation of the sexes in incubation. The dullest male sparrow may never take a turn on the eggs; the elegant male Rose-breasted Grosbeak often does so.

It had long been known that tropical birds of many families lay smaller sets of eggs than do the most closely related species at higher latitudes. The observations supporting this generalization had been made chiefly in warm lowlands. Would it be valid for birds of cool tropical highlands? As I looked into nest after nest, I became convinced that, although latitude may strongly affect the size of bird families, altitude has little influence. In every zone, hummingbirds and pigeons rarely, if ever, lay more than two eggs, and the latter very often only one, so these families may be excluded from consideration. Among the families in which the number of eggs is more responsive to environmental influences are the finches. Those on the Sierra laid only two or three, as those in Central American lowlands most often do. Ruddy-capped Nightingale-Thrushes laid only two eggs; Orange-billed Nightingale-Thrushes of much lower altitudes lay two or sometimes three eggs. The Mountain Trogons laid only two, although lowland trogons often lay three. The Blue-throated Green Motmots laid three eggs; lowland members of the family have three or four. The one woodpecker's nest that I could reach, that of the Red-shafted Flicker, held four eggs, the number that frequently occurs among woodpeckers of tropical lowlands. Southern House Wrens on the Sierra laid four eggs, as they most often do at all altitudes in Central America. Four eggs were also incubated by the Bushtits, Black-capped Swallows, Eastern Bluebirds, and one exceptional Pink-headed Warbler. The largest sets that I found were those of the Banded-backed Wren, consisting of five eggs. With these exceptions, all the nests of passerine birds that I examined on the Sierra held only two or three eggs or nestlings. Taken as a whole, the birds on the Sierra laid only about half as many eggs as one might find in a similar sample from the northern United States or Europe.

Since the average temperature falls about three degrees Fahrenheit for every increase of one thousand feet in altitude, it is evident that temperature hardly influences the number of eggs in a set. A more important factor appears to be the length of the day from dawn to dusk, which determines how many hours diurnal birds can devote to gathering food for their young and, therefore, how many they can adequately nourish if food is available in sufficient quantity. Day length varies greatly with latitude but, except as deep and narrow valleys decrease its effective duration and high, exposed summits increase it, it is everywhere the same at the same latitude on the same date. If day length powerfully influences the number of eggs that birds lay, this should be about the same on high mountains as in neighboring lowlands.

Although the birds of the Sierra laid sets of about the same size as their closest relatives in the lowland did, on the whole they did not try to raise as many broods. Most of them started to nest around the beginning of April, when I noticed the last of the heavy nocturnal frosts that had whitened open fields on almost every clear, windless night since the preceding November, after the dry season began. The main breeding season continued for six or seven weeks, while pastures were still brown from the prolonged drought, but many trees wore full new foliage, shrubs were ripening their berries, and insects flourished. After the wet season broke in mid-May, and cold, drenching rains fell almost daily, the number of active nests rapidly diminished. Parents still feeding nestlings continued to attend them as well as they could, but few started another brood. The ground-feeding thrushes and finches nested later than most other birds, evidently because the insects and other small invertebrates that they sought in the ground litter became more abundant, active, and easy to find after rain soaked the soil. The young of some of these late nesters died in their nests, apparently as a consequence of the inclement weather that prevented the parents from both feeding and brooding them adequately.

After July, I discovered no active nests on the Sierra until late October, when the wet season ended and bright sunshine, falling upon a mountain that retained much moisture in its soil after long rainy months, called forth a profusion of nectar-bearing flowers that helped hummingbirds and Cinnamon-bellied Flower-piercers to form their eggs and nourish their young. These nectar-drinkers continued to breed until drought and heavy nocturnal frosts greatly decreased the abundance of flowers in January and February. As far as I could learn, not one of them nested with all the other birds in April and May. Each species nested when food for its young was most abundant, despite such seemingly unfavorable weather as the boisterous, chilling winds and frosty nights of the winter months, when hummingbirds and flower-piercers incubated their eggs and attended their young in open nests on exposed mountainsides, or the heavy rains of late May and June, when ground-feeders nested.

With the exception of a White-eared Hummingbird who fed a juvenile while she incubated her second set of eggs, I found no undoubted case of a bird attending a second brood. With small sets of eggs, a short breeding season, and few broods, these mountain birds had a reproductive potential lower than that of many species of neighboring lowlands, and much lower than that of many birds at higher latitudes. However, their nests were more successful than I have known nests to be elsewhere in the tropics. Of eighty-two nests of twenty-eight species that I found, I learned the outcome of sixty-seven. Thirty-seven of these nests, or 55 percent, produced one or more living fledglings. Below three thousand feet in Central America, I have rarely found nesting success as high as 40 percent, and frequently, especially in forest, it has only been about half as high.

I attribute the relative freedom from predation of nests on the Sierra largely to the rarity of snakes, which in warmer lands devour so many eggs and nestlings. Perhaps the chief mammalian predators were the Indians, who, to diversify their diet, pillaged many nests near their huts. Inclement weather was evidently responsible for a number of failures. Although fairly high nesting success compensated for their small broods and short breeding season, these mountain birds appeared able to maintain their populations only because their mortality was low. Resident the year around in the same locality, or at most moving up and down the mountains, they avoided the great hazards of long migrations; they had few natural enemies; they dwelt amid woods that were perpetually green and provided abundant berries throughout the year. Prolonged cold rain, rather than snow and ice, made the worst weather that they had to confront.

Sometimes, as I lay in bed, none too warm under several heavy Indian blankets, I wondered what measures the mountain birds took to protect themselves from the penetrating nocturnal chill. Surely, I thought, they must make greater use of snug dormitories than do birds in warm lowlands. But, as I studied the sleeping habits of birds in this and other elevated regions, I learned, to my surprise, that sleeping in dormitories is no more prevalent among highland than among lowland birds. With few exceptions, I found birds between five thousand and ten thousand feet above sea level sleeping in enclosed spaces only if this was a habit general in their family, followed by lowland no less than highland species. Neither on the Sierra de Tecpán nor elsewhere have I discovered finches, wood warblers, vireos, thrushes, jays, cotingas, hummingbirds, trogons, and pigeons roosting anywhere except amid sheltering vegetation. The only flycatchers, icterids, tanagers, and honeycreepers that I have found sleeping in dormitories or snug niches were at low or medium rather than high altitudes. On the other hand, wrens, woodcreepers, and woodpeckers sleep in enclosed spaces wherever they live, and this habit is widespread among swallows, ovenbirds (Furnariidae), and barbets.

The most conspicuous dormitories on the Sierra were the bulky covered structures with a side entrance that Banded-backed Wrens built well up in trees. I found from two to eleven of these big wrens sleeping together, snug and warm. Probably it is to these commodious nests that these wrens owe their ability to thrive in habitats so diverse as lowland rain forests and cypress forests nearly 10,000 feet above sea level. After the dispersal of their young brood, adult Southern House Wrens slept singly in shallow niches in roadside banks. At lower altitudes I have found them sheltering in such diverse sites as holes in trees, beneath the eaves of a house, and in the midst of a bunch of green bananas hanging where it grew. The related Rufous-browed Wrens slept, singly or in pairs, in niches in banks, old nests of Banded-backed Wrens, and amid moss-covered boughs high in cypress trees. On a mountain where Highland or Gray-breasted Wood-Wrens were more abundant than on the Sierra de Tecpán, I found pairs sleeping in globular nests that they had built. Apparently, they slept together to keep each other warm, for adults of the Lowland or White-breasted Wood-Wren always sleep singly in the slighter dormitories that they make in warmer forests.

Spotted-crowned Woodcreepers roost alone in crannies in trunks, as do all their lowland relatives whose sleeping habits I know. The cavity may be open above, permitting rain to enter, and suggesting that these birds seek concealment rather than a dry lodging. Like many other woodpeckers, Hairy Woodpeckers sleep alone, male and female in separate holes, that of the more industrious male being generally newer and sounder than the female's. On the Sierra, I found up to three Acorn Woodpeckers passing the night in the same hole, and in Costa Rica I have found five in a cavity. On frosty mornings, they emerged from their bedroom very late, after the rising sun had begun to warm the air. But they did not delay so long as eight Black-capped Swallows who lodged in a deep burrow in a roadside bank, situated on a windy shoulder of the mountain at an altitude of nine thousand feet. Here, while I watched, growing colder and colder, they lingered until past the middle of a morning with bright sunshine.

While the Bushtits' exquisite, lichen-encrusted, downy hanging pouches held eggs or nestlings, the two parents and one or two of their helpers used it as their dormitory, which at times sheltered as many as eight of the tiny birds, old and young. Although the pouch provided excellent protection during the clear, cool nights of the breeding season, it became sodden and doubtless unhealthful after the rains began, at about the time the fledglings took wing. Now all the Bushtits abandoned the nests to roost in trees, as they continued to do through the wettest and the coldest nights of the year.

The outstanding exception to the rule that the birds of the Sierra did not depart from the sleeping habits prevalent in their families was the Blue-throated Green Motmot. Although all motmots nest in burrows, none of the eight lowland species, as far as I know, uses them as dormitories—not even the Blue-diademed Motmot, which digs its burrow four or five months before it lays its eggs there but leaves it vacant in the interval. But, apparently as an adaptation that enables a member of a heat-loving family to reside as high as 9,500 feet above sea level, Blue-throated Green Motmots slept by pairs in long, crooked burrows in roadside banks, through the rainy and the frosty months when they did not breed, and even while they incubated their three white eggs and raised their nestlings. Less protective of their young than wrens and certain woodpeckers and barbets, they left the newly emerged fledglings outside beneath the cold nocturnal rains of late May and June. Yet the adults often continued to sleep in the old nesting burrows until, in late June or early July, they dug new ones nearby. If all went well, they continued to occupy these new burrows, for sleeping and then nesting, throughout the next year.

Although, despite the cold night air, the birds of Central American mountains seem rarely to depart from sleeping habits widespread in their families, the situation is different in the much more rigorous climate of the high Andes of Ecuador and Peru. There, far above the tree line, where at night the thermometer may fall well below the freezing point and snow and ice are frequent, birds as diverse as geese, hummingbirds, flycatchers, ovenbirds, finches, hawks, and owls roost in caves, old mine shafts, and whatever sheltering nooks are available.

The Migrants and Their Resident Companions

In the midst of the rainy season, winged travelers from the north began to arrive on the Sierra. By this time nearly all the resident birds had ceased to nest and sing, and the possibility of meeting unexpectedly some pretty migrant that I had not seen in months added greatly to the interest and pleasure of my solitary walks over the mountains. Since I did not know just when to expect the common winter visitors, nor what rare wanderer I might encounter, I enjoyed that indefinite expectation of a welcome event which is the most pleasant form of anticipation.

The autumnal migration began with a surprise. While descending through the oak woods on the lower slopes of the Sierra on August 9, I met a mixed flock of small resident birds. With them was a single Black-throated Green Warbler, a male in full breeding plumage, who sang his small, far-away song while he foraged with his newly found companions. He was two months early, for Black-throated Green Warblers are among the last of the wood warblers to arrive. I saw this species only once more before early October, when it became abundant.

After my premature meeting with the warbler, I continued downward to the plateau, where I found other recent arrivals that were not unexpected. Spotted Sandpipers had returned, and along the Río Chayá I saw at least five. Each year they are among the first of the northern migrants to reach Central America, as they are among the last to depart in the spring. Many arrive before they have changed their spotted summer attire for their winter dress with immaculate white breast.

Black-and-White Warblers reached the Sierra in late August, the third species to arrive during that month; but migrants did not become abundant until September. Then the warblers that were most numerous during the winter—Townsend's, Wilson's, MacGillivray's, Hermit, and Red-faced—appeared on the mountain and daily became more abundant. Wilson's Warblers, which reappeared on September 3, had been absent only three months and eleven days. Two days after I noticed the first arrival, they had become too numerous to count. Townsend's Warblers, which also returned on September 3 and in a few days became abundant, had been away exactly four months. I wondered why these birds chose to come to the Sierra at this time, for in whatever region they began their long journey, the weather could hardly have been less pleasant than it was here, when rain fell every night and often through much of the day, and a chill dampness pervaded the air. Certainly, they had not set out in search of sunshine or warmth!

In October other wanderers arrived. Solitary Vireos appeared on the tenth, and Rose-breasted Grosbeaks on the nineteenth. The Yellow-bellied Sapsucker did not return until November 3. The Hermit Thrush, which in the spring had departed a day later, also returned a day later than the sapsucker. Both of these birds had been away for more than six and a half months, the longest absence of any of the more regular winter visitors to the Sierra, except Audubon's Warbler and the Cedar Waxwing, which had not reappeared by the year's end. Although I have seen Audubon's Warblers in other parts of Guatemala in September, I have not found waxwings until January, and they are birds which are not easily overlooked because they perch conspicuously in large flocks in treetops.

In addition to the birds that came to pass the winter, a few traveled over the Sierra on their way to other regions. In September I noticed two Yellow Warblers, a single American Redstart, and a lone Hooded Warbler, all of them birds that prefer a warmer climate and did not remain among the chilling mists which then enveloped the mountain. In October I met a single Olive-sided Flycatcher, a lone Olive-backed or Swainson's Thrush, and a solitary Indigo Bunting in brown winter plumage. The first was evidently on its way to South America, but the other two may have descended only a few thousand feet to their winter homes. The number of transients that I recorded fell far short of what I might have seen in the lowlands at the same season; it seems that most migrant birds prefer to travel through lower and warmer regions.

By September, when the warblers arrived in numbers, many of the small resident birds of the Sierra roamed through the woods in mixed flocks, of which Crescent-chested Warblers formed the nucleus. The more sociable of the newcomers immediately joined these parties, as though they had never been absent. They were received amicably, with a ready companionship that must have compensated for their long, hazardous journeys. Townsend's Warblers from the western United States and Canada, olive-green on the back, prettily marked with black and yellow on head and breast, soon became more abundant in these flocks than all the other birds together. They were not only the most common migratory species on the Sierra but the most numerous bird of any kind during their eight months' residence there. Despite their beauty, I was frequently exasperated, after I had tried until my neck ached to identify some small, elusive bird that flitted through high treetops, to find at last that it was just one more Townsend's Warbler. There was always another of the same kind much lower among the branches that I might have seen to better advantage!

As I wandered through the woods toward the end of the wet season, when few plants flowered and few birds sang, they seemed lonesome and deserted until I met one of the motley flocks of Townsend's Warblers and their friends. Then there was no lack of life and animation, a medley of small voices and a crowd of active figures. Perhaps the Slate-throated Redstart in the party would sing a brief snatch, or the gorgeous Painted Redstart utter his mellow *weecher weecher weecher*. The charming little Tufted Flycatchers, of which a single pair was usually present, continually repeated their confiding *chee chee cheet* between pretty flouncing flights to catch small insects. At intervals the Hutton's Vireos, also represented by a single pair, called *cheerie cheerie* in loud, clear voices. Very rarely, at this season, a Crescent-chested Warbler delivered his insectlike buzz. If a single

Greater Pewee had joined the flock, his oft-repeated, resonant *wic wic wic*, voiced as he returned to an exposed perch from an aerial sally, added variety to the chorus. The rather high, screeching call of the Spotted-crowned Woodcreepers, of which the flock never contained more than two, was another frequent and distinctive note. Occasionally a dozen to a score of Bushtits joined the party and redoubled its chatter with their lisping twitters. Near the summit of the range, resident Golden-crowned Kinglets replaced the Bushtits.

What drew these so different birds together? They were not attracted by a local abundance of food, as when frugivorous birds of many kinds gather in a generously fruiting tree, or when insectivorous birds of a dozen species crowd around a swarm of army ants to snatch up fugitive insects, spiders, and other small creatures that the ants drive from concealment and make readily available. All the members of these mixed flocks on the Sierra were primarily insectivorous, and the small invertebrates that they hunted by diverse methods were scattered through the woodland rather than concentrated in particular spots. Possibly these birds unintentionally helped one another to forage, as when an insect driven from a trunk by a woodcreeper, or shaken from foliage by a warbler, was caught in the air by a flycatcher. However, such occurrences were hardly frequent enough to account for the continued cohesion of the group.

More probably, as Edwin O. Willis (1972a) has maintained, the birds felt, and were, safer from surprise attack while in the group. Undoubtedly, such a noisy party was far more conspicuous than scattered individuals or pairs; but the many watchful eyes, the many voices ready to sound the alarm at the first hint of danger more than compensated for this heightened conspicuousness and increased the birds' chances of survival. Probably, too, the flocking birds were held together by a desire for companionship that was independent of utilitarian motives. We cannot dismiss this possibility simply because, the minds of birds being closed to us, we cannot prove it. The cries of these flocking birds reveal an innate altruism; one of them might increase its personal safety if, on spying an enemy, it discreetly hid, leaving companions unaware of danger to become targets of the predator's attack. I never saw one of these flocks menaced by one of the few hawks that I noticed on the Sierra—the Red-tailed, the Marsh Hawk, the Sparrow Hawk or American Kestrel.

These animated mixed flocks were the key to the social organization of a large part of the birds of the Sierra in the season when they did not nest. It was interesting to notice the varying degrees of sociability of the different species. The most sociable species were represented by a number of individuals, a flock within a flock. After September, Townsend's Warblers invariably formed the largest group; but Crescent-chested Warblers, Hermit Warblers, and sometimes Olive Warblers were present in smaller numbers. Other species, which remained mated through the year, were represented by a single pair, almost never by more than two individuals. One pair each of Spotted-crowned Woodcreepers, Tufted Flycatchers, and Hutton's Vireos was to be found in almost every large flock, and sometimes a pair of Pink-headed Warblers temporarily joined the party. Species intolerant of the company of others of their kind, yet not wholly devoid of social impulses, were represented in each flock by a single individual. The Slate-throated Redstart, Painted Redstart, Red-faced Warbler, Black-and-White Warbler, Greater Pewee, and Solitary Vireo belonged to this group, and it was rare to find more than one individual of each species in a flock. If two Red-faced Warblers, evidently both males, joined the same flock, they sang against each other until one drove his rival away. Slate-throated Redstarts behaved in the same fashion.

The same three degrees of sociability, at least with reference to their own species, were exhibited by birds that did not often join the mixed flocks. Among those that usually went in parties composed of their own kind alone were Banded-backed Wrens, Bushtits, Steller's Jays, Black-throated Jays, Gray Silky-flycatchers, Cedar Waxwings, Band-tailed Pigeons, White-winged Doves, Barred Parakeets, Green Parakeets, Rose-breasted Grosbeaks, Black-capped Siskins, Black-headed Siskins, Yellow-backed Orioles, Black-capped Swallows, and a few others. Sometimes flocks of two of these species mingled, as when Steller's Jays foraged with Black-throated Jays, or Gray Silky-flycatchers perched with Cedar Waxwings, or Bushtits joined one of the large mixed flocks of warblers and other small birds. The relations between the two groups were usually amicable; but they were held together by no strong attraction, such as bound the members of the mixed flocks, and soon they drifted apart.

Among the birds which usually remained in pairs that kept to themselves were Yellow-throated Brush-Finches, Chestnut-capped Brush-Finches, Highland Wood-Wrens, Rufous-browed Wrens, Pink-headed Warblers, and Golden-browed Warblers. Sometimes, however, a pair of Yellow-throated Brush-Finches accompanied a pair of Chestnut-capped Brush-Finches, a pair of Pink-headed Warblers joined one of the mixed flocks, or a pair of Golden-browed Warblers stayed near a flock of Common Bush-Tanagers, which became abundant in July, evidently having migrated upward after nesting at lower altitudes. Most of these species did not repel other kinds of birds whose paths happened to cross their own, but they would not tolerate a third adult of their own kind.

Although swans, geese, and cranes remain in pairs or families on long migrations, I have never seen any indication that wintering migrants of any species maintain pair bonds in Central America. Migration or winter wandering, with the consequent dissolution of pairs, is responsible for many of the differences between tropical and northern birds that we earlier noticed.

A few of the birds on the Sierra appeared to live quite alone after the close of the breeding season. All hummingbirds are essentially solitary. They may be drawn together in numbers by a local abundance of flowers; and the males of many species gather to sing within hearing of one another to attract the females; but they lack a true group spirit. Hawks, too, lead lonesome lives. I almost always saw the Scaled Antpitta, Yellow-bellied Sapsucker, and MacGillivray's Warbler alone. Wilson's Warblers not infrequently associated singly with mixed flocks, but as often remained quite alone. Birds that are truly solitary, and pass the season when they do not breed without any company at all, appear to be in the minority.

The resident Eastern Bluebirds kept largely to themselves until the Audubon's Warblers arrived. These handsome warblers that breed in the west from Canada to Guatemala so closely resemble the Myrtle Warbler that the two are now placed in the same species, known as the Yellow-rumped Warbler. Nevertheless, the adult male Audubon's Warbler is readily distinguished by his bright yellow rather than white throat. He has five patches of yellow, on the crown, throat, two sides, and rump. I found Audubon's Warbler abundant on the Sierra from mid-January until April, but, strangely enough, it did not return with all the other migratory warblers in August and September, and none had arrived by the year's end. Yet, in the middle of the following September, it was numerous among pine and alder trees on the Sierra Cuchumatanes, nearly a thousand feet higher than the summit of the Sierra de Tecpán. The males, resplendent in their full nuptial attire of yellow, white, and black, were still singing enchantingly. Probably they nested in this remote region.

Audubon's Warblers are versatile foragers. Sometimes, from the top of a tall tree, they darted out on long, intricate sallies to catch insects on the wing. Twisting about in the air, they spread their tails to reveal the prettily contrasting areas of black and white. At other times they foraged on the ground, like Myrtle Warblers, a habit that brought them into contact with the bluebirds, likewise arboreal birds that frequently hunted on the ground. On the Sierra de Tecpán, I almost always found these two species together in close-cropped pastures with scattered low oak trees. This association was too frequent to have been accidental but evidently resulted from the mutual attraction of two kinds of birds quite different in appearance and lineage. Both were exceedingly wary as they hunted on the ground and flew up into the trees whenever they saw me approaching, even at a great distance. Probably because they so often enter open, exposed places, where they are conspicuous and far from shelter and must exercise great caution not to be surprised, Audubon's Warblers were by far the shyest and most difficult to approach of all the warblers on the Sierra, resident or migratory. This was true whether I found them on the ground or in trees.

In the evenings, foraging over the ground as they advanced, Audubon's Warblers and bluebirds went to bathe together in one of the little streams that flowed through the pastures. After splashing vigorously in the shallow water, they would fly up together into the Raijón bushes, shake the drops from their feathers, sometimes wipe their wet faces against the branches, and arrange their plumage. The last Audubon's Warbler that I saw in the spring was a lone female, who foraged with a pair of bluebirds in the open pasture. She must have appreciated the companionship of the bluebirds more than ever, after all of her own kind had departed for higher mountains in Guatemala, or possibly for Canada—I did not learn whether these birds belonged to the Guatemalan or a northern race.

Rose-breasted Grosbeaks lived in flocks of their own kind. They frequented the garden and its vicinity, where I first found them in November, 1930, and again when I returned at the beginning of 1933, when about twenty were present. By March some of the males had acquired full nuptial plumage and were resplendent in black, white, and rose. The last member of this flock left on April 6. They remained away for six and a half months, returning on October 19, when I noticed three in the hedgerow at the far end of the garden, in almost the same spot where I saw the last birds of the spring. Two were females clad in buffy brown and grayish white. Their companion was a male attired almost as plainly as they, with only a tinge of rose on his white breast to remind me of the warm rosy shield that covered it in summer. His wings were conspicuously marked with black and white, in striking contrast to the general dullness of his dress. I had little doubt that they were the same individuals who had passed the preceding winter here; but I could not tell in what far northern land they had nested, or what route they had followed on their long southward journey, or what adventures had befallen them, or how many days their journey had taken.

The three grosbeaks began at once to eat their favorite seeds, those of the euphorbiaceous shrub *Stillingia acutifolia*. The foliage of this bush is poisonous to cattle, deadly if eaten in quantity; but the grosbeaks seemed never to suffer any ill effects from its seeds. To extract the three small seeds, they crushed the thick, three-lobed pods in their heavy bills, making a noise audible at a distance. They were also fond of the garden peas, to obtain which they perched beside one of the long pods, pecked a hole in it, and removed the fat green seeds one by one. Extremely fastidious, they deftly removed the germ from the tender green seed-coat, which they dropped to the ground. Sometimes they managed to extract the germ without detaching the seed, leaving the empty seed-coat in the empty pod. I could well understand their addiction to these peas, for I have never tasted any sweeter than these grown at a high altitude.

To save the peas, the old Indian gardener devised a scarecrow, consisting of an inverted tin pail with a white rag tied around it for a head and an old garment draped over a crossbar for a body; but the grosbeaks were not deterred by this palpable deception. With praiseworthy patience, the gardener stretched long strings completely around and diagonally across the pea patch. To these strings, at intervals of a foot or less, he tied long, thick leaves of the yucca, so that, dangling from their tips, they might sway in the wind and alarm the thieves; but this arrangement also failed to serve its purpose. Having enjoyed the Rose-breasted Grosbeaks' delightful song in the north, I deemed them worthy of their epicurean fare; but I found it difficult to persuade those who had never heard the grosbeaks sing to be indulgent with them.

Just as most of the resident birds of the tropics have definite altitudinal ranges, so the visitors from the north prefer certain altitudinal zones as their winter homes. Although while migrating they may be found at almost any altitude, after they have settled down they are seen only within more narrow limits. Some, like Townsend's, Audubon's, Hermit, and Red-faced warblers, remain in the cool highlands when they come to Guatemala. Townsend's and Hermit warblers are most abundant between 5,000 and 10,000 feet; but where, as on the Pacific slope of Volcán Atitlán, pine woods occur locally at lower altitudes, they descend as low as 3,400 feet, although they avoid the neighboring broad-leafed woods. MacGillivray's Warbler also favors cool highlands, but it has a wider altitudinal range and is often found from 10,000 down to 2,000 feet. Species that prefer higher altitudes are all from western North America. Wood warblers from east of the Rocky Mountains seek a warmer climate. The Magnolia, Yellow, Kentucky, Hooded, and Mourning warblers, Common Yellowthroat, American Redstart, and Yellow-breasted Chat are all fairly abundant in Central American lowlands during the winter months but are rarely found above 5,000 feet.

A few of the winter residents spread over a very wide range of altitudes. Perhaps none is more adaptable to extremes of height and temperature than the black-capped Wilson's Warbler, which winters from near sea level up to 10,000 feet, although it is less abundant at low than at high altitudes. From September until May, its emphatic, nasal *chip* is a familiar sound amid dooryard shrubbery, tangled thickets, and the more open woods over all this great vertical range. During the winter, Black-and-White Warblers avoid their own kind and spread over such a vast range, on the continent and in the Antilles, at sea level and up to about 8,500 feet in the mountains, that they seem nowhere to be numerous. The Black-throated Green Warbler and Solitary Vireo are good examples of birds that winter chiefly at middle altitudes; they spread over a wide range of elevations but tend to avoid extremes. In northern Central America, I have found the warbler from 1,000 to 8,500 feet; the vireo from 2,500 to 9,000 feet.

The warblers that winter at higher altitudes are much more gregarious than those that winter in the lowlands. All over the higher parts of Guatemala, large flocks of Townsend's Warblers, joined by a variety of other warblers and small birds of other families, were a familiar sight during the years when I traveled widely there. We have already noticed how flocks of Audubon's Warblers associate with Common Bluebirds. At middle altitudes, Tennessee Warblers form the nuclei of flocks that contain a number of other species. But at the lowest elevations the wintering warblers, even when numerous in both species and individuals, are more solitary; here I have never seen flocks comparable to those I so frequently met in the mountains. Myrtle Warblers are exceptional in flocking even when they winter near sea level, but they often forage on open ground where none of their neighbors care to join them.

The Black-and-White Warbler was the first of the migrants to disappear from the Sierra de Tecpán. I saw none after late February, although at lower altitudes they may linger until toward the end of April. The Red-faced and Hermit warblers left in March. In April the northward movement became stronger. The last of the Rose-breasted Grosbeaks disappeared on the sixth, the American Kestrel on the ninth, the Mourning Doves on the following day, the Yellow-bellied Sapsuckers on the sixteenth, the Hermit Thrushes on the seventeenth, and Audubon's Warblers on April 23. After singing their beautiful, clear songs loudly and often through most of the month, the Solitary Vireos followed northward; I saw the last on April 28. Townsend's Warblers repeated their weak, dreamy little lays before they departed, the last on May 2, and left a void among the trees by the withdrawal of their myriads. Black-throated Green Warblers, never very numerous, began to utter a very similar song and were the next to go, the last of them remaining until May 6. MacGillivray's Warblers continued to sound their sharp *tuc tuc* amid low, dense vegetation until May 10. Cedar Waxwings, which nest late in the north, lingered in large flocks until the twelfth. Last of all to go were Wilson's Warblers, who sang a simple but cheerful refrain before they vanished, the final stragglers on May 22. Long before these late-lingering visitors had gone, the majority of the resident birds with whom they associated had built their nests and laid their eggs.

I saw few transient wanderers during the spring migration. Two Swainson's Thrushes passed over the Sierra on April 12, but they did not sing, as I have often heard them do at this season in Costa Rica. At the end of the month I met a solitary Canada Warbler, pausing for refreshment on his long aerial voyage from Peru or Colombia to Canada. On the morning of May 3, a flock of thirteen Eastern Kingbirds, returning northward from South America, rested in the tops of some oak and pine trees standing in a pasture, whence they made long, graceful sallies to snatch up insects, all in perfect silence. No chance encounter with an old friend could have given me greater pleasure than this meeting, for these far-wanderers formed a living link between all the lands that I knew best. They delayed for only a day, then departed as quietly and unobtrusively as they had come.

CHAPTER 3

The Charm of Hummingbirds

White-necked Jacobin

To those who have the happy ability to find adventure among little things, I recommend the hummingbirds. In no other warm-
blooded animals, perhaps in no other living creatures of any kind,
has nature managed to compress so much beauty, vitality, animation, and complex behavior into so small a compass. The distinction of being the smallest of the world's birds is generally attributed to the elegant Bee Hummingbird of Cuba, only two and a
quarter inches long, including bill and tail. The biggest member

of the family, the plainly attired Giant Hummingbird of the central and southern Andes, measures about eight and a half inches from tip of bill to tip of tail. Intermediate in length are the approximately 318 other species of a family that has no close living relatives.

Although hummingbirds are often placed in the same order as the swifts, their classification is controversial, and certain recent authors have given them a separate order, all their own. Who could confuse a dull-colored, stubby-billed swift, perpetually circling above the treetops in pursuit of volitant insects, with a brilliant, slender-billed hummingbird that stays down amid the vegetation where it finds the flowers that supply its principal food, nectar? Both hummingbirds and swifts have exceptional powers of flight, but they use them in very different ways; and the similarities of the anatomical structures that support their flight may result from evolutionary convergence.

The uniqueness of hummingbirds makes them easy to recognize. Although we are often doubtful in what family to place a bird new to us, this rarely happens with hummingbirds. In early childhood, from untutored observation of the dashing little birds that hovered before the spreading blossoms of my mother's old-fashioned hollyhocks, I formed my concept of a hummingbird. Since that distant time, in years of wandering through the tropical lands where hummingbirds chiefly abound, I have watched a hundred kinds. Nevertheless, my early picture of a hummingbird, based upon familiarity with a single species, remains essentially unchanged. To me, a hummingbird was, and is, a fairylike bird, with a tiny body of slender grace, that hovers, miraculously suspended between two broad sectors of misty light, like the separated halves of a halo, giving forth now and then a bright glint of green from its back, and sending out a low, murmurous humming from those wings vibrated into an unsubstantial haze, while it probes the cool depth of some bright corolla with a long and delicately slender bill. I have since learned that the green scintillations from the back are not an essential feature of hummingbirds, although most kinds display them; but otherwise this early image remains unchanged, and whenever any feathered creature conforms to it, I am sure that I behold a hummingbird. For few other great families of birds could I give, in so few words, a description adequate for the recognition of all their species, with so little danger of its misapplication.

Perhaps, before leaving this description, it may be well to add one caveat. Be sure that the sprightly creature that hovers before the flowers on vibrant wings is covered with feathers and not with powdery scales, and that its bill is rigid, not capable of being coiled into the semblance of a spring. Some hawk moths, compact of body and swift of wing, superficially resemble hummingbirds as they poise before a flower to sip the sweet secretion from its center, and not a few of the more casual observers of nature have been deceived by the likeness. But hawk moths begin their visits in the twilight, when hummingbirds seek their leafy bowers and repose. Some small birds of other families may flutter beside a blossom that they cannot otherwise probe, but they can sustain themselves so only momentarily, not as long as hummingbirds do, and their wings produce no hum.

Hummingbirds are confined to the Western Hemisphere, where they are most abundant in the tropics, and only a few species range much beyond Cancer and Capricorn. All the vast area of the United States and southern Canada east of the Great Plains has only a single kind of hummingbird, the Ruby-throat. The mountainous West has about a dozen kinds, several of which extend northward little beyond the Mexican border. Compare this with the rich variety of hummingbirds in a tropical land. Costa Rica, with an area considerably less than that of the state of West Virginia, has fifty-one species.

The Neotropical region has the world's richest bird life, among which hummingbirds can claim to be the most distinguished family. We have in the Western world no family of large or middle-sized birds, peculiarly our own, that rivals in splendor of plumage the birds of paradise and the pheasants of the Eastern Hemisphere. Our orioles, our motmots, and our jacamars seem ornate enough to satisfy the most exacting eye; but should some bird-loving Paris be assigned the difficult task of awarding a golden apple to the Earth's most gorgeous family, I would not trust any of these to win the beauty prize. With greater confidence, I would support some of our exquisite miniatures, our multihued wood warblers, our little gemlike tanagers, or our scintillating hummingbirds, in the belief that they alone could bring the trophy to our own hemisphere. Our perfection lies in little things.

Nevertheless, the brilliant colors of hummingbirds are not easy to see. If one can be satisfied by delicate grace of form, swift movement, and superb mastery of flight, the first view of a hummingbird is a thrilling experience; if one demands color, too, it is likely to be disappointing. The hummingbirds' most intense colors are not produced by pigments but by the reflection and diffraction of light by minute parts of the feathers. They are in the same category as the colors of the rainbow, the prism, and a thin film of oil spread over water. The color sensation that we receive from a body whose coloration results from structure rather than a pigment depends wholly on the angle from which we see it; viewed from an unfavorable position, it may appear black or colorless, according to its opacity and its background. Seen well above eye level, especially against the sky, the most brilliant hummingbird, like the greenest parrot and the bluest bluebird, is a drab disappointment.

The most intensely brilliant colors of hummingbirds usually flash from the throat. The male's gorget may be coldest green or warmest red, brightest blue or deepest purple, shining gold or glittering magenta. The forehead and crown may bear some metallic color different from the vivid green that is the most frequent color of the hummingbird's upper plumage. But to see a hummingbird's throat and forehead in their full splendor often demands the greatest patience, not unmixed with a measure of skill, and some knowledge of the bird's habits. As a rule, the intense coloration is apparent only to one who views the bird from directly, or almost directly, in front; seen from a point too far to the side, the most vivid gorget may appear a dead black. The hummingbird guards his chief splendors for the privileged eyes that he chooses to favor; he does not display them carelessly to all the vulgar world.

To add to the difficulty of properly seeing the metallic colors of a hummingbird, some kinds are, despite their small size and rapid movement, shy and distrustful of man. Often I have found it more profitable not to try to maneuver myself in front of a perching hummingbird, but to sit or stand quietly before some flowering plant whose blossoms attract him, with the sun behind me, and wait patiently for his return. Sooner or later, unless I have worse than average luck, he will poise before a flower whose position obliges him to assume the precise angle most favorable for displaying his splendors to me. Then, in a sudden burst of effulgence, like the light of some great revelation, what was previously black and lusterless stands unveiled in its true brilliance and glory. For it is with hummingbirds' colors as with all true revelations; they resist eager importunities and cannot be compelled. We must bide our time, humbly and patiently, until the divine afflatus, or whatever it is that leavens and uplifts the spirits of men, finds it convenient, out of the fullness of its time and the vastness of its resources, to inspire us; and it is more likely to do this when we are quietly receptive than when we go bustling about, intent upon the immediate achievement of our own narrow aims.

It is in our intervals of alert passivity, amid surroundings that invite the spirit to expand (and in such surroundings hummingbirds are usually found), that we experience most deeply and reap the richest harvests from time's swift flight. As I pass in retrospect years of a naturalist's roving life, devoted to the pursuit of this fact and that specimen, I find that it was those hours and half-hours when I suspended active endeavor and waited expectantly for something to happen that have left the most vivid and treasured impressions.

Once, while wandering through the dark cypress forests that crowned some of Guatemala's higher mountains, I became aware of an endlessly reiterated *squeak squeak squeak* that seemed to arise from all sides. After much searching and stalking, I located the origin, or one of the origins, of those tireless squeaks, a hummingbird somewhat above average size, who perched upon a naked twig in the undergrowth and repeated his melancholy note with mechanical regularity. I noticed the rather dull green of his upper plumage, the whitish stripe behind each eye, the slight downward curvature of his long, black bill; but from every angle at which he would permit me to view him, his throat persisted in appearing lustreless black. It was useless for me to strive to gain a position relative to the bird from which the gorget would reveal any other color. Yet I could not accept this negative testimony, for I was certain that the throat could not be wholly devoid of metallic coloration.

At the edge of the forest where these hummingbirds squeaked the trees had been thinned by lumbering, and where sunshine reached the ground a variety of flowering shrubs flourished. Prominent among them was a Salvia that displayed a profusion of blossoms with long, furry, deep crimson corolla tubes, each with a liberal drop of nectar at its base. These deeply colored, richly laden flowers strongly attracted the hummingbirds, who flew to them from the neighboring forest, sipped nectar from a number, then darted away again. I resolved to wait in sight of one of these crimson-flowered shrubs for the appearance of the hummingbird with the white mark behind each eye that squeaked in the deeper shade beneath the cypress trees.

I sat on the grass, close-cropped by goats, upon the steep slope above a Salvia shrub that flowered profusely. The mountain rose toward the west, and the sun, which had already fallen through half of its descending course, sent a few mild rays slanting down the slope behind me. At these great heights the thin air quickly relinquishes its heat, and already a chill was falling over this eastern slope. About me grew the Mexican Lappula, a low herb with pale blue, forget-me-not flowers, and the little Alpine Clover. From down the slope came the hum, softened and tranquilized by distance, of the small sawmill that cut the cypress logs.

Hummingbirds darted up to the Salvia flowers, probed the depths of as many as they needed to satisfy them, then sped away until lost to vision among the trees. Among these visitors the kind that I most wanted to see was prominent; but it was long before one of them hovered in just the position that would reveal his brightest colors to me. The sun, meanwhile, dropped lower above the crest of the mountain behind me; the chill grew sharper in the air. At last, a hummingbird flew up to the bush that I watched and began to make the rounds of the crimson flowers. Among others, he visited one that made him poise with his bill pointing straight toward me and the westering sun. A gleam of the most intense amethyst overspread his tiny throat, played there an instant, then, with a slight shift in the bird's orientation, was extinguished as swiftly as it had appeared. My vigil on the mountain slope had been fruitful; I had had my revelation.

To be sure, had I belonged to the school which holds that the most valuable thing a bird can yield is a stuffed skin with an exact record of locality and date, I might have shot my Amethyst-throated Hummingbird, picked up his limp, lifeless form, turned it this way and that in my hands, and scrutinized at my pleasure the play of colors over his blood-stained plumage—all in far less time than it had taken me to glimpse fleetingly the brilliance of the living bird. But there is nothing more pitiful, more charged with disillusion, than a dead hummingbird. No, I should rather say that there is no such thing as a dead hummingbird. I have never killed one; but I have extracted their dead bodies from house screens, against which they had flown at full speed, never suspecting that anything could bar their swift approach to the tree they so clearly saw through the corner of the screened veranda. So hard and deeply did they plunge their slender bills into the meshes of the metallic network that they could not pull away, and they hung helplessly until a speedy death brought release from agony—unless one of the occupants of the dwelling happened to notice their plight. I have more than once plucked their lifeless bodies from a house screen, but they never seemed to correspond to the living hummingbirds who had dashed against the hardware cloth. All that vibrant life, all that intense animation, all that which was essentially hummingbird in them had somehow evaporated along with the water from their desiccating bodies, leaving them smaller and less brilliant than they had been, little lumps of flesh and feathers that evoked pity more than admiration.

In a later year, when the Inga trees that shaded the small coffee plantations in the Costa Rican valley where I then dwelt were densely covered with white, fluffy stamen clusters, I glimpsed a kind of hummingbird very different from any I had hitherto seen. At first I had only the most fleeting view of it, as I walked along the edge of a coffee grove, but a gleam of white on its forehead revealed that it was new to me. Early on a sunny morning in November, I waited on the eastern side of the lowest flowering Inga tree in the plantation, hoping for a better view of the diminutive hummingbird as it probed the stamen clusters for nectar. Several times one came in sight just long enough to reveal that he was exceptionally ornate, but each appearance was abruptly terminated when some bigger hummingbird, of the many that hovered around the Inga trees, darted toward him. For a long while, my expectation of enjoying a satisfactory view of this unfamiliar bird was cheated by the pugnacity, or the playfulness, of the others.

Finally, I noticed that, between visits to the flowers, my white-fronted gem perched and preened his feathers on an exposed twig, scarcely head high, of a coffee bush that grew beneath the Inga tree. By stationing myself in view of this shrub, I could examine him at my leisure. Although one of the smallest of birds—his length, from the black tip of his slender, coral red bill to the end of his rounded, chestnut-rufous tail, was barely three inches—he bore such a variety of colors and adornments as one will only exceptionally find on a much larger bird.

Just behind his coppery bronze forehead rose a plumed tiara, broad of base but narrowing rapidly to an attenuate apex that projected above his crown, and all of snowy whiteness. Above each ear was a longer tuft of plumes, green at the broad base but appearing black on their stiff, threadlike tips, which extended well behind his head. His upper plumage was chiefly glittering green, varied by a conspicuous band of white across the rump—a color pattern unusual in hummingbirds. His cheeks and throat appeared black as long as he kept his bill pointing directly toward me, but, if he turned so that I viewed these regions from the side, they became intensely green—a reversal of the hummingbird's usual scheme of color visibility. His chest, below his green or black throat, was pure white, and the remainder of his under plumage was cinnamon, tinged with green upon the sides. He was my first male White-crested Coquette.

When, from a distance of several yards, I had satiated my eyes with his miniature elegance, I was encouraged by his apparent indifference to his observer to find how near he would permit me to approach. As I advanced slowly, step by step, he calmly watched me. When, finally, he decided that I was too close and darted away with a suddenness of which only a hummingbird is capable, I raised a hand and, without changing my position, touched the spot where he had perched. Never before, in a long experience with many kinds of hummingbirds, had any adult consciously permitted me to come so near.

Despite the contrary statement of so competent an authority as

W. H. Hudson, the hummingbirds that I know display no insect-like insensibility to danger, and most of them appear to be aware that man is to be feared. These plumed hummingbirds were not seen in the valley throughout the year, and I suspected that they had wandered into it from the vast, uninhabited forests that then covered much of southern Costa Rica, where they lacked experience of man and the destruction of which he is capable. Others of his kind, that I tested later, were almost equally tolerant of my near approach; but the hummingbirds who resided in the valley throughout the year were all very wary.

Most of my closest encounters with adult hummingbirds have occurred when I, not they, have been the object of close scrutiny. While passing laboriously through the low, densely tangled, second-growth thickets which cover so much of the deforested lowlands of Central America, I have often become aware of a low humming that arose very near me. If I stood quite still, I could usually discover the source of the sound. It was a tiny brownish hummingbird with long, white-tipped central tail feathers and a long, downcurved bill—a Little Hermit. It hovered all around me, suspended motionless, in the intervals between its sudden changes of position, between wings that beat too rapidly to be seen, while it subjected me to a lingering examination from various angles. More than once the tiny hermit has hovered so near that my cheeks, hot in those torrid lowlands, have been fanned by its vibrant wings. The inspection terminated to our mutual satisfaction, the elfin sprite uttered a sharp *cheep* and shot away through the vine-entangled bushes, where I could follow only by laboriously cutting my path with my long-bladed machete. Or any slight, sudden movement that I made would cause the precipitate retreat of my little inspector, who seemed aware that the satisfaction of his curiosity was not unattended by danger. Other rather dull hummingbirds of low, dense vegetation, including the Long-tailed Hermit and the Band-tailed Barbthroat, have frequently scrutinized me in similar fashion.

Hummingbirds cannot subsist wholly upon the sweet liquid that they draw from flowers through their long, slender, white, tubular tongues. They find it necessary to supplement their diet of nectar with sources of protein. This is supplied by minute spiders plucked from webs, tiny insects gleaned from foliage, bark, or among flowers, and small winged insects caught in the air. In this last activity hummingbirds display consummate mastery of minutely controlled flight. What keenness of vision, swiftness and accuracy of movement it must require to grasp an elusive winged mite that flits and darts erratically through the air, with no better instrument than a slender forceps about an eighth of an inch broad!

Many kinds of hummingbirds capture part of their food in this manner, but the flycatching of some is especially spectacular. None that I am familiar with catches insects with more brilliant technique, or more sustained effort, than the White-necked Jacobin, a hummingbird elegantly attired in green, blue, and white which dwells in the forested lowlands of Central America. An opening in the woods or a clear space above the rocky channel of some limpid, swiftly flowing stream, where swarms of tiny gnats or other insects hover in the still, warm air, is often the scene of its aerial maneuvers. Frequently I have paused beside some wild stream to watch with unbounded admiration as it twists and turns, darts and hovers, shoots back and forth with wondrous skill, weaving in the air the most intricate trajectory, as it snatches up its (to me) invisible prey.

Hummingbirds have a reputation for pugnacity, but I am not sure how well it is deserved. One need only watch for an hour, here in the tropics, before any bright-blossomed tree which proves attractive to them, to be convinced that they are endlessly darting at and pursuing each other. The individual who finds himself the target of another's swift onslaught almost invariably flees in time to avoid impact; pursuer and pursued go streaking off over the treetops at a speed that baffles the human eye. Rarely, the object of the attack stands his ground. Among the Inga trees in the coffee plantation where I met my first White-crested Coquette, a larger hummingbird suddenly darted at him while he perched on a high twig. The plucky little bird refused to budge, with the result that the assailant's green breast struck him squarely. The two hummingbirds bounced apart as lightly as two fluffs of cotton, apparently none the worse for the collision. In all the countless times that I have watched hummingbirds chase other hummingbirds, I have never seen one injure another seriously. They seldom clinch and pull feathers from each other, as other kinds of birds sometimes do. Indeed, the hummingbirds' long bills and small, weak feet make it difficult for them to engage in such rough combats. They may be the most sportive rather than the most pugnacious of feathered creatures. Although, like other birds, they frequently defend the sources of their food, their animated attacks and dashing pursuits may often be undertaken in a playful rather than an angry mood, as an outlet for exuberant vitality.

Certainly, in their courtship assemblies, hummingbirds give ample proof that they do not injure their neighbors, even while competing with them for the opposite sex. With one or two possible exceptions that require further study, the male of no species of hummingbird regularly helps to build the nest, incubate the eggs, or feed the young. As far as we know, only in a few unusual species, including the Bronzy and Rufous-breasted hermits, does he remain attached to the breeding female and guard her nest until the young fly. If not based upon faulty observation, the reports of male hummingbirds feeding young that we from time to time read refer to aberrant behavior in species of which the males nearly always take no part in rearing their progeny. Typically, the male hummingbird's role in reproduction is simply to make himself readily available to females whose eggs are ready to be fertilized.

The males of many kinds of hummingbirds advertise their presence and availability to the females by means of their voices. Usually a number of such males gather in some spot congenial to their habits—on a bushy mountainside, in a garden, in the treetops, or in the depths of a humid thicket—and form what we may designate as a singing assembly. In these assemblies, each participant has his own perch, or several of them within a small radius, where he is to be found hour after hour, day after day, week after week, sometimes through many months continuously, tirelessly repeating his little chant. While performing, he is within sight, or hearing, or both, of one or several of his rivals for the attention of the females. Although the members of an assembly from time to time chase each other, on the whole they refrain from interference with their neighbors, and rarely, if ever, do they attack each other with destructive fury. Indeed, the very existence of this system of courtship implies a high degree of respect for the rights of neighbors and the unwritten rules of the assembly, without which it would soon disintegrate.

The utterances by which male hummingbirds try to attract females are mostly simple and tuneless. They may do nothing more elaborate than reiterate a single squeaky note, in the manner of the Amethyst-throated Hummingbird that I heard among the cypress trees in Guatemala; or they may repeat short, simple phrases which, with few exceptions, are hardly melodious. These little songsters seem to try to compensate for their lack of tunefulness by persistence. Among the most tireless performers are the Green Violet-ears, who inhabit the Andes and high mountains of Central America and southern Mexico. Each adult male violet-ear chooses a perch that is usually high and exposed, preferably a dead twig, and repeats his squeaky little refrain from dawn to dusk. He interrupts his singing only long enough to draw nourishment from the bright flowers that grow below him, to snatch up an insect that now and then flies temptingly near his perch, to chase intruding rivals, and at intervals to preen his glittering plumage.

One Green Violet-ear, whom on a high mountain in Guatemala I watched for several months, had a peculiar catch in his voice that served to distinguish him from all his neighbors. Toward the end of the dry season, when the flowers from which he sucked nectar had succumbed to the drought, he and all his rivals withdrew from the mountainside where their singing assembly was situated, and for eight months I failed to find them there. But after the long wet season, when bright sunshine fell again on slopes that were still moist from months of rain and covered them anew with blossoming herbs and shrubs, the violet-ear returned, I know not whence, to the same spot on the mountainside, and resumed his singing with the same catch in his voice.

I have walked or ridden horseback for miles over the higher mountains of Guatemala and Costa Rica with the *squeak squeak squeaky squeak* of the Green Violet-ears almost constantly in my ears. It is a sound as characteristic of these lofty mountains, where the forest is not too heavy, as the chirruping of crickets is of summer fields in northern lands. Later, in the Andes of Ecuador, I found the squeaks of the violet-ears equally prevalent.

At least one hummingbird, among those that I have heard, has a song that I so designate without reservations. This is the Wine-throated Hummingbird of the highlands of Guatemala and Chiapas, a very small species whose scintillating magenta gorget has elongated lateral feathers that give it a shape suggestive of a swallow's tail. Once, upon a bushy mountain slope nine thousand feet above sea level, I found a singing assembly containing four of these gifted little songsters, each of whom had his own special perch, the exposed dead twig of a shrub, from which he always performed. His voice, although small like himself, avoided the disagreeable squeakiness of many small voices, and his song was so richly varied, so sweetly phrased, so long-continued and earnest, that he needed only to treble or quadruple his volume to earn for himself a place among the world's renowned songsters. Sometimes the pitch of the Wine-throated Hummingbird's voice rose above my range of audition, so that I could assure myself that he still sang only by watching the vibrations of his tiny throat, over whose polished surface the colors rippled from magenta through green to black, then back again to the flashing magenta of the full frontal view. I could only surmise what delightful melodies, audible to hummingbirds alone, he poured forth while he appeared to sing in silence.

Not all male hummingbirds are content to wait passively while they try to attract the females by voice alone. Some, more dynamic, take more active measures to win a mate, engaging in spectacular flight displays. Such dynamic courtship is the prevalent mode among the hummingbirds of temperate North America but rare in the forested regions of tropical America, where most of the species whose courtship habits are known favor the singing assembly. The only display on the grand scale that I have seen in the tropics is that of a species which ranges from the Rocky Mountains southward to the loftier elevations that rise above the high plateau of Guatemala—the Broad-tailed Hummingbird.

When flying, the adult male Broad-tailed Hummingbird attracts attention by the peculiar, high-pitched, imperious buzz, quite different from the low hum made by the wings of many hummingbirds, which he emits even as he goes about the commonplace activities of his day. His courtship rarely begins until the rising sun has dispelled the piercing chill that falls every night over the high altitudes where he lives, and it ends as soon as the westering luminary once more permits that swift chillness to descend. It is in the golden sunshine and genial warmth of the middle third of the day that he is most active in his wooing. How often, then, on a lofty mountainside where scattered trees stood above pungent herbs and shrubs bright with bloom, have I watched the dashing atom of a bird rise almost vertically up and up, through the thin mountain air, until he poised for a moment at the level of the treetops. Then, a thin, dark streak against the blue, he shot downward so swiftly and so straight that one who watched for the first time might suspect that he dropped with suicidal intent and would knock out his intense little life against the ground. But, just in time to save himself, he swerved, swung through a narrow arc whose lowest point was only a few feet above the ground, then soared swiftly upward again, tracing a high, narrow U in the air and always emitting his insistent buzz as he flew. At the summit, he reversed his course, and shot again through his orbit in the opposite direction; but this time, instead of turning so sharply upward after his abrupt drop, he might incline his course more gently, and fly off to a perch and needed rest. Whenever I could pick out her for whose approval these wild flights were undertaken, I noticed that she rested quietly and inconspicuously on some low twig, at the very perigee of her suitor's orbit, and hardly deigned to turn her head as he shot gallantly in front of her.

CHAPTER 4

Among Ecuadorian Forests

Magpie-Tanager

What naturalist familiar with the books of Wallace, Bates, and Spruce has not dreamed of visiting Amazonia, the heart of South America, where the earth's most extensive tropical rain forest is drained by the mightiest of all rivers, where vegetation is most exuberant and varied, where more species of birds, insects, or almost whatever kind of terrestrial life most interests one are to be found than anywhere else? After a decade in Central America,

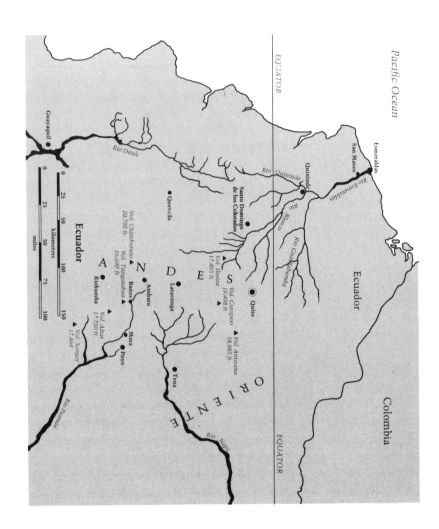

studying its birds and plants, I could resist the call of the Amazon basin no longer. From Costa Rica, where I was then stationed, the easiest way to reach it was by a coasting vessel from Puntarenas down the West Coast to Guayaquil. Thence a journey over the Andes, by rail and automobile, brought me to Baños, the "Gateway to the Oriente."

Although comparatively easy of access, the Oriente of Ecuador is in the wild heart and center of South America. To the west, it is walled off from the Pacific by the immense Andean rampart; on the east, two thousand miles of untamed forests separate it from the Atlantic; to the north are the vast llanos of Colombia and Venezuela, themselves shut off from the Caribbean Sea by a mountain barrier; to the south lie the equally wild forests of eastern Peru and Bolivia. The Napo, the Tigre, the Pastaza, the Morona, and the Santiago, which drain these extensive equatorial forests, are among the principal northern tributaries of the Amazon and its uppermost reach, the Marañón.

At the time of my visit, in 1939, the Oriente of Ecuador was perhaps best known to the outside world as the home of the headhunting Jívaro Indians. By a process peculiar to themselves, they dried and shrank the heads of defeated enemies to the size of an orange. Perhaps only a psychiatrist can explain why these ghastly objects proved so attractive to collectors of curios that they found their way into the homes of apparently civilized people at a great distance, and to supply the demand for them became a lucrative business. For me, the Jívaros were one of the reasons for not visiting eastern Ecuador. But on the other side of the balance was all the wonderful life of the Amazonian region, birds and other animals and plants that I had long wanted to see in their native setting—and this was the most accessible region where I could see them. Moreover, the experienced traveler is aware that, in many parts of the world, dangers which some of his less conscientious precursors have exaggerated to embellish their narratives shrink upon his arrival, in the same air and the same sunshine that he knew at home.

Baños is the "Gateway to the Oriente" in a quite literal sense. At this point the Río Pastaza, with waters collected from the peaks of Chimborazo, Cotopaxi, Iliniza, and many another Andean summit crowned with eternal snow, and laden with all the volcanic silt collected in the high inter-Andean valleys by its tributaries the Patate and the Chambo, has with millenial toil hewn a deep and narrow portal in the outer ramparts of the Andes. The old town of Baños lies on a fairly level terrace at the bottom of a profound and narrow valley, with rocky walls rising up for thousands of feet on either side. Above the barrier on the right one catches glimpses of the snowy volcanic peak of Tungurahua, nearly seventeen thousand feet high. On the opposite side of the town, the terrace ends abruptly at the edge of the chasm through which the brown, turbid current of the Pastaza foams and roars, between vertical cliffs of the most fantastically fractured black and gray rock, as it hurries impetuously toward the Atlantic Ocean, six thousand feet lower and nearly three thousand miles away.

Looking up toward the lofty plateau whence these waters come, one beholds only slopes and summits, crowding one behind the other, as barren and treeless as those that hem the narrow cultivated terrace. Turning one's face toward the rising sun, one gazes down a long valley whose sides are corrugated by the tremendous abutments of the Andean foothills—foothills that in many countries would be mountain ranges famous for their height and steepness. These interlocking spurs rise one behind the other like the headlands of a high and dangerous seacoast. Those in the foreground sweep up to barren grayness, but those in the distance are clothed with the deep green of the forest that clings tenaciously to their precipitous flanks. These are the uplifted fringes of a vast carpet of trees that formerly covered the land in almost unbroken continuity over immense areas almost as level as the carpet on a drawing-room floor, here crumpled into innumerable creases and folds over the eastern approaches of the Andes.

The hot springs that issue from the foot of one of the mighty spurs of Tungurahua draw many visitors to Baños, to take the baths that give the town its name. As a resort, it has a number of hotels and pensions, the best of which, at the time of my visit, was the Gran Hotel Termal. From this hostelry as a center, I made excursions up the slopes of the volcano and down the valley of the Pastaza as far as the Hacienda Río Negro. I could not at first go much farther in this direction, for I lacked the special passport re-

quired of all who entered the provinces of Napo-Pastaza and San-
tiago-Zamora, which together included all the trans-Andean forests of Ecuador.

This document was to be obtained only from the military authorities in Quito. All these eastern territories of the republic
were under military administration, partly because of the generally primitive character of the widely scattered population, even
more in consequence of the long-standing dispute with Peru,
which claimed nearly all of the forested territory at Ecuador's
back door, and succeeded in holding as much of it as could be patrolled by shallow-draft gunboats ascending the great waterways
of the region. On these rivers the Ecuadorians had no fighting vessels, for they could not be brought here without ascending the
Amazon through territory controlled by their rivals. Accordingly,
the government at Quito actually held dominion over only as
much of the eastern lowlands as could be reached from the Andean highlands about as easily as by way of the navigable rivers—
only a small part of the national territory as it appeared on maps
published in Quito and Guayaquil. This situation gave rise to occasional clashes between Peruvian and Ecuadorian troops garri-
soned at the border outposts, spilling a little blood and much ink
in the presses of the two sister republics.

A dozen miles or so below Baños the valley widened slightly.
From the roadway, as it twisted around a sharp spur, high above
the muddy, turbulent river, one enjoyed a vast prospect eastward,
over the lower foothill country. Flowing wavelike over hill beyond rounded hill, the dark green forest purpled into misty distances. The river, rushing through its narrow chasm far below,
glinting here and there in the morning sunshine, broadened and
flowed more placidly as it passed between the lower hills, to vanish at last amid the welter of wooded ridges. What a scene to stir
an adventurous spirit, and sharpen its thirst to explore the vast
unknown!

Into the Oriente

After nearly a month of travel in northern and western Ecuador, I
returned to Baños early in August, 1939, bearing the passport

necessary for travel in the Oriente, but with no definite plan for my visit to this wild region that had no hotels or public conveyances. Naturalists who collected in this territory often traveled with their own caravans; but I had neither the means nor the equipment to outfit an expedition. I had only the hope that some less costly way of going there would turn up. Fortunately, it did, sooner than I expected.

One evening, a few days after my return to Baños, the manager of the Gran Hotel called me to his desk. He had just received a letter from Puyo, a military post on the river of the same name, near the western edge of the Oriente. Here a young German couple named Jansen had settled; they had a big house and wished to receive paying guests to augment the meager income from their newly started farm. The letter went on to specify some of the primitive features of the place, lest a guest arrive with a false notion of the accommodation he would find. There was no plumbing and no bathroom, save the river that flowed in front of the house; no butter and rarely fresh vegetables; no electricity; beds without springs; and so forth. I liked the frankness of this letter with its catalog of limitations, which did not dismay me. I had already lived for years under conditions similar to those described, and I decided to set forth without delay for Puyo.

Arranging for the journey was not easy, but finally I found a citizen of Baños who, for thirty sucres, undertook to transport me and my impedimenta down the valley to Puyo. He needed another day to have his animals shod and prepare provisions for the trip, but solemnly promised to call for me at six o'clock on the morning of August 8. A month of travel in Ecuador had already taught me that early starts were not in high favor, and departures at the specified hour in exceedingly bad form, only the railroad, with its foreign traditions, making an earnest attempt to follow a fixed schedule. Hence I was most agreeably surprised when my muleteer arrived at the hotel before I had finished my early breakfast. He roped the light baggage on the packsaddle while I struggled with a cup of hot chocolate. In a somewhat unusual arrangement, the horse bore the luggage, while I rode upon the little mule. The *arriero*, a small, active man, traveled upon his bare feet.

The highway from Ambato in the high Andes to Canelos in the

Oriente was at that time passable by automobile as far as Machay, ten or twelve miles down the valley from Baños. Construction was proceeding actively over the next six or eight miles, or as far as the Río Lopo. Beyond this there was a good mule trail, with light suspension bridges over the larger rivers, to Mera, a full day's journey by pack animal from Baños.

It was good to be riding through the cool morning air, to hear the shod hoofs strike ringingly against the hard roadway, and to feel that at last I was drawing nearer to those great forests which I so greatly desired to explore. Our route that first day lay entirely through the deep valley—or perhaps, more properly, gorge—of the Río Pastaza, and the scenery was magnificent from beginning to end. The turbid river, which already at Baños had considerable volume, rushed and tumbled down its rocky bed over countless rapids and low cascades, with here and there a vertical drop of impressive height. Its numerous tributaries, racing through deep and narrow valleys or plunging abruptly down wooded mountainsides, contributed many a white column of falling water to enhance the wild splendor of the scene.

Beyond the Río Ulva, the road crossed the Pastaza by a high, narrow bridge to its left side, along which we continued all the way to Mera. Now for considerable stretches the road was a narrow shelf cut into the precipitous rocky wall high above the river. In many places, the stony precipice actually overhung the highway, so deeply had the shelf been carved into its flank. Water flowing down the almost vertical face sprayed the middle of the road. To avoid a drenching, the wayfarer took the inner side, against the fractured wall of rock, where he was sheltered by the projecting roof. On the right, the mountainside fell away, by dizzy slopes hundreds of feet high, to the impetuous torrent far below. Here and there a landslide had scraped all soil and vegetation from the abruptly inclined rock strata; a traveler, stepping carelessly from the edge of the narrow road, would hurtle down the naked face of the cliff into the river below, without the slightest possibility of saving himself. This highway, with its sharp curves at the verge of an abysm from which no parapet shielded the careless, seemed a perilous road to travel; yet, compared to some of the automobile roads I saw later in the Peruvian Andes, it was as tame and unexciting as a country lane.

Across the gorge of the Pastaza, the wooded slopes swept steeply up into the clouds that seemed always to veil the lofty summits. Small tributary streams descended swiftly through the narrow, trenchlike ravines that furrowed these slopes, then flowed gently through little hanging valleys, to plunge at length in vertical columns of falling water into the river below. These little triangular areas of comparatively level land, at the end of the course of each mountain stream, seemed to represent an earlier level of the bed of the Pastaza, from which they are now separated by an upright wall of rock of imposing height. Each of these tiny hanging valleys was the site of one or more rustic dwellings, surrounded by areas of cultivation that reached far up the abrupt enclosing slopes. The agricultural population, forced outward from the crowded highlands, preferred to stop here and wrest a precarious livelihood from tiny farms, rather than venture another day's journey down into the forests, where vast areas of unoccupied land were available. One wondered how they managed to enter and leave their homesteads, tucked so securely away in this mountain fastness, with a vertical cliff in front, a towering peak behind, and precipitous slopes on either side. Some seemed to make their way by narrow paths that ran along the slopes above the river gorge, while others passed over the chasm itself, pulling themselves along in little boxes suspended beneath a cable that stretched from brink to brink. Doubtless they did not often venture into the outer world!

At noon we paused at the Hacienda San Francisco for a hasty lunch, then at once resumed our journey. The Pastaza now became broader and less precipitous in its descent of the eastern face of the Andes. Its valley was also somewhat wider, allowing the highway, here still unfinished, to run farther back from the channel, traversing in places broad, level terraces, over which the work of construction was less difficult and costly. But ever and again a projecting spur of the enclosing mountain wall would make it necessary to cut a shelf for the road. At one of these points we met a motley band, men, women, and half-grown boys, mostly Indians, toiling with shovel and pick to carve the highway from the stubborn mountainside. As the traveler approached, they needed no urging to interrupt the shower of loose earth, rubble, and large boulders that they sent rattling down toward the river, that he might pass in safety. How severe must life in the high Andes have been, when women came to these dripping outer slopes and engaged in tasks like this!

The mountain slopes that rose steeply up on either side of the river were clothed with broad-leafed forest of moderate height. Tall, slender feather palms, exceedingly abundant over all these slopes, held their graceful crowns well above all the other trees, as though to shade and protect them. In no other mountain forest have I seen palms more numerous, or taller and more graceful. The branching trees, and frequently also the unbranched trunks of the palms, were burdened with mosses and a great variety of flowering epiphytes. One of the interesting plants of this valley, from the Hacienda San Francisco at least as far down as Puyo, was a giant begonia with slender, branchless, canelike stems sometimes fifteen feet high, huge coarse leaves, and small white flowers in great panicles a yard broad—the tallest but by no means the most attractive begonia that I have seen. The following year, I found the same vigorous begonia in wet forests near Santo Domingo de los Colorados, on the opposite side of the Andes.

The chief product of this rainy valley was the Naranjillo de Quito, an orange-colored fruit about two inches in diameter, produced by a big-leafed, thorny shrub related to the potato plant. Its slightly acid juice is the base of a deliciously cooling unfermented beverage, highly esteemed in Ecuador and worthy of wider fame. On the return journey, we saw many sacks of these fruits being taken up the valley on horses and mules, to be picked up by the automobile truck at Machay and hauled to the weekly market at Baños.

After ten hours of travel, we arrived at sunset at the unattractive little village of Mera, situated near the edge of a broad shelf of level land which here falls off in a high, abrupt cliff. From the edge of the precipice we looked over the Pastaza, now a wide, shallow stream flowing diffusely, far below, over a shingly bed. The Hotel Pastaza, situated at the entrance to the village, was far from luxurious; but its crude accommodations were welcome in so wild a district, after a hard day's journey. I was surprised to see an automobile in Mera and wondered how it had arrived over the narrow trail, with numerous bridges only half its own width. It had been transported in parts and reassembled on the spot, for service in highway construction. On the trail that day we had passed a squad of Indians toiling along with the machinery of a sugar mill, each ponderous iron part lashed to a stout pole and borne over the rough path on stalwart shoulders.

The fine weather that had favored us on the first day now forsook us, and we set forth from Mera in the early morning beneath a slow rain. As we passed through the weedy open square in the center of the village, a policeman inspected my military passport for travel in the Oriente. The muleteer doubted whether in this rainy weather we would be able to ford the small river not far beyond the village; but, more fortunate than many a traveler, we were able to ride through the swift current and suffered no delay.

The character of the country we now traversed was abruptly different from that of the preceding day. At Mera we had emerged from the high, steep, outlying ridges of the Andes and entered an extensive region of low hills and gentle, even-topped ridges—a rolling foothill country still 3,500 feet above sea level. The trail, which had once been well constructed of stones and gravel, with long stretches of corduroy over the swampier ground, had been allowed to fall into a miserable state of disrepair, with deep mud holes and broken corduroy, which of all road surfaces is the most perilous for the legs of horses. Half-rotten bridges with gaping holes spanned numerous small watercourses. The nearer we drew to Puyo, the worse the trail became. A narrow belt of land along the roadway had been cleared for cultivation; but on our left the forest rose up a few hundred yards away, while to the right we here and there caught glimpses of the Pastaza, sprawling over a wide bed at the foot of a precipice hundreds of feet high. In the middle of the morning we veered away from the river and saw it no more.

The attempts at agriculture along the trail were unpromising. The pastures had the appearance of swamps, with sedges seeming to predominate over grasses. Sugar cane was the chief, almost the only, crop; but the leaves were narrow and rolled, and the stand uneven. A number of the little wooden dwellings displayed signs announcing that the property was for sale. Evidently the proprietors had learned that farming in such a rain-drenched region was a losing struggle. Even the land at the very edge of the high precipice above the Pastaza appeared poorly drained; but what ground can dry with so little sunshine and so much rain? The average annual rainfall at Mera was 187 inches.

Halfway between Mera and Puyo, we passed the landing field of an aviation company, then engaged in making an aerial survey of parts of the Oriente, as the first step in a search for petroleum. At the edge of the field a large and substantial dwelling—the most commodious that we saw in all this region—had been built as the temporary residence of the aviators and their families. It appeared that they would lack none of the comforts to which they were accustomed in the United States. Through an open door, I even glimpsed a big porcelain refrigerator, undoubtedly brought here by air. Thus North Americans carry their mechanical contrivances with them wherever they go, as migrating Atta ants bear the spores of the fungi that they raise on their gardens of finely divided leaves. I cannot decide whether northerners succeed in spreading "good will" and a sense of fraternity among their neighbors to the south, or whether the disparity between their wealth and mode of living and those of the people among whom they come creates a feeling of aloofness and distance, if not actual envy.

As we struggled over the broken corduroy and ruinous bridges, the sky gradually cleared, until at noon we rode into Puyo under a bright sun. It was an uninviting village, composed of a handful of thatched dwellings and a big, barracklike, unfinished wooden church, fronting the square of bare ground intended to be the plaza. A sinking feeling came over me as I arrived, tired and hungry. But we soon learned that the Jansens lived across the river. Since horses could not reach their dwelling, I paid my muleteer, left my baggage in a shop, found a boy who knew the way, and continued afoot. We crossed the swiftly flowing Puyo River by a suspension bridge, walked over a path of logs through a swamp whence even at midday arose a chorus of frogs, and climbed a low hill through a small coffee plantation. From the crest of this my young guide pointed out the dwelling, at the top of the opposite elevation, which after crossing a rivulet I ascended by a long flight of log steps.

Among German Refugees

My arrival, necessarily unannounced, took Frau Jansen by surprise. But she was equal to the occasion, and soon had me seated before an appetizing meal, while she put in order the room I was to occupy. The house was unlike any that I had seen north of Ecuador, but it was admirably adapted to local conditions. The floor was raised high above the ground on palm trunks; and the great, wide, high-peaked roof, thatched with fronds of the chonta palm, was supported above it by a second set of longer palm trunks. I was told that if the huge palm fronds are set with their massive midribs close together, such a thatch will last for eight or ten years, even in a climate as wet as this. The main floor was divided into six compartments, three on a side with a narrow hall between them. The handsawn wall boards were not nailed in place, but set loosely in upright slots or grooves, between parallel cleats, so that as they dried and shrank in seasoning they would sink down under their own weight and remain in contact, leaving no gaps.

But what appeared to me most curious in the Jansen house was the glass windows. The combination of window glass and palm thatch was novel to me, although not rare in the Oriente of Ecuador. My chamber at a corner of the house was more comfortable than I expected. Never before had I slept in a room with a *curtained* window that gave view of so much wild forest, so close at hand. Indeed, there were double curtains, red and white, and a scarf on the table, and a rug on the floor—delicate feminine touches that my own abodes in forested regions had always lacked.

Frau Hilda Jansen, my charming hostess, was small and blonde; Herr Ludwig, her husband, tall and dark. He spoke little Spanish and no English; and, as my vanishing German had always been of the textbook variety, our conversation was perforce limited and formal. But Frau Jansen's Spanish was fluent, and from her I learned the strange story of this young couple. Theirs was a true romance, of the sort that in these prosaic times one rarely meets outside story books; a romance which tyranny and bigotry had tried to blight, yet succeeded only in demonstrating its earnestness and depth. She had been employed in a department store in

Berlin; he was an artist from the Rhineland. They fell in love and wished to marry, but learned to their dismay that the Nazi government frowned upon the union of the blond "Aryan" girl and the dark man with Mediterranean blood—it offended Hitler's notions of "racial purity." They decided to emigrate and marry abroad; but the Nazi government, which prohibited their marriage in their native land, also made it difficult for them to depart. Moreover, it would not permit them to take their small savings in marks from the country. They could finance their intended emigration to Ecuador only by arranging an exchange of moneys with a Dutchman who needed marks to do business in Germany, delivering their German currency to him in that country and receiving an equivalent in pounds sterling in Holland. Then twice, after they had paid for their steamship passage by a Dutch line, the Nazi government forbade them to leave Germany, and they forfeited the price of their reservations. Finally, on their third attempt, they were successful in crossing the German frontier.

Arriving in Ecuador, the young couple lived first in the highlands, where Herr Jansen made many paintings, especially portraits of Indians. Then they came down to Puyo, where already a few of their expatriate countrymen had settled, and bought the land on which I found them established. A neighbor provided lodgings for them while their own house was being built. Evidently they passed through a trying period and suffered much from the deficient diet, for they told me that they lost energy and became fatigued by slight exertion, and a blackness would come over their vision when they arose from working in a stooping posture. Even at the time of my visit, two years later, most of their food came down from the highlands by truck and then by muleback over the long trail. Cereals in various forms made up the bulk of it, and potatoes were brought in large quantities. Fruits were almost completely lacking; occasionally we had a pineapple; and once in a great while a few oranges found their way down from the interior—a great and unexpected luxury. Green vegetables there were none, save the leaves of the Pokeweed, which springs up in new clearings and may be used as a substitute for spinach, and of the *col de monte*, a small tree of the papaya family that grew in the forest.

In 1939, Ecuador was full of refugees from Central Europe. Few other countries in the Western Hemisphere had admitted them so freely. From Guayaquil to Quito the hotels, the restaurants, the railway coaches were full of foreigners; German was heard on every side. Under the conditions of their admittance, these immigrants could not engage in business or the professions (although some did so clandestinely) but were obligated to devote themselves to agriculture. Most of them were obviously not farmers, and it was distressing to see so much humanity uprooted and aimlessly drifting.

A few of these Europeans ventured into the outlying regions and settled on the land, some of them in the Oriente. About half a mile farther up the river, two other families of German émigrés lived in a big thatched dwelling, with walls and floor of split bamboo, which yielded in a manner somewhat alarming to one who had no previous experience in walking over such floors, for the ground was far below. These were also people of considerable culture; one of the men had been a lawyer in Königsberg and spoke good English; their children had charming manners. It was strange to find them dwelling here in these primitive surroundings, where a horse could not even arrive for lack of adequate bridges over the brooks with steep banks that intersected the narrow woodland trail. Although the Río Puyo washed the foot of the bluff upon which the dwelling stood, it was so shallow and swift as to be scarcely navigable even by small canoes.

I was interested to learn how these new settlers would fare in this setting so strange to them. The Jansens had planted several acres of cacao, although the altitude of Puyo, about three thousand feet, is greater than that at which this crop is usually produced. In this cloudy land, the shade trees provided for cacao elsewhere appeared to be unnecessary; yet occasionally the sun shone so brightly that it burnt the tender leaves. Although the altitude was that generally considered more appropriate for coffee than for cacao, the former was said not to do well; the bushes grew large but yielded little, probably because the climate was too continuously wet for abundant flowering. In August and September, even steep hillside pastures were swampy.

One evening I heard the lawyer from Königsberg dickering with a laborer who asked an exorbitant price for planting bananas. "You are rich," said the brown man; "it will not hurt you to pay me that." I have often wondered how long these people continued to be rich, even in the estimation of the nearly penniless laborers whom they employed, and whether they were in the end able to make their farms yield a meager living, learning by trial and error what would grow in this wet region. Or perhaps, after the American republics entered the war, they were all thrown into concentration camps, and their agricultural perplexities came temporarily to an end.

Aside from these recent immigrants from Europe and a few white officers at the neighboring military post, the sparse population of the region consisted almost wholly of mestizos who had lately come down from the highlands. The aborigines had already retreated deeper into the forests. I saw at close range only one Jívaro, under somewhat curious circumstances. Living with the Jansens was a young Dutchman whom they had known in Europe. At the time of my sojourn there, the director of the German school in Quito came to spend his vacation at Puyo; and these two, together with another German, arranged a voyage down the Río Puyo by canoe. Two days after their departure, the Jívaro boy arrived. He was small, black as a Negro, with the darkest, most penetrating eyes I ever saw. He had come with a letter from the departed voyagers. Their canoe had capsized in rapids, with the loss of much of their equipment and provisions. They had sent the young Indian to bring them matches, a cooking pot, rice, and a few other necessities. A week later the three men returned, each with his head of normal size upon his own shoulders. They had received hospitality in a Jívaro dwelling and from all accounts had been well treated.

Snowy Peaks and Dripping Forests

The clouds which hovered about the eastern approaches of the Andes did not often permit a view of the magnificent snow peaks that rose up to the west of us. But in mid-September we enjoyed two consecutive bright days without rain—a truly remarkable occurrence in this region of gloomy weather. Encouraged by the starry night, I went out before dawn to visit a Long-tailed Flycatcher nesting on a distant hillside, and at daybreak enjoyed the best view of the Andes I ever had from this side. As the sky slowly brightened, the huge, snowy bulk of El Altar stood revealed in the west. It was a broad, massive mountain, miles long at the topmost ridge, above which rose a number of sharp pinnacles, all covered with snow. On the gentle eastern slopes were vast snowfields; but on the northwestern side I saw grim, jagged masses of exposed black rock. While all the nearer, lower peaks and all the intervening miles of forested foothill country still lay in the shadow of the earth's convexity, the broad snow fields of El Altar gleamed whitely in the sun's earliest rays. Above them the slender, jagged pinnacles were joined together by long, tenuous wefts of clinging white mist, stretching from point to point like gossamer strands spun between the dewy blades of meadow grass.

Forty miles away, to the south-southwest, rose the great volcanic cone of Sangay, only partly veiled by clouds, its plume of smoke, as always, drifting westward. The eastern profile of the volcano was a long, straight, unbroken line, sweeping up from the tropical forests that covered its foot to the snowy Arctic wastes of the summit—an epitome of all the earth's climates. The huge gap that broke the symmetry of the cone on the northwestern side lay in black shadow, while the mile-long snowclad slopes on the orient face shone with unstained whiteness. Sometimes, on the rare occasions when the summit was visible, a huge puff of dense smoke, suddenly appearing, grew slowly upward until it formed a towering, somber column, rising high above the volcanic crest until it tilted, then drifted away to the west. And on clear nights we sometimes saw glowing masses of lava near the summit, more rarely long red streaks coursing down the northwestern flank, where there was little snow.

Stretching between El Altar and Sangay, but more in the foreground, the long, irregularly serrated summit of a lofty range was darkly silhouetted against the sky, while all the mountainside stood up blackly like a vast, featureless wall. As the sun rose higher, its rays threw into bold relief the deeply sculptured eastern face of this range: long, sharp ridges leading up to the craggy crest; profound ravines between them; the lower, rounded summits in the foreground casting black shadows upon the flanks of the higher mountains beyond; here and there the long, vertical white streak of a cascade. The growing daylight revealed also the colors of the range: the yellowish-brown of the páramo covering the thin soil that clung around the rocky summits; the somber green of the forests mantling the lower slopes.

In the foreground, almost at my feet, the plumy crowns of tall, slender palm trees stood up above the gray mist that filled the valley, seeming to float upon the fog, while through a gap in the vapors gleamed a quiet reach of the Río Puyo. But the vast, glorious panorama did not long remain revealed; soon rising mists veiled the distant snowy peaks, which were rarely for long exposed to our view.

Then, from this inspiring spectacle of great snow peaks at dawn, I turned to another, on a far smaller scale, which delighted me no less. A Coppery-chested Jacamar—a dainty, slender, long-tailed bird, with resplendent metallic-green upper plumage and rich chestnut under parts—emerged from a tangled thicket down the hillside, bearing a large moth in his long, sharp bill. Coming to rest upon a low branch, he struck his prey many times against it, then passed the insect to a fledgling who had been waiting expectantly on a vine at the edge of the thicket. The young jacamar with difficulty gulped down the great meal, then delayed long in the same spot, digesting it, until at length its parents called it back into the tangle of vegetation.

The forest that began a hundred yards from the house stretched on and on for distances too great to be pictured by the human mind. A monkey able to swim the many wide rivers as well as he could swing through the treetops might have begun at this point and extended his arboreal journeys to Colombia, Peru, and Brazil, without ever being obliged to walk over the ground. Most of the land about Puyo was covered with forest, through which the paths were infrequent and often poorly defined. While watching birds or collecting plants, I had to be careful not to stray too far from the trails without blazing one of my own, for the topography was irregular, and by going a hundred feet out of the way, even in the right direction, it was easy for one not thoroughly familiar with the lay of the land to become hopelessly confused. Once I was on the verge of losing myself and wandering to Peru instead of back to Puyo. It was no pleasant experience.

Most of the forest in the district appeared to be primeval. Certainly, if it had formerly been shorn away for cultivation by Indi-

53036

an tribes now vanished from the region, it had enjoyed tranquil centuries through which to re-establish itself. Yet it was not a particularly heavy forest. The trees, although tall, were nearly all slender. Giants of imposing size were rare, and even those of the second order of magnitude were thinly scattered. Full, wide-spreading crowns were exceptional. Certainly it was not lack of moisture that prevented the development of a more impressive stand of timber. Perhaps the very superabundance of rain kept the forest trees from attaining truly grand dimensions. Tropical forest cannot reach its full development without a liberal precipitation —eighty to one hundred inches per year is the probable minimum —yet excessive rainfall may be detrimental. The superfluous water leaches soluble salts from the soil, especially on sloping ground; and the longer the rains continue, the less sunshine there will be. Trees, no less than crops planted by man, require sunlight and a fertile soil, as well as sufficient moisture, to reach perfection.

Stately palms were abundant in these forests about Puyo. The predominant kind had crowns of great pinnate fronds at the summit of tall, slender trunks propped up by spiny roots that descended obliquely from points two or three yards above the ground. They held their heads proudly aloft, yielding nothing in height to the taller of their dicotyledonous neighbors, and in many areas they almost dominated the forest, as they do in the lowland and foothill forests on the opposite side of the Andes, in northwestern Ecuador. On the soils best suited for general agriculture, palm trees usually play a subordinate role in the forest, becoming abundant only in swampy hollows and on dry, sterile ridges, for they are ill adapted to compete for a place in the sun with wide-branching trees when these are growing in the most favorable conditions. Hence the fertility of a humid region may be in inverse ratio to the number of beautiful palm trees it supports. In was interesting to find that the local people called these palms with spiny prop roots *chontas*, a name applied to species of similar appearance at least as far north as Nicaragua.

For the rest, I was singularly unsuccessful in learning the names of the forest trees and other plants. The Spanish-speaking inhabitants, recent arrivals from the highlands, had hardly any names for them; while the Indians, who doubtless had a designation for each tree, shrub, and herb, had vanished from the region. It was typical of the inadequacy of the vocabulary of the actual inhabitants, in relation to the environment in which they now found themselves, that they lacked even terms to distinguish the second-growth thickets from the heavy forest, calling both indifferently *monte*—a word which I have elsewhere heard applied to the former alone. Since in August and September few trees were in flower, they were not in the proper stage for botanical determination.

But the forests about Puyo, if not developed upon the grandest scale, were beautified by a wealth of flowering epiphytes, as well as by the profusion of stately palms. The aerial vegetation which flourished upon the trunks and upper branches of the larger trees was here developed to a degree that one rarely finds at so low an altitude, save on ridges exposed to moist sea breezes—and here the sea whence the breezes blew was more than two thousand miles distant. Indeed, I have hardly ever, even in regions far more elevated, seen trees more heavily burdened with mosses, lichens, and ferns, with foliage, flowers, and fruits not their own. The heath family, the melastome family, the orchid, pineapple, and arum families were all well represented in these treetop gardens. The gesneria family was exceptionally prolific here; one of the unexpected features of the local vegetation was the profuse growth upon the ground of shrubs and herbs belonging to this family, including types which in other regions I have rarely seen except on trees. Sometimes these shrubby members of the gesneria family formed rather close stands in the shade of the forest, and with their big, bright blossoms, red and yellow, or white and purple, and their often gaily colored bracts as well, were delightful to behold.

Growing with these low plants beneath the forest were ground ferns, dwarf palms, and a variety of flowering shrubs. Among the most interesting of these were *Miconia barbicaulis* and related species of the melastome family, low shrubs whose strongly veined leaves bore a pair of hollow lobes at the base of each blade, where it joined the leafstalk. Each hollow lobe was provided with a tiny orifice, opening upon the lower surface of the leaf; and nearly all of these cozy green chambers were inhabited by colonies of small, inoffensive brown ants. Another noteworthy shrub of the region, at home in swampy openings rather than in the forest, was the sanchezia, a member of the acanthus family whose yellow blossoms are displayed in compact heads surrounded by red bracts. It is often planted as an ornamental in tropical regions.

Birds of Andean Foothills

The birds that dwelt in these mossy forests and the clearings among them were noteworthy for their diversity and beauty rather than for their size and abundance as individuals. Above all, the tanagers were present in amazing variety. They almost bewildered the newcomer with their numerous species, as they captivated him by their gorgeous colors. The biggest of the local tanagers was the most unexpected of all, a veritable giant among tanagers, approaching a large thrush in size, long-tailed, clad in black and white in much the pattern of a magpie—a magpie in miniature, aptly named the Magpie-Tanager. These golden-eyed birds roamed through the bushy clearings in active pairs or small flocks; unhappily, like most other birds, they neither sang nor nested at the time of my visit.

Next in size came the Silver-beaked Tanager. The male is beautiful in a unique fashion, quite distinct from any other bird I know. Glancing at him hastily, especially in a dull light, one would say his plumage is wholly velvety black. More attentive examination reveals that his whole head, neck, shoulders, and breast are a deep, rich, subdued purplish red. In sunshine, this color is seen to extend over much of his belly. The bird's upper mandible is black, but his swollen lower mandible is silvery white, contrasting strongly with his dark plumage. Although the female Silver-beak differs much from the male, she is also beautiful, with rich chestnut-brown rump and under plumage and brownish olive head and back. These tanagers were abundant, flocking through clearings and thickets, but very shy. Both this species and the Magpie-Tanager are widespread in western Amazonia; later, I met them repeatedly in eastern Peru.

Here I also found the wide-ranging Palm Tanager and the Blue Tanager, distinguished by its white wing-patches from races of the Blue Tanager so abundant and familiar west and north of the

Andes. A little euphonia wore the colors typical of his kind, with blue-black upper plumage and throat, bright yellow forehead, breast, and belly. But most abundant of all were the small, gem-like, multicolored tanagers, of which I found six species at Puyo, each, when it first flew into my ken, seeming lovelier than the last. Yet the most gorgeous and brilliant of all was certainly the Paradise Tanager, often called *siete colores* ("seven colors"), although only six are obvious on the bird in the tree: black on the back, hindhead, tail, abdomen, and much of the wings; bright red on the rump; golden-green on the head; purple on the wing plumes; light purple on the chin and throat; turquoise blue on the breast, sides, and flanks. These enameled beauties foraged among the trees in flocks of from four to eight individuals, among which it was impossible to distinguish the males from the females. Often they went in company with other small and brilliant tanagers.

Most abundant of the smaller members of the family was the Blue-necked Tanager, which might with equal accuracy be called the Blue-headed Tanager. The remainder of its plumage was predominantly black, with the rump greenish-yellow, and patches of deep blue and purple on the flanks. These little birds usually traveled through the treetops in pairs, of which the sexes were alike. The equally beautiful Green-and-Gold and Golden tanagers had backs streaked with black. All these brilliant tanagers seemed to find much of their nourishment among the moss that covered the branches of trees. Clinging to the side of the bough, they would hang head downward to examine the lower surface. At this season they sang rarely or not at all; and their voices, so far as I heard them, were disappointing.

The family of birds represented by the greatest number of species was the flycatchers, of which I found fourteen kinds in the vicinity. Many were old friends that I had long known farther north. Of all the birds of tropical America, excepting only the vultures, the Tropical Kingbird is probably the most widespread and conspicuous; it is the small bird that the traveler notices in more localities than any other, and it was not lacking here. Gray-capped and Vermilion-crowned flycatchers darted up for insects in the clearings. Little Black-fronted Tody-Flycatchers trilled softly from the edges of thickets. Tiny Torrent Flycatchers, tutelary spirits of clear rushing waterways, flitted from boulder to boulder

Paradise Tanager

along the river, snatching minute insects from the air, or daringly plucking them from rock surfaces momentarily left uncovered by receding surges. I found one of their nests, a neat mossy cup attached near the end of a long streamer of moss that dangled from a branch overhanging the channel. With a mirror attached to a long pole, I glimpsed the two whitish eggs that swung well beyond reach, thirteen feet above the water.

In a hillside clearing, I found a pair of Long-tailed Flycatchers, black and whitish in plumage, with two long, slender tail feathers that fluttered gracefully when they darted out for insects. They were nesting in an old woodpecker's hole in a dead palm tree, too high to be reached. Of all the birds, the little Olive-chested Flycatchers of the thickets appeared to be breeding most freely. Their nests were mossy cups attached by their rims to horizontal forks, vireo fashion. I discovered five of them, one empty and each of the others with two eggs or nestlings. At dawn, these flycatchers sang more than other birds at this season, repeating tirelessly a monosyllable that was low and soft but full and far-carrying and sounded something like *chite* (rhymes with *white*). One of these flycatchers repeated his monotonous note at the rate of sixty times a minute and continued the performance for about twenty minutes. During the remainder of the day, these small flycatchers uttered slow, clear trills and low, soft whistles with grave and deliberate accent, but almost never the note peculiar to their dawn song.

From time to time, a flock of oropéndolas would trail through the clearings; but these big relations of the orioles were always shy and difficult to approach. *Cucupachos*, they were called here. There were two kinds, the Green and the Crested oropéndolas. The plumage of the former was prevailingly an olive color difficult to describe, becoming a peculiar, oily yellowish-olive-green on the head and neck. The rump was chestnut, like the under tail coverts, and the outer tail feathers bright yellow, in typical oropéndola fashion. The long, slender feathers of the crown, usually held flat, were easily seen when the big male bird bent far forward to deliver his liquid call. The Crested Oropéndola was black, with deep chestnut at the base of the tail both above and below, and on the flanks; it had the usual yellow outer tail feathers, conspicuous as the birds flocked overhead. The male had a pale yellow bill,

blue eyes, and a clear, liquid call. With the oropéndolas sometimes flocked Yellow-rumped Caciques, smaller birds clad in
black and gold, the males with clear blue eyes. At Puyo I found no
nests of any of these hang-nests; but higher up the Pastaza Valley,
in October, I watched two female Green Oropéndolas weaving
their long pouches at the ends of the fronds of a small spiny palm
tree, while a third nest, nearly completed, swung from a neigh
boring palm.

In the tops of forest trees lived the Tropical Parula Warbler, the
shining blue Spangled Cotinga, the black-and-white Masked Tityra, the brilliant Red-headed Barbet, several kinds of woodpeckers, and the big Yellow-ridged Toucan, locally called the *predica-
dor* ("preacher"). Its plumage was mostly black, with a white
chest, bright yellow upper tail coverts, and red beneath the tail.
Its huge beak, less colorful than that of many toucans, was largely black, with pale yellow at the base of the upper mandible and
bright blue at the base of the lower. The naked skin around its
eyes was also blue. Woodcreepers of several kinds hunted over the
trunks of the forest trees. The most abundant of these was the
smallest, the Wedge-billed Woodcreeper, which much of the time
kept up a rapid pecking movement of its short bill, apparently
plucking from the bark objects too small to be seen from the
ground. One of these diminutive brown birds retired in the evening to sleep alone in a hole at the top of a soft Burío stub in a
clearing. Lower in the same stub was a nest of the Golden-fronted
Piculet, smallest of the woodpeckers. Two female piculets and a
male slept each night in the neatly carved chamber with two tiny
white eggs.

Three kinds of hummingbirds were fairly abundant in the lower regions of the forest, where there was no lack of bright flowers
to point the way to nectar. The largest was the Green Hermit,
with a long, curved bill and long, white-tipped tail. The smallest
was the brownish Little Hermit. The brightest of these hummingbirds was the Fork-tailed Woodnymph, resplendent in scintillating green and purple. Of the manakins, the most abundant was
the White-crowned, whose pure white cap contrasted boldly with
his uniformly blue-black dress.

At the very bottom of the forest were two birds which, paradoxically, speedily attracted attention despite reticent habits.

One appealed most to the eye, the other to the ear. The first was the Orange-billed Sparrow, whose bright bill and bold black-and-white markings flouted the "law" that birds of the forest undergrowth must be soberly attired to escape detection by their enemies. These finches went in pairs, uttering a little tinkling song. The other was the Lowland or White-breasted Wood-Wren, a diminutive bird that also displayed much black and white in its plumage, which on the upper parts was a deep, rich brown. These short-tailed wrens lurked so well concealed amid the ground cover and litter of fallen branches that they were difficult to see despite their rather striking coloration; but their exquisite songs, clear and forceful all out of proportion to the size of the instrument that produced them, commanded instant attention. One version consisted of a prelude of trilled notes, leading up to three loud, ringing whistles. Although the wood-wrens went about in pairs during the day, at night male and female retired into separate dormitories. I found one of these little lodges, situated a yard above the ground, in the vertical fork of a small sapling. It was roughly globular, with a round entrance in the side, its walls composed of dark, fibrous roots, moss, and a few skeletons of leaves. At nightfall, I watched a single wood-wren go to rest in it.

Birds seemed rare in the undergrowth of the forest until I chanced to meet a foraging swarm of army ants, with their attendant feathered camp-followers, ever alert to seize the cockroaches, spiders, small frogs, and other diminutive creatures which, until the approach of the ravaging horde, had lurked in quiet concealment among the ground litter or in crevices of the bark. Driven into the open by the ants, these creatures fell an easy prey to the birds. Numerous kinds found a comfortable living in this manner, relieved of the necessity of patiently hunting out for themselves the well-hidden creatures upon which they subsist. At the advancing head of the deployed battalion of ants, one found movement, sound, and a general sense of eager activity that contrasted sharply with the prevailing stillness of the understory of the forest.

It was at one of these gatherings that I made the acquaintance of a remarkable little antbird, with a frontal crest of stiff, elongate white feathers standing upright at the base of the bill and a little white mustache. These facial decorations at once served to distinguish the White-plumed Antbird from the general run of ant-birds, which, although varied in coloration, lack ornamental plumes. For the rest, it had a black head, dark gray back and wings, a rufous-chestnut collar about the neck, and under plum-age, tail, and rump of the same warm color. There were two of these distinguished antbirds at the gathering, probably a mated pair, although the sexes wore exactly the same garb. I watched for several hours while they clung to low, upright stems, flagging their long tails deliberately up and down, and ever and again dart-ing momentarily to the ground to snatch up some fugitive from the ants, in typical antbird fashion. They never broke their si-lence the whole time I watched them. A pair of Spotted-backed Antbirds that foraged with them were more vocal, often repeating their small, high-pitched *pe-de pe-de pe-de pe-de*, and at times uttering weak, sharp monosyllables, in measured cadence. They were an affectionate couple; and while they perched on a fallen branch a few inches above the ground, the male preened the plumage of his mate's back. With them were antbirds of two other kinds and a lone Spotted Nightingale-Thrush—a blackish bird, with black-spotted, buffy breast—who hopped over the ground on long orange legs, picking up fugitive insects and spiders with a bright bill of the same color.

When I arrived at Puyo in early August, few birds were singing; and, contrary to my expectation, they grew more silent as the weeks passed and the sun entered the Southern Hemisphere. By far the most gifted of the songsters that made themselves heard with some frequency during August and September was the Low-land Wood-Wren. When I first arrived, the Tropical Parula War-bler often sang its animated little lay among the treetops, but it became less songful in September. Along the watercourses, the River Warbler at times lifted his ringing crescendo; and in the grassy clearings the Yellow-browed Sparrow occasionally uttered his dry, buzzing song, consisting of two equal parts with a mo-mentary pause between—an insectlike performance that remind-ed me of Savannah Sparrows in meadows thousands of miles to the north. The Bananaquit sounded his somewhat more musical lay among the boughs of the trees, but became more silent as my sojourn lengthened. Sometimes, when the sun shone brightly, the Olivaceous Siskins sang in an animated chorus from some tree standing apart in a clearing. A number of other birds sang out briefly on rare occasions—just enough to suggest of what melody they were capable, and to give rise to the wish that I had come into their homeland at a more propitious season. Yet all the birds together produced very little volume of song; and the forests and clearings along the Río Puyo would have been dismally silent had it not been for the frogs, which in this rainy region were all day long proclaiming their feelings of contentment, some of them in clear, appealing voices.

As with song, so with nesting; my visit was timed at the wrong season. I had expected, from analogy with what I knew of conditions on the opposite side of the Equator, that here, in the second degree of southern latitude, the main breeding season would begin in September, the beginning of spring in the Southern Hemisphere. Actually, it seemed that the nesting season for the majority of species was just ending when I arrived in August. A number of birds were then feeding fledglings already a-wing, among them a flycatcher, a tanager, an oropéndola, and a wren, for which I could discover no indications of continued nesting. The decrease rather than increase of song at the approach of the September equinox bore testimony in the same sense. During six weeks, I found only twelve occupied nests of eight species, including four of the Olive-chested Flycatcher, which obviously was in the midst of its reproductive season. Since so little is understood about the influences that cause the majority of tropical birds, resident the year around in a fairly equable climate, to nest only in certain months, I had hoped here almost on the Equator to make observations that would throw light upon the subject. But my sojourn was too brief and at the wrong season.

An Agricultural Colony

The narrow road from Mera crossed the river at Puyo by a light suspension bridge and wound through the forest among the hills north of the stream. This was a beautiful walk, through varied tropical vegetation; but to enjoy it properly the pedestrian required a spider's complement of eyes, one pair of which might serve to guide the feet over the rough going, leaving the others free to gaze about and above. Much of the way was covered with logs laid transversely to form a corduroy, which provided a firm and dry but by no means smooth footing. Where this arboreal pavement was lacking, the mud was on most days deep and treacherous, for the soil was by nature soft, and the frequent rains rarely allowed it to dry out.

An hour's walk over this winding way brought me to the military encampment, where the soldiers of the garrison were quartered in rustic shelters thatched with palm fronds. I found them splitting wood and engaged in other wholesome rural activities; but doubtless, like most of the highlanders, they felt strange and ill at ease here among the lowland forests. From the encampment, I followed narrow trails through the forest to the *colonia civil*, or civilian agricultural colony, then passed through several of the farms by muddy, log-encumbered paths, crossing rivulets precariously by fallen tree-trunks.

Most of these new clearings had already been abandoned. Four years earlier, the government had settled here fifty indigent families from Quito and other parts of the highlands, promising to each a tract of forest land and a daily subvention of half a sucre (about 3.5 cents in U.S. currency), to enable them to subsist until their farms became productive. These colonists must at first have passed through difficult, discouraging times: the continual rain and relative warmth was depressing to people accustomed to a drier and cooler climate, the struggle with the forest difficult for men from a region devoid of natural woodland. During a period of about eight months the promised governmental subsidy failed to arrive. Of the fifty families, only six survived the trying initial period and succeeded in establishing themselves somewhat securely on their lands; the remainder returned to the capital and surrounding districts "to endure again the same privations they had wished to escape," as one of the survivors put it.

This man, a native of El Quinche, northwest of Quito, seemed to be quite comfortably settled, and expressed himself as contented with his lot—far better off than he had been in the Sierra. He possessed a large tract of land—to which the government had still not given him legal title—a big cabin with thatched roof and wooden floor, and productive stands of bananas, cassava, and coca. He received me courteously and offered a plate of savory bean soup, a welcome gift to an appetite sharpened by clambering over fallen logs.

The experiment of settling indigent families from an overpopulated region in a wilderness area, with government aid, had, then, been 12 percent successful. Possibly, if the small subvention had been regularly paid, the number of families that struck root would have been somewhat higher; but I doubt that the difference would have been great. In the first place, the indigenous highland populations of tropical America have rarely showed themselves adaptable to the lowlands: from Mexico to Peru, one sees men trying to scratch a living from sterile, rocky slopes so steep that they must, it seems, hang on by their teeth as they labor, while great areas of more fertile soil in the neighboring lowlands remain uncultivated. Difficulties in communication are not the root of the situation, but rather the result: it was difficult enough to construct roads through the mountains, but, because the people lived there, roads were built.

It is a fallacy productive of much unhappy maladjustment to suppose that every able-bodied man will make good as an independent farmer. He might be able to dig the soil and sow seeds; but a successful farmer requires a longer apprenticeship and a more careful cultivation of his judgment than a carpenter or a mechanic—I almost said a physician or a lawyer. An alert intelligence is especially needed in a region where standard agricultural practices have not been evolved, as here at Puyo. A large proportion of those who call themselves agriculturists but mock the name. The state will not allow a man to practice medicine, pharmacy, or law, or even to drive an automobile, until he has demonstrated by passing adequate tests that he knows what he is about. But it does permit any incompetent agricultural bungler to do just as he pleases with the soil, a substance as complex and delicately balanced as any of the living organisms it supports, easily ruined but slow and difficult to regenerate, and the ultimate foundation of the nation's prosperity and continued existence.

The new immigrants from Central Europe, driven hither by intolerance and political upheavals, were certainly people of higher education than the fifty highland families that had tried their luck at agriculture in the same region. They had the advantage, too, of possessing a little capital; but I wondered whether, after all, a greater proportion of them would be successful at farming under conditions so new and strange to them. At home they had engaged in business, finance, and the professions—almost everything but farming.

The Cock-of-the-Rock

At the end of September, I returned to Baños in company with yet another of these immigrants, who had come down to Puyo to buy land. When hardly more than a boy, he had been a lieutenant of artillery in the imperial Austrian army, and after serving two years in the First World War, was captured by the Russians and sent to Siberia, where he spent five years. Then he returned to Prague and entered the insurance business, but this was ruined by the German occupation of Czechoslovakia. Besides, he was a Catholic, so he decided to emigrate; and Ecuador was the only country in the Americas that would admit him for permanent residence. I asked why he had decided to farm in a region whose agricultural potentiality had never been demonstrated. He replied that he had no other choice; the productive plantations of cacao and rice about the Guayas Estuary and the fat dairy farms in the inter-Andean valleys were beyond his means. He rode the sorry nag our muleteer had provided for him like an officer on parade.

Although there was no good reason why we should not have started earlier, it was past ten o'clock before Egidio, the stout *arriero* who drove pack and riding animals between Puyo and Baños, set his little caravan upon the road. Early starts were peculiarly difficult to make in this country. It seems that the weather has much to do with local practices in this matter. In southern Costa Rica, where morning rains are rare and almost never hard, but an afternoon downpour is to be expected during most of the year, the people habitually set out on their journeys at daybreak. To travel dry, one must travel early. But in eastern Ecuador the rains keep no predictable schedule, and showers at dawn are frequent. One is as likely to enjoy fair weather in the afternoon as in the forenoon, and no premium is placed upon an early setting forth.

But finally we began to move along the way to Mera, under a

bright sun but over a road wet from the morning rain. While a single horse had sufficed to bring my baggage down, I needed two pack mules for the return journey. One bore my botanical collections; and, when I saw the terrible condition of the poor beast's back, I was glad that wet weather had kept them light. I did not know at the time that the back of the horse who carried me was almost equally raw; for I had told Egidio that I would not ride a horse with saddle galls, and he had brought the animal already accoutered, solemnly assuring me that it was in perfectly sound condition. Perhaps the conscientious traveler should personally inspect the back of his hired animal before he mounts; but, if he makes a point of sitting only on sound horseflesh, I fear that in regions without mechanical conveyances he must go afoot more often than not.

It rained during the afternoon, but fortunately the shower did not continue long; and the sky was clear when we rode into Mera at sunset. Rain fell again during the night. Mera was proving to us that it could live up to its reputation of being the wettest spot in Ecuador. In 1925 the rainfall amounted to 5,274.3 millimeters—more than seventeen feet of rain in a year!

Next day we made a fairly early start under a cloudy sky. As we wound up the Pastaza Valley we enjoyed a little sunshine; but from ten o'clock to past noon we rode through rain. The trail was a mere shelf cut into the precipitous forested slopes high above the river. At one point, a pair of Coppery-chested Jacamars flew up from the high cut bank ahead of us, uttering sharp calls. It appeared that they were digging a nest-burrow, or at least prospecting for a site. Leaving my horse around a bend in the trail, I returned to watch them. Although they flew several times above the bank, they would not dig in my presence. Higher up the valley I later discovered a pair of jacamars incubating two white eggs, which lay upon a bed of glittering regurgitated beetle shards, at the end of a short tunnel in a bank beside a footpath.

At about noon occurred what was for me the unforgettable event of the journey—and for my Czechoslovakian companion doubtless the convincing demonstration of what he had begun to suspect when I found the jacamars, namely, that he rode with a man not quite sane. For again I abruptly jumped from my horse, leaving it standing in the middle of the trail, and rushed ahead of the ex-lieutenant of artillery, motioning to him to stop, and at the same time drawing my binoculars from the case that hung from my shoulder. I had glimpsed a heavy-set, brilliant bird, as big as a pigeon, as it flew across the trail in front of us, to alight in a low tree on the outer side, high above the foaming river. I knew at once that it was my first Andean Cock-of-the-Rock, one of the feathered denizens of Ecuador that I most wanted to meet.

Obligingly, the bird rested motionless in the tree beside the trail, giving me a satisfying view of himself, while he reciprocated my scrutiny with large, brilliant orange eyes. He was an adult male in perfect plumage, clad in an unbroken expanse of pure orange color. Does any other bird display so much orange plumage, of so bright a shade? His head was adorned with a crest of the same delicious hue, forming a high ridge that projected forward above his short, rather stout bill, partly concealing it. His black tail and wings set off the brilliant plumage of his body; only the innermost wing plumes were gray, and remarkably broad. His strong feet were bright yellow. He held my delighted gaze until he darted down into the chasm through which the river roared. Then I recovered my horse and apologized to my companion for my abruptly rude behavior. He was not an ornithologist, and unless he knew what it was to grow enthusiastic over some hobby of his own—whether etchings or antique china or postage stamps—I fear that he could not sympathize with my elation.

Later, I returned from Baños to this section of the Pastaza gorge, chiefly to learn more of the ways of the Andean Cock-of-the-Rock. The man who gave me lodging described graphically how these birds "danced" on the bare shores of the river; but, although I visited the point where he had seen this rare display, I did not have the good fortune to witness *el gallo de monte* in action. Yet I found another brilliant male among the trees that fringed the river. He was tame; turning his elegant, crested head from side to side, he viewed me intently while I watched him at a distance almost too short to use field glasses. So we examined each other until some Indians coming along the trail frightened him away. Like the first of his kind that I saw, he was quite silent.

Along the shore of the river grew a number of trees belonging to the melastome family, whose broad, glossy leaves, before falling, turned a bright orange, almost the color of the cock-of-the-rock.

From a distance, a leaf might be mistaken for a bird, or a bird for a leaf—what a case for the school of naturalists who cannot rest in peace until they have proved that all creatures, from the green caterpillar on its leaf and the brown moth resting on the bark of a tree to the flamingo and the tiger, are "protectively colored"!

I could not agree with a friend, an accomplished naturalist, who contended that the cock-of-the-rock surpasses the Resplendent Quetzal in beauty. He lacks the quetzal's rich variety of coloring, his wonderful iridescence, his long train, his grace of form and carriage. Still, the orange bird of the Andean torrents is a rarely beautiful creature, and made September 27, 1939, one of the memorable days of my visit to Ecuador.

Traveling without a pause for lunch, we reached Machay in time to catch the motor truck that was drawn up at the bridge, waiting to receive the sacks of juicy *naranjillos* brought on horses and mules from points lower in the valley. When the cargo had been all stowed away, the human passengers crowded into the scant remaining space, as closely packed as the *naranjillos* in their sacks. We made the final stage of our journey much less comfortably than the first, but consoled ourselves with the reflection that we no longer weighed upon the raw backs of the horses, and that we moved far more swiftly. Darkness had fallen before we rolled into Baños. I believed that I had said a last good-bye to those wet forests east of the Andes; but such are the unexpected turns of fortune that the following year I traveled through them and over them, by river boat and airplane, from the Río Huallaga to the Río Pilcomayo. On this later journey, described in Chapter 6, I saw something of their varying aspects and vast extent; at Puyo, I was settled in one spot long enough to penetrate a few of their intimate secrets.

CHAPTER 5

The Cotingas: A Study in Contrasts

Turquoise Cotinga (female)

The birds of tropical America have lacked publicity. I suppose that nearly everyone with a smattering of natural history, or a more than local interest in birds, has heard of the birds of paradise, those profusely ornate inhabitants of New Guinea and neighboring islands. But how many have heard of the cotingas, a family twice as large, and certainly no less remarkable from any aspect?

The ninety species of cotingas are practically confined to the wooded regions of continental tropical America, from northern Argentina to Mexico. One species, the Jamaican Becard, is endemic to that island, and one, the Rose-throated Becard, reaches the extreme south of the United States, from Texas to Arizona. This family of passerine birds, related to the American flycatchers and the manakins, exhibits an unusual range in size, its largest members being as big as crows, while the smallest are among the most diminutive of birds. Although the coloration of the cotingas is exceedingly diverse, they are less lavishly adorned than the birds of paradise. Frills and flounces would only detract from the chaste loveliness of the snowy cotingas of the genus *Carpodectes* or the restrained beauty of the glossy blue cotingas of the genus *Cotinga*, which seem like bits of sky come down to the treetops. Other species display brilliant red, orange, yellow, glittering green, rich purple, or bright cinnamon-rufous, while some are clad in modest gray or somber black. In addition to colorful plumage, many cotingas have areas of bare skin, red, scarlet, or bright blue, on the cheeks, or covering much of the head and neck. Although special adornments are exceptional in the family, the ornamentation of certain cotingas verges on the fantastic, as in the big, black umbrellabirds of the genus *Cephalopterus*, with their helmetlike crests of forwardly directed feathers extending over their bills, and a long, fleshy appendage, covered with overlapping feathers or largely naked, pendent from their forenecks.

The cotinga family includes the four species of bellbirds of the genus *Procnias*, famed for their ringing calls. The male White Bellbird of the Guianas and Amazonia, who has a single fleshy wattle hanging, stringlike, from his forehead, utters a *kong kang* that sounds like hammering on an anvil and a resounding *kaaaaaaaaaang* said to be audible at a distance of three miles. The male Three-wattled Bellbird of the highlands of southern Central America is a stout bird a foot long, elegantly clad in a rich shade of brown, with pure white head and neck. From the base of his bill hang three long, flexible wattles which are not, as sometimes depicted, erectile. With his mouth gaping widely to reveal a black interior, he emits loud notes that may have either a wooden or a metallic quality. The females of the bellbirds, as of most of the more strikingly attired cotingas, are clad in duller and less revealing shades and are devoid of wattles.

Not only have the cotingas lacked publicity agents to make them known as widely as they deserve; along with other birds of tropical American forests, they have lacked enough dedicated field observers to disclose their remarkable habits. Certainly many surprising discoveries await naturalists with the patience and hardihood to watch these birds that spend so much of their lives in treetops where they are difficult to see, in woodlands too often teeming with mosquitos and other pests and by no means free from venomous snakes.

A foretaste of what is in store for diligent watchers of cotingas is provided by Barbara Snow's (1961; 1972) studies of the Calfbird or Capuchin Bird in Guyana. This big cotinga, about thirteen inches long, is chiefly chestnut-brown, with black tail and wing feathers and bright orange under tail coverts. The bare skin of the face is bluish gray. The sexes are alike. These birds sometimes display communally in nearly leafless trees, on branches from which they snap off twigs to increase visibility. In the most striking of these performances, two Calfbirds perch side by side, facing the same way and leaning forward, with their tails cocked up and their orange under tail coverts conspicuously puffed out. Gradually elevating their bodies in unison, they utter a growling *grrr* which changes to *aaa* and finally, when they have passed the upright posture and are leaning slightly backward, to the far-carrying *moo*, like the lowing of a calf, for which they are named. The meaning of this unique display has not been clarified.

Cotingas subsist on a mixed diet of fruits, insects, spiders, and the like. They perch well up in trees, turning their heads from side to side until their keen eyes detect a suitable item, often a green insect inconspicuous against a green leaf. Then they dart out, snatch the insect from the foliage without alighting, and carry it to a perch, against which they may beat it before swallowing it. Some cotingas concentrate on larger prey. A pair of Bright-rumped Attilas that I watched nourished their nestlings chiefly with small lizards and frogs. Whether these active, vociferous birds should be classified with the cotingas or the flycatchers is a question that has not been finally settled.

The nesting habits of cotingas are no less diverse than their appearance and voices. Their nests range from the slightest to some of the bulkiest of structures built by birds of their size. Some breed in holes in trees, which they appear never to carve for themselves. In certain species the nesting female is quite solitary, while in others she is attended by a faithful mate. In no cotinga, as in no American flycatcher, is the male known to incubate or brood, but he may help build the nest and do his full share in feeding the young. Perhaps I can best convey the diversity of habits in the family by telling about three species resident on our farm in the Valley of El General in southern Costa Rica.

Of these three cotingas, the Masked Tityra, which ranges from Mexico to Bolivia and Brazil, is the most conspicuous and familiar. As one of these stout, eight-inch birds flies overhead, he appears to be almost wholly white. Closer scrutiny through binoculars, after he has come to rest on some high perch, reveals that his upper plumage is mostly pale bluish gray. His wings are largely black; his pale gray tail is crossed by a broad black band; and his bare cheeks are bright red, framed in black feathers. The female, who also has naked red skin around her eyes, is browner above and grayer below. In pairs or small flocks, tityras roam widely through the treetops, not only in the forest but also in plantations and pastures with scattered trees. Their curious low grunts and dry, insectlike notes contrast with the stentorian proclamations of certain other cotingas.

In the dry season, pairs of tityras prospecting for the cavity they need for their eggs frequent the forest borders and new clearings where early-nesting woodpeckers are carving their holes or already rearing their broods. They annoy the woodpeckers by filling their holes, in which incubation has not yet been started, with dying or dead leaves and other litter. Sometimes, tiring of throwing out the steadily accumulating trash, the woodpeckers relinquish their newly made cavity and begin another for their own eggs. Tityras may even dispossess a flock of much larger araçari toucans of the cavity where they sleep, by filling it with leaves and twigs until the toucans no longer fit into it. As far as I have seen, tityras always gain possession of a nest hole by indomitable persistence rather than by violence. Practically all of the nest material is brought by the female. Her mate makes a great show of carrying leaves and twiglets but drops most of them outside.

In regions with tall trees, tityras' nests are commonly from forty to one hundred feet up, usually in decaying trunks whose questionable stability makes a prudent man hesitate to climb. I shall never forget my first visit to a tityra's nest. Years ago, when the coves and backwaters of Gatún Lake in the Panama Canal Zone were studded with the gaunt skeletons of forest trees that had been drowned by the rising water of the impounded Río Chagres, I saw a tityra enter a hole thirty-five feet up in a massive rotting trunk about a hundred yards from shore. I would never have dared to climb such a trunk on dry land, but I decided to risk a fall into the water in order to examine eggs of which I had seen no description. From a cayuco, my helpers and I threw a cord over the top of the broken-off trunk, then drew over a rope, with which we pulled up a heavy rope ladder. My determination to climb the trunk dissolved as great chunks of rotten wood, dislodged by the rope, splashed into the water around us; but my helpers urged me on and I was ashamed to abandon the project. On the way up the ladder, I passed a large cavity containing two ugly naked nestlings of the Blue-headed Parrot. At the very top of the trunk was an irregular hollow, descending obliquely into a short decaying stub. When I peered in, nothing was visible except a loose litter of leaves, but beneath them my fingers encountered two eggs. They had a most peculiar aspect, dark buff or *café au lait*, heavily marbled with brown, especially on the thicker end, and spotted here and there with black; they were typical cotingas' eggs.

Many years passed before I found a tityra's nest that could be reached with only moderate risk. This nest was only eleven feet up in a hole in which Red-crowned Woodpeckers had raised young, in a slender, badly decayed trunk standing in the midst of a cornfield, a short flight from the forest. By propping the trunk at the back and setting a ladder nearly upright against the front, I could reach the hole without toppling over the trunk. Since the doorway was too narrow to admit my hand, I illuminated the interior with an electric bulb and looked in with a mirror, with a dark cloth over my head like an old-fashioned photographer. During the approximately three weeks that the female incubated in this nest, I made numerous visits of inspection without once glimpsing an egg. Whether she departed spontaneously or fled as I approached, she always left her eggs completely buried in the loose litter for their better protection. From time to time she brought additional pieces of leaf to the nest.

Then came a day when my light and mirror revealed half of an empty shell lying above the leaves. I heard infantine *peep*s and saw the leaves move, as they had never done before, but I could not see a nestling. On the following morning, however, I glimpsed parts of two nestlings before they vanished beneath the leaves. The few tufts of gray down on their heads, backs, and wings failed to conceal their pink skin. Their eyes were tightly closed. On my inspections during the following days, I sometimes saw the leaves move and rarely heard a week *peep peep peep*; but mostly the nestlings lay so still beneath the leaves that only the parents' continued attendance convinced me that they were still there. Beginning on their tenth day, the young tityras were sometimes found with their heads exposed but their bodies covered. From their fifteenth day onward, however, they rested on rather than beneath the litter, their bodies wholly exposed. Their plumage developed slowly, and they were not well feathered until they were three weeks old. When they were twenty-four days old, their mother called persistently, apparently urging them to leave the nest, but they were not yet ready to go. One remained in the cavity a full four weeks, the other a day or two longer. When finally they emerged, their plumage resembled that of the adult female.

Throughout the long nestling period, both parents brought food, the mother somewhat more often than the father. At first the nestlings were given only insects, which became larger as the days passed. Soon fruits were added to the diet, especially the green, olivelike fruits of a tree of the laurel family, each with a single large seed that the nestlings regurgitated. Occasionally they received a spider, a tiny land snail, or even a small lizard. The parents also continued to bring leaves to the nest. They seemed to be stimulated to do so by any exciting event, such as hatching, my visits to the nest, or the imminence of a fledgling's departure. The first two articles that I saw the female take to the nest after the eggs hatched were leaves rather than food; and just before the first nestling flew, its mother, clinging outside the doorway, dropped a billful of leaves before its open mouth.

A less conspicuous neighbor of the Masked Tityra, over much of its wide range, is the White-winged Becard, a bird hardly bigger

White-winged Becard

than a wood warbler, but with a stouter body and a larger head. The male's upper plumage is largely blackish, with gray on the rump and conspicuous white areas on the wings and shoulders. Below, he is dark gray, paler on the abdomen. The very different female is prettily attired in delicately blended shades of greenish olive, pale yellow, cinnamon, and buff. These cotingas are most often seen, singly or in pairs, along the forest edges and in the crowns of trees scattered through pastures and other clearings. In contrast to those of many other cotingas, their voices are soft and melodious. At daybreak in the nesting season, the male repeats over and over, hundreds of times with hardly a pause, an arrestingly beautiful song consisting of about eight dulcet notes.

The female builds the bulky nest, which is usually far out on a thin branch high in a tree standing apart from other trees. The male, who does not work, often perches close by, from time to time singing sweetly, or driving away an intruding bird with a loud clacking of his short, thick bill. Of the many becards' nests that I have seen, only two were accessible to me. These were roughly globular and about seven inches in diameter. A round doorway in the side, one and a half inches in diameter, gave access to a chamber about three inches wide and high. These nests were composed chiefly of long skeins of more or less shredded bast fibers, with dry leaves and grasses lining the chamber all around. One nest contained four eggs and the other three, which appears to be the more usual number. In coloration they resembled the tityra's eggs, but they were much smaller.

Only the female becard incubates, and she sits very inconstantly, apparently depending on the thick walls of her nest to keep her eggs warm while she is absent. In ten hours of watching, one female never remained in her nest longer than thirty-eight minutes at a stretch. Her average session was only fifteen minutes, and she was in the nest only 45 percent of the day. She continued to add much material to her nest until her eggs hatched, after eighteen days of incubation.

The tiny, blind, pink-skinned nestlings were devoid of the sparse down typical of newly hatched passerine birds. Although I had not seen the male look into the nest to learn whether the eggs had hatched, somehow he discovered within a day or two that he was the father of nestlings and helped his mate to attend them, bringing food almost as often as she did. As far as I saw, the nestlings received only winged insects and larvae, which were nearly always of substantial size—never any fruit. When, at the age of sixteen days, the young were well feathered, they gave fair imitations of the male's day song, sometimes answering when their father sang in the distance. Their soft notes, filtered through the nest's thick walls, sounded much weaker than those of the parents. At the age of three weeks, the young left the nest, wearing a plumage much like that of their mother. Now, as they roamed with their parents through the treetops around our house, they revealed their presence by little songs and soft notes constantly repeated, but they were most difficult to glimpse amid the clustered foliage.

Unlike the tityra and the becard, the Rufous Piha rarely ventures beyond the forest, where it stays well up in the tall trees, betraying its presence by its sudden, sharp, powerful whistles. Any loud sound, such as the snapping of a dry branch underfoot, a shout, a handclap, a peal of thunder, or the whir of the wings of a startled Great Tinamou rising suddenly from the ferny undergrowth, may be answered by the piha's whistle; but usually one must look long before spying the plain, bright rufous bird, as big as an American Robin, amid the clouds of verdure far overhead. The male and female are exactly alike, and both can whistle loudly, although apparently the male does so more persistently. The whistle is often a disyllable that suggests the bird's name. Sometimes it is prolonged into a musical trill.

I had found many nests of the tityra and the becard before I discovered one of the piha. One day, while walking along a woodland path, I noticed a piha resting on a slender branch about twenty feet up in a small tree, in an attitude that excited my curiosity. When, after sitting motionless for a long while, the bird flew away, she left exposed a nest so diminutive that it had been largely hidden beneath her. It was a nearly flat mat or pad about three inches in diameter, composed almost wholly of coiled tendrils, and supported by two horizontal twigs, each no thicker than a lead pencil. Looking up through the meshes of this incredibly slight structure, I could see that it held—most precariously, it seemed—a single egg that was smoky gray, heavily mottled with dark brown.

Of the five pihas' nests that I later found, four were similarly situated on two or more slender twigs, one on a single stouter branch. All were in the lower story of tall woodland, from seventeen to thirty-five feet up, where they were sheltered from the wind that often sways the crowns of the higher trees and that might roll the egg from so shallow a nest. The slightest arboreal nests that I have seen, they had been reduced to the absolute minimum compatible with their function of supporting a single egg or nestling. What a contrast between these skimpy structures and the bulky nest of the much smaller becard!

Many hours of watching during building, incubation, and rearing the young failed to disclose that the female piha was ever helped by a male; pihas, like bellbirds and blue cotingas, appear not to form pairs. While at their nests, all the pihas that I watched ignored me, even when I walked directly beneath the lowest of them. It was surprising to see so big a bird, after incubating quietly for an hour or two, spread her wings and fly right up from her egg, just as a hummingbird does. This method of departure reduced the danger of shaking the egg from its shallow receptacle. One egg took twenty-five or twenty-six days to hatch, which is about one day shorter than the incubation period of the Calfbird but twice as long as that of thrushes and finches of about the piha's size. I am aware of no other passerine, except the far bigger Superb Lyrebird of Australia, whose eggs take so long to hatch. Probably the poor insulation afforded by the thin, open meshwork on which the piha's egg lies contributes to the length of the incubation period.

Nourished by its mother with insects, spiders, fruits, and an occasional small scorpion, the nestling piha develops slowly. Still largely naked at the age of eleven days, it is feathered at seventeen days. Nevertheless, the careful parent continues to brood it; one nineteen-day-old nestling was covered almost half of the morning. At night, and when rain fell, it was brooded until at least twenty-seven days old. A very restful nestling, it took its meals with a restraint that contrasted with the eagerness of young birds that must compete with nest mates for food and reduced the probability that it would fall from its narrow platform. When, at the age of twenty-eight or twenty-nine days, it finally left the nest, it resembled the adults in coloration but had a stubby tail. In certain other cotingas, including the Bearded Bellbird and the Purple-throated Fruitcrow, the solitary nestling stays in its nest even longer—up to thirty-three days.

From the beginning of nest building to the fledgling's departure, the piha takes about nine weeks to rear her single offspring. This is about twice as long as Gray's Thrush, which nests in our Costa Rican dooryard beside the forest where the piha dwells, takes to raise a brood of two or three in a far more substantial structure.

Yet, despite its slow rate of reproduction, the piha is the most abundant bird of its size, or larger, in our forest, and I hear its musical call as I write this sentence. No less surprising than the leisurely pace of development is the fact that egg and nestling remain for so many weeks on the rimless platform where they lie so precariously. They owe their survival to the deliberateness of the parent bird, who is not easily frightened into an abrupt departure that might knock out the egg, no less than to the restrained movements of the solitary nestling.

A peculiar habit of the piha and certain other cotingas is that of dismantling their empty nests. Whether the piha's nest had been pillaged by some predator or the fledgling had left it at the proper age, unless I promptly collected the structure I always found its materials scattered a few days later. I watched one piha tear pieces from her unoccupied nest and carry them off in various directions, while the stubby-tailed fledgling that evidently had recently flown from it rested nearby. When a female Lovely Cotinga returned to her high nest and failed to find her still flightless nestling that a toucanet had driven from it, she scattered the materials in what appeared to be a gesture of anger or desperation. Similarly, a Blue Cotinga that Frank M. Chapman (1929) watched in Panama dismantled her nest after her nestlings vanished prematurely. But becards seem never to tear apart their much bulkier nests, unless they need the material to build another.

These are some of the contrasts that the wonderful cotinga family presents. Doubtless others equally surprising await discovery by diligent naturalists.[1]

1. More details are given in my *Life Histories of Central American Birds* (1954–1969), vol. 3.

CHAPTER 6

Through Peruvian Amazonia by Gunboat

Hoatzins

Over the Andes

The airplane that carried us across the high, barren Andes, from Chiclayo on the desert coast of northern Peru to Yurimaguas amid the ever-verdant forests of the Amazon basin, seemed to have transferred us in four hours from one world to another. The impression that we had been taken to another, more prolific, planet was heightened by the circumstance that for a long inter-

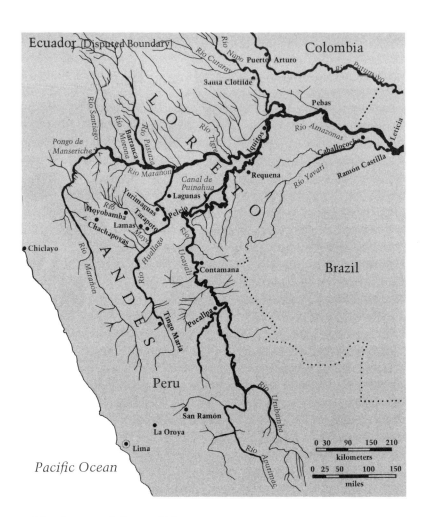

Northern and Central Peru

val we lost all visual contact with this one. Leaving Chiclayo at seven o'clock on the misty morning of September 13, 1940, we flew for miles over the coastal desert's bare sands, scattered cacti, and thorny scrub. Soon we began to rise above the long, barren slopes of the Andean foothills. Here and there a tiny hamlet of white-walled houses, roofed with red tiles, perched on the broad back of a ridge. We flew high over the Río Marañón, a big mountain torrent of muddy water rushing along the bottom of a V-shaped trench, thousands of feet deep—how different from the Marañón of broad, smooth water and endless low shores that we were soon to navigate!

Then we passed above the clouds and lost all contact with the earth. We knew that jagged peaks reached up toward us, but, save for a rare, imperfect glimpse through a rift in the vaporous masses, we saw nothing of them. As we flew on and on, three miles above the level of the sea, and the white clouds continued to stretch ahead of us in unending, unbroken ranks, we began to speculate upon their physical properties, especially their ability to sustain a weight. So soft and fleecy they looked, it was easy to fancy that we might jump upon them with no more danger to our bones than if we fell upon a mound of hay, and continue to lie at ease upon a yielding couch, in this world of blue and white and softly blended grays, in philosophic calm and high communion with the mysteries of space and time.

But reason, contradicting the suggestions of the senses, told us that we would fall swiftly through this unsubstantial blanket, and crash upon some remote peak where only the condors would find us. So we felt more at ease when the pilot, his practiced eye detecting a narrow fissure in the clouds that would have passed unnoticed by us, dived boldly through—and we found ourselves, as if by magic, high above a green valley. As we circled to descend, the tilted wing of the airplane seemed almost to brush the feathery crowns of palm trees that grew upon the wooded crest of a flanking ridge. A minute later we were bumping along the grassy landing field of Moyobamba, on the Río Mayo, a tributary of the Huallaga. We were safely across the formidable barrier of the Andes, and it was only half-past nine in the morning!

We saw nothing of the town of Moyobamba; but the lush vegetation, the vigorous growth of weeds along the edges of the airstrip, told us that we had entered a region of ample rainfall. Soon we were called back to our airplane, which took us down the valley of the winding Río Mayo to Lamas, a village of low, red-tiled houses built upon a dry ridge above the river. Here half the population seemed to have gathered at the airstrip to see the weekly plane arrive. A local resident accosted us in English, a language that was, to say the least, unexpected here in the remote hinterland of a Spanish-speaking country; but I left my companions to converse with the stranger, and tried, in the few minutes at my disposal, to make friends with the strange plants that surrounded me.

Those small, nearly leafless trees that stood amid the thickets around the landing field, all gloriously covered with lovely reddish purple blossoms—could they possibly be a species of *Lagerstroemia*, the "queen of flowers"? There was not time to gather a specimen before we took to the air again, passing over many more of these beautiful flowering trees as we continued down the valley to Tarapoto, a flight of a few minutes only. Here the low woods again abounded with the purple-flowered trees, and also with a vine of the bignonia family that displayed superb trumpet blossoms of the same color. Again our stop was too brief to allow me to reach a specimen; but months later, back in Lima, Dr. Weberbauer, an authority on Peruvian flora, told me that the trees were *Physocalymma scaberrimum*, the Brazilian Rosewood tree, a relative of the "queen of flowers" that deserves to be equally well known.

In a few minutes we were in the air once more. After a short flight we dropped down over the last low foothill and were gliding over a vast level plain, all covered with forest, that swept onward as far as we could see. We could trace the course of one long, low escarpment that marked an abrupt but slight change in the level of the plain; aside from this, it all seemed as uniform as the surface of the ocean. The symmetrical crowns of palm trees occupied a prominent place in the canopy of the forest that spread like a green carpet beneath us, over land that appeared to be poorly drained and in many places swampy. Before us meandered the Río Huallaga, broad and muddy. At a few minutes before eleven o'clock we were set down on the outskirts of Yurimaguas.

That afternoon, in the little rustic hotel, we met a man who had come from Tarapoto on horseback; he described to us the hardships of the three-day journey over muddy forest trails. He placed our aerial voyage in its true perspective. If Tarapoto, which seemed to us to be next door to Yurimaguas, was so difficult to reach by terrestrial travel, how many weeks of toilsome overland journeying would it take us to return to the coast, were the air service suddenly to fail!

Spread over a group of low hills of sandy clay beside the river, Yurimaguas, in Peru's huge eastern province of Loreto, was a big, straggling village, composed of palm-thatched cabins surrounding a central nucleus of more substantial buildings. The outskirts of the village were bright with the great yellow blossoms of a small tree with palmately compound leaves, a species of *Cochlospermum*, among which grew the "sanang," a low shrub (*Faramea anisocalyx*) of the coffee family whose whole inflorescence, including the little flowers, unopened buds, and the stalks that bore them, was deep blue, and adorned with pale blue, leaflike bracts. After the damp, misty coolness of coastal Peru, where the climate is moderated by the cold Humboldt Current, we found sun-flooded Yurimaguas almost insufferably hot, and were glad to learn, the day after our arrival, that the *Amazonas* had come up from Iquitos, and we could install ourselves on board.

The *Amazonas* was a gunboat of the Peruvian navy—or perhaps it would be more correct to say one of the Peruvian navies; for, in an insecure world, a country with well over a thousand miles of exposed oceanic coast on one side and several thousand miles of navigable waterways on the other, with a mighty mountain range and the length and breadth of a continent isolating the two, needs to support two navies, one maritime, the other fluviatile. The *Amazonas* was a neat little vessel of 250 tons and very shallow draft, which permitted it to push far up the tributaries to the Amazon. Built at Groton, Connecticut, when the Leticia episode of 1933 threatened to cause war between Peru and Colombia, it had arrived too late to serve in that unfortunate but happily transitory dispute. We wondered how a vessel of so shallow a draft had weathered the open waters of the Atlantic on the long voyage from the northern shipyard to the mouths of the Amazon.

Now, under the command of Captain Texiera and Lieutenant Delgado, the *Amazonas* patrolled the broad, far-reaching waterways of the Peruvian Montaña peacefully enough, yet seeming somehow out of place as, in its coat of battleship gray, with swivel guns mounted fore and aft, it brushed along forest-shaded shores inhabited by creatures no more warlike than parrots, monkeys, tapirs, jaguars, and anacondas. For the present, the ship had been commissioned by the government at Lima to convey our party of six while we explored this vast, sparsely inhabited region for *Hevea* rubber trees growing wild in the forests and for lands where they might be cultivated in plantations. The Second World War was already raging in Europe, and, fearing that the Western world might be cut off from the Far Eastern plantations which were then the principal producers of natural rubber, the government of the United States had sent out a number of parties to survey the actual and potential sources of this essential commodity in tropical America.

Now that we had become fresh-water sailors, we had to learn to adapt ourselves to living in a confined space—at least while we were not ashore wandering through those limitless forests. I shared a cabin, measuring little over two yards in each dimension, with Marion Striker, the soils expert of our party, a massive, rubicund six-footer from North Dakota. Since the combined equipment for collecting plants and taking samples of soils occupied rather more than a fair share of the available space, we had to take turns getting up and dressing in the morning. Dr. Elvin C. Stakman, the plant pathologist, a professor from Minnesota and leader of our party, shared an equally small cabin with Earl Blair, the rubber expert, who had settled in California after retirement from long service on Sumatran rubber plantations. The four of us had been sent to Peru by the Department of Agriculture in Washington. Our party was completed by two agronomists representing the Peruvian government, Bernardo Moravsky and Manuel Sánchez del Aguila.

The Huallaga

Through our first night on board, the *Amazonas* drowsed beside the high river bank at Yurimaguas. Early next morning the moorings were cast off, and the ship began to vibrate with the revolu-

tions of the Diesel engine and nosed out into the muddy Huallaga, still veiled beneath the mists of night. We had begun our odys-
sey over the upper waters of that great river system, the world's
grandest, which drains the heart and core of the American tropics.
Ever since my student days, I had nourished vague projects for
voyaging upon the Amazon; and now, less than two months after
an unexpected radiogram from the Department of Agriculture in
Washington had sent me southward from Costa Rica as botanist
of the expedition, I was floating upon one of its principal tributaries!

Turning upstream, we soon passed beyond the last of the clearings that surrounded Yurimaguas. Since the *Amazonas* was not
a passenger vessel, there was no sign warning of "certain persons
excluded from the bridge." I promptly discovered that Del Aguila,
the little silent pilot, would tolerate my presence there, and that,
aside from the crow's nest—which I did not pluck up courage to
invade until a later date—it was the vessel's best point of vantage
for watching the life along the shores. All morning we wound up
the broad channel, breasting the smooth, strong current, brown
with silt from the high Andes. The banks were everywhere of almost uniform height, between ten and twenty feet at the present
stage of low water. Long stretches that appeared to have been
freshly cut by the river were nearly or quite vertical, with little or
no vegetation to mask the brown or reddish soil.

Nearly everywhere the forest pushed down quite to the land's
edge, save where, here and there, it had been destroyed to make a
small clearing, devoted to pasturage or to the cultivation of plantains, bananas, cassava, barbasco, or sugar cane. In each clearing
stood the thatched hut of the farmer, or more rarely the iron-
roofed dwelling of sawed boards belonging to some more affluent
planter. This forest was not quite so lofty and dense as I had expected to find it, although subsequent experience showed that it
was a fair sample of the woodland along many hundreds of miles
of this and other tributaries of the upper Amazon. There was no
lack of trees of noble stature—prominent among them the Silk-
cotton, with tall, massive, high-buttressed trunks and far-flung
branches reaching horizontally above their neighbors' heads; and
the Capirona, very lofty and slender, easily recognized by its
smooth brown or cinnamon bark—yet these magnificent trees

grew scattered among many others of inferior size. The result was a broken rather than a uniform high canopy, with interspaces between the big trees that were frequent and wide, occupied by palms, lower trees, shrubs, and vines. I have seen more uniformly tall stands of cypress or of oaks far up on the mountains of Central America. Yet perhaps it was only because imagination had formed such an exaggeratedly grand prevision of this forest that it disappointed. A woodland whose dominant trees are well over a hundred feet high is not to be despised in any zone.

What are those stout, big-headed, blackish little birds that perch in pairs upon the topmost naked twigs of tall, dead or dying riverside trees? Their short black bills taper from a thick base to a sharp, downcurved point; the tips of their long wings reach almost to the ends of their short tails. The rump is pure white, contrasting sharply with the otherwise somber upper plumage; the belly is cinnamon, shading off to pale gray beneath the tail, as may be plainly seen when they sally far out to catch some insect flying above the river, then return to their lofty perch to devour it and wait for another. From time to time the mates call to each other with weak, appealing whistles. Flycatchers, their mode of earning a living would seem to proclaim them. Yet in bill and general form they do not resemble flycatchers, and in coloration they are strikingly different from any flycatcher I have seen farther north. Well, perhaps they are becards; yet, as a rule, becards snatch their insect prey from the foliage rather than the air. This was three decades before Meyer de Schauensee gave us his guide to the birds of South America, and it was not until I returned to the United States and looked through the illustrations in Goeldi's *Album de aves amazonicas* (1900–1906) that I found these birds depicted and learned that they were neither flycatchers nor becards but puffbirds. Swallow-wing is their book name, which is no more than a literal translation of the first part of their Graeco-Latin scientific name, *Chelidoptera tenebrosa*. We found them widespread along the rivers of Loreto and met them in Andean foothills up to nearly three thousand feet above sea level.

So these alert, swallow-winged creatures of the treetops are puffbirds, those proverbially "stupid" birds of the collectors! The bird watcher, no matter how well acquainted with the avifauna of the North American continent, even its tropical parts, has many

a surprise when he reaches the Amazon country. It was surprising, too, to read in Cherrie's "Ornithology of the Orinoco Region"
(1916), where also this far-ranging species is abundant, that the
Swallow-wings descend from their high treetops to dig their nesting burrows in the ground. They may choose either a stream bank
or a level surface, in which they excavate a downwardly inclined
tunnel, a yard or two in length, that widens at its lower end into a
chamber where the two white eggs repose on the bare ground or a
few bits of dead grass. The birds apparently carry away in their
bills all the earth that they excavate, for Cherrie found no loose
dirt about the tunnel's mouth. The little Swallow-wings hatch
perfectly naked, and after their pinfeathers sprout they creep out
to the entrance of their burrow, where they bask in the sunshine
while they wait for their parents to bring food. If suddenly
alarmed, they scuttle backward into their subterranean nursery,
never pausing even long enough to turn around.

If I made some very wide guesses about the identity of the
Swallow-wing, I console myself that I did not go wrong with the
big blue-gray herons that we met every mile or so, perching solitary above the shore or fishing alone in the shallows. The black
forehead and crown, the white under plumage with a broad black
streak on either side of the breast, the two converging and joining
on the center of the abdomen, make it easy to recognize. From
Goeldi's *Album* I learned that this distinctively marked species is
the Cocoi Heron, which is W. H. Hudson's (1920) translation of
Ardea cocoi. For this bird, now called the White-necked Heron,
ranges over most of South America and Hudson knew it in Argentina, and described its ways in *Birds of La Plata*. Here he stated
that these herons pair for life; but if the Cocoi Herons that we
met along this and all the other rivers of Loreto indeed had mates,
they were widely separated from them.

Equally abundant and equally solitary along all these rivers was
the Streaked Heron, similar in appearance to the Green Heron of
North America, but distinguishable by the gray rather than chestnut of its face and the sides of its neck. Here at last was an old
acquaintance, for I knew the bird in Panama. Even more familiar
were the kingfishers: the big Ringed Kingfisher with slate-blue
upper plumage, strongly barred wings, and rich chestnut under
parts; and the middle-sized Amazon Kingfisher, deep green above,

white below with a chestnut breast band, at least in the male. These far-ranging birds were living proof of the unity of the Americas. And the Spotted Sandpipers that teetered over the sandbars and exposed muddy shores, now with immaculate breasts, had been hatched and reared perhaps some fifty or sixty degrees to the north.

Although all the South American kingfishers range into Middle America, the swallows that flew tirelessly over the Huallaga and other rivers of Loreto were different from any to be seen north of Panama. These included the White-banded Swallow, steel blue with a conspicuous white band on its breast and a deeply forked tail, and the White-winged Swallow, blue marked with white, very prominently on the wings.

But the great thrill of that first day of voyaging on the rivers was provided by the Hoatzins. I had never seen a Hoatzin, not even, to my recollection, the stuffed skin of one. But who that has read William Beebe's (1918) inimitable account of these unique fowls, or has seen them pictured, can fail to recognize them in the flesh? We had not traveled far up the river when I noticed a flock of big, dark-colored birds, almost as large as a hen pheasant, resting among the branches of a fallen tree stranded in the shallows by the shore. The passage of the gunboat scarcely perturbed them —why should they, who had flourished along these rivers for long ages before man appeared on the scene, permit themselves to be driven, even temporarily, from their ancient abode by this upstart monster of his invention? As the ship plowed noisily past, they merely shifted to somewhat higher perches in the same tree, deliberately, one or a few at a time, in no hurry to escape it. Their long, skinny necks, their slow and loose-jointed, clumsy flight, their long, loose crests which gave them an aspect of alertness that their habits belied—all were so characteristic of the bird that it was hardly possible to confuse it with any other. At the end of each short flight they held their wings outstretched, displaying a beautiful chestnut area in the center of each.

Hoatzins were abundant along this stretch of the Huallaga. We saw numerous flocks, each containing from ten to about fifty individuals. Their favorite resort was among the branches of a dead tree fallen along the shore, or the boughs of a living one projecting above the water. How I regretted that I could not stop to search for their crude nests of sticks built above the marginal waters, and perchance see the alarmed nestlings drop into the river at my approach, then, when all was quiet again, scramble back to their nursery, climbing not only with feet and bill but also with the claws on the forward edge of their wings, a primitive character that most birds have lost. Years after this, Drs. Charles Sibley and Jon Ahlquist (1973) showed convincingly, from analysis of their egg-white proteins and other evidence, that Hoatzins are related to cuckoos rather than to the gallinaceous birds, as we once supposed. Indeed, they resemble overgrown Guira Cuckoos; and, as in these and the related anis, their nests are attended by more than a single pair of parents.

About the middle of the afternoon we tied up to the bank at Pelejo, a hamlet of thatched huts whose name means "sloth" —the hairy animal of the treetops, not the besetting sin. This was as far upstream as the *Amazonas* could proceed at the present stage of low water. I enjoyed a long, solitary walk along a trail that led through the forest along the river, saw Green Oropéndolas, black Yellow-rumped Caciques, and araçari toucans of a species I was not sure about, but not as many birds as I had hoped or expected to find.

Early next morning we set off upstream in the ship's lifeboat, propelled by an outboard motor and manned by two sailors. We hung close to the shore to avoid the strong current's full force. Little clearings with thatched huts, small patches of cultivation, and weedy pastures were frequent along this reach of the river. As we were slowly chugging upstream close to the marginal vegetation, two brilliant birds flew out from the shore, winged upstream ahead of us, then dived in among the bushes and vanished. They were the size of a large finch, had bright red heads with yellow eyes, black upper plumage, wings, and tail, and the under parts all pure white, except the black throat. How I wondered what they could be, to what family they belonged! When a new bird flies into the field of vision of an ardent bird watcher, he feels much as the astronomer does when a new planet swims into his ken—and especially so when the strange bird is so brilliantly colored, so strikingly different from any that he has seen before. Later we met birds of this kind among the marginal vegetation of other rivers, nearly always in pairs. Near Iquitos I watched one tearing

apart a cocoon attached to a low twig on the shore of the Morona-
Cocha. Months passed before I learned that this finch is the Red-
capped Cardinal. It belongs to a genus, *Paroaria*, widespread in
South America but unknown farther north. W. H. Hudson's moving story "Cardinal" is about another species of this genus.

About midday we saw a big, colorful coat-of-arms of the Republic of Peru displayed on the front of a large thatched building
which, perched high upon massive posts, stood in a clearing fronting the river. Landing, we sat on the porch of this rustic school-
house to lunch on provisions brought in the boat. All along the
rivers of Loreto, sometimes in the wildest and most unlikely
places, we found similar schools, easily recognized by the shield
bearing the cornucopia, tree, and llama. These rural or, perhaps
better, sylvan schools, together with the agricultural experiment
stations, gave the traveler the impression that the republic was
not neglecting the welfare of its citizens, even in the most remote
and sparsely settled parts. Behind the school was a fine grove of
Capirona trees. I greatly regretted that I nowhere saw them in
flower. If they make a display at all comparable in snowy whiteness to that of the related Madroño of the drier parts of Central
America, they must be a very fine sight.

After our repast we continued upstream afoot, by a path that
led along the bank, leaving the boat to work up the river alone.
Even lightened as it was, it could hardly make headway against
the swifter parts of the current. As we watched from the shore,
we wondered whether it would reach our destination. We walked
through some very imposing stands of lofty trees. Here, as at
many other places along the rivers of Loreto, we noticed that the
land sloped gently downward from the river bank, so that the
farther inland one went, the lower and marshier the ground became. Doubtless it was for this reason, no less than for the easy
transportation that the waterways afforded, that most of the settlements and clearings clung so closely to the banks.

About four o'clock in the afternoon we reached Navarro, a collection of thatched dwellings on the stream's left bank. Here we
invaded a big, clean double cabin belonging to the village carpenter and settled down to await our boat, which arrived not long afterward. Since it was too late to continue our journey, the eight of
us remained in the carpenter's house for the night. I do not recall

that he invited us to stay; we simply took his hospitality for granted, as one must so often do in the wilder parts of the world, in a way that would be considered outrageous in any town or city, or even in a well-populated rural district. Although we turned the poor carpenter's household upside down, he was good-natured about it, even courteous. My companions inflated their air mattresses and slept on the ground. Since fortunately I had none, I occupied a hammock. Many a time on this expedition, I had reason to be grateful that the man who packed our equipment in Washington had provided only three air mattresses for a party of four! However it may be in northern regions, in tropical lowlands it is best to sleep somewhat above the ground. A folding canvas cot is preferable to an air mattress and hardly weighs more.

Next morning we crossed the Huallaga in our lifeboat and walked through a forest of tall, slender, clean-boled trees growing close together. Arriving at the Río Chipurana, we crossed it precariously upon a slender fallen trunk that stretched from bank to bank high above the water. Then we continued through lower vegetation with many tall palms, where we found the Brazilian rubber trees that we sought. There was hardly time to see anything else—but if one finds what one seeks, I suppose one should be satisfied. In the afternoon the outboard motor and the current, uniting their forces, took us swiftly downstream. At sunset we reached Pelejo and the *Amazonas*, which was promptly set in motion and continued down the Huallaga through the night.

Late the following morning we tied to the bank at Oromina and went ashore to examine a neglected rubber plantation. Here low hills bordered the river, instead of the usual level, often swampy, land. Four porpoises played in the river beside the ship. Later they were to become a familiar sight along the Amazon and its wider tributaries. One hardly expects to find porpoises in fresh water, in the middle of a continent. Some were blackish, others pink. Because of the prevailing turbidity of the water, they were visible only when they leaped above the surface to breathe. I never saw them line up ahead of the prow to race the ship, as their deep-sea relatives often do, probably because, in these muddy waters with reduced visibility, the game would be less exciting, with more danger of a collision, than in the clear water of mid-ocean. If, like their marine relatives, these inland porpoises use echolocation, it must be even more serviceable to them, for avoiding obstacles and finding food, than to the porpoises of more transparent seas.

That night, while we were moored beside the bank, I watched bats dipping into the surface of the river in the moonlight. They stirred memories of another moonlit night, years before, when, gliding through the placid water of Gatún Lake in Panama, the great ornithologist Frank M. Chapman called my attention to the fishing bats. The two great classes of winged vertebrates, the birds and the bats, both include fishers, but they ply their trade in very different manners. Fishing birds catch their prey with their bills, and many kinds dive far beneath the surface. Bats fish wholly at the surface. The fish-eating hare-lipped or mastiff bat (*Noctilio*) of tropical America has extraordinarily large hind feet with stout, heavily clawed toes that might well serve for seizing small fry, perhaps after first scooping up the fish from the water's surface with the membrane that joins the hindlegs and tail.

Next morning we continued downstream. The Huallaga now meandered excessively. At one point we saw the river directly ahead, through the trees on a narrow neck of land; yet we went far, around a sharp bend, to reach this water that appeared so near. Doubtless the river has since cut through the narrow peninsula and shortened its course. A brief excursion ashore at the village of Lagunas, situated on another area of higher land beside the river, was made memorable by a splendid plant new to me and my first meeting with a bird of which I had read so long before that it already seemed an old friend. The road from the landing up to the village was brightened by a shrub, four or five yards high, that displayed generous clusters of small blossoms of a mauve or pinkish violet. It obviously belonged to the coffee family—a group that in the Amazon country contains so many handsome members—and was evidently a species of *Palicourea*, but the experts back in Washington were dubious about its exact classification.

It was while passing through a grassy clearing beyond the village that I saw the bird. No one not entirely blind, or color blind, could have failed to see him, for, perched atop a low shrub, his crimson breast turned toward me, he was a sight to catch the eye from afar. Elsewhere he was nearly everywhere black, except only a brilliant red patch at the bend of the wing, which became apparent when he flew. In size and form he much reminded me of his northern relative, the Meadowlark, but his song was inferior, a mere metallic buzz. "Huanchaco," volunteered one of the lads who had followed us from the village; "policia ingleza," said Goeldi in his *Album*; Red-breasted Blackbird it is called in recent lists, which is certainly a name as concisely descriptive of *Leistes militaris* as the English language can provide.

At Lagunas we visited our first plantation of barbasco—the derris root of commerce—whose cultivation had assumed great importance in the Amazon country, and of which we were to see so much lower on the rivers. *Barbasco* is the name applied in Spanish-speaking countries to any plant, whether tree, shrub, or liana, which when pounded into a pulp and thrown into the river stupefies or kills the fish, making them easy to catch. But in eastern Peru the name appeared to have been securely captured by the leguminous vine *Lonchocarpus nicou*, from the root of which a valuable insecticide is extracted. In early life, up to the age of a year or two, it is shrubby rather than vinelike. After attaining a height of four or five feet, the stem becomes slender and reveals scansorial propensities; but at this stage the plant is pulled up and its roots dried, baled, and shipped down the river on the first stage of their long northward journey.

The Marañón and the Pongo de Manseriche

Through the afternoon we continued, between low shores, down the winding course of the Huallaga until we emerged from this broad tributary upon the far broader Marañón, which, after it joins the Ucayali about two hundred miles below, becomes the Amazon.

In spite of all I had read about the magnitude of these mighty rivers, I was not prepared for the actuality of their vastness. Here, nearly three thousand miles from the Atlantic, this main affluent of the Amazon had an estuarine aspect—the breadth and sweep of open water, the deepness of the bays, which a lesser river assumes only as it broadens at its mouth and meets the salt water of the ocean. The Mississippi at New Orleans, the Hudson at New York cannot compare in grandeur with the Marañón while it has not yet become the Amazon. As we emerged upon the larger river and turned upstream, a school of porpoises played in the mouth of the Huallaga, and many terns winged over the wide waters, all helping to create the impression of a seascape. The day ended with a glorious sunset, to be followed by a night of brilliant moonlight. The Marañón had prepared a regal welcome for us.

We turned upstream on the Marañón and in the night passed the mouth of the Río Pastaza, which flows down from the highlands of Ecuador. Early next morning we went ashore at Barranca, climbing to reach the military post and village perched upon a bluff a hundred feet above the river. Thence we made another excursion into the forest, passing through two large clearings planted with cassava. The forest was again much lighter than we had expected to find it, and the soils expert declared this to result from the poorness of the soil. We had scarcely found a rubber tree before a drenching shower sent us back to the *Amazonas* in a pitifully bedraggled state. As we passed the officers' quarters at the military post, a captain courteously invited us to come in and have some refreshments; but I had already reached the saturation point, and, excusing myself by alleging fear of a cold, I hurried down the bluff to my cabin and dry clothes.

We resumed our voyage up the Marañón in the rain. By the middle of the afternoon a clearing sky permitted us to see the first blue hills rising far in the west—over our stern! Soon we rounded a bend in the river and beheld them over the bow, where they seemed to belong. A Swallow-tailed Kite soared easily above the stream, and these birds that I had long known made the Amazon country seem more homelike. Since navigation became more dangerous as we approached the mountains, the pilot deemed it prudent to tie up for the night in front of a hut and a pile of cordwood. The low range of hills, the last outlying foothills of the Andes, was now plainly visible in the west. Pilot Del Aguila told me that this was the Cerro de Campanquiz, and pointed out a shallow, V-shaped notch in the summit, which was the site of the Pongo de Manseriche,[1] dreaded by early explorers of the region. Again we enjoyed a lovely sunset.

Early next morning we started upriver through the mist. The

---

1. *Pongo*, a word peculiar to Peru and Ecuador, signifies a narrow stretch in a river.

approach to the Pongo was through a maze of channels separated by low islands covered with light, open, vine-entangled woods and cane brakes. High, rocky banks began to border the river only a few miles below the entrance to the Pongo, for the low plain extends nearly up to the foot of Cerro de Campanquiz. The vegetation on the cliffs was extraordinarily beautiful; a shrubby *Warszewiczia*—another member of the coffee family that deserves a poetic and more easily pronounced name—made a vivid display with its brilliant red, leaflike calyx lobes.

In mid-morning we went ashore at the military post of Borja, situated at the foot of the Pongo de Manseriche, and promptly pushed back into the forest on the broken limestone hills to search for rubber trees. We found a few, some shedding their old leaves, which before falling turned a bright coppery red that made the trees fairly easy to locate amid the almost uniform verdure. Others were putting forth bright green new foliage at the same time that they displayed little pale yellow flowers in many-branched panicles. When, early in the afternoon, we returned to the *Amazonas* with our specimens, it was announced that we would proceed downstream at once. I was astounded! To visit Borja without seeing the Pongo de Manseriche would be equivalent to going to the town of Niagara Falls, New York, without looking at the Falls, or visiting Washington without even glancing at the Capitol—nay, worse, for Niagara Falls and Washington are fairly easy of access from most parts of the world, but few people ever reach this far-off wilderness even once in a lifetime. Happily, the plans for a prompt departure were altered.

A rough, little-used path led up from Borja along the steep, rocky side of the limestone ridge that rises above the Pongo—evidently it had few visitors. After walking several miles, we came to a point where the path skirted the brow of a precipice, and we enjoyed an outlook over the great rapids. Far below, the broad, muddy river flowed, swift and broken, between high cliffs and long, steep slopes all covered with luxuriant verdure. It was a scene wild and grand, yet it lacked that impressive quality conferred by great volumes of water thunderously falling, for the Pongo is not a waterfall but a long series of rapids. When the river is high, small ships of shallow draft can work up through the gorge; when it is low, shooting the rapids in a dugout canoe can be dangerous. Fully to appreciate the Pongo de Manseriche, one must view it with the geographical perspective as well as the sensuous eye. Here the headwaters of the greatest of all rivers burst through the last outlying ridge of that stupendous mountain range where they arise; before them lies only a vast lowland through which they will flow, calmly and deliberately, to the ocean on the opposite side of the broad continent.

Incidentally, along the sides of the gorge the soils expert and I found more rubber trees than our party saw at any other point we visited on the Marañón. The moral seemed to be that it does not pay to concentrate too strictly upon business!

Next morning, September 22, we started downstream from Borja. Making several short stops along the way, we passed the mouth of the Pastaza at seven o'clock the following morning. The broad, muddy stream, flowing out into the wider Marañón between wooded capes in the midst of the wilderness, carried my thoughts far up into the Ecuadorian Andes, where I knew it in its impetuous childhood, a dashing young river taking daring leaps and rushing boisterously through profound chasms, where White-capped Dippers built their mossy nests in niches in cliffs of intricately fractured volcanic rock, above the surging torrent. Later that same morning, we met a wood-burning river boat tied up along the bank, and stopped to talk to one of its passengers. This was the only machine-driven boat of any kind that we passed on the Marañón above the mouth of the Huallaga.

Passing the Huallaga, we entered the Lower Marañón and began to see a new kind of tern. Two species of terns are widespread along the rivers of Loreto. The smaller, the Yellow-billed Tern, which we had already met on the Huallaga and the Upper Marañón, is a delicate, graceful little bird, with bluish gray upper plumage, white under parts, deeply forked white tail, black outer wing feathers, and black cap. The other is the much bigger, more heavily built Large-billed Tern. Its back and shallowly notched tail are dark brownish gray, its under plumage white. Its wings when spread reveal on the upper side three contrasting shades in longitudinal bands. Next to the body they are gray, on the middle third white, and on the outer third abruptly black. Like the smaller tern, this big species wears a black cap and has a yellow bill.

We frequently saw these big terns resting in companies on exposed sandbars or perching on floating logs, riding downstream; often they were in pairs. One evening after sunset, I watched one flying high above the treetops, catching insects from the air. I never saw either this or the smaller tern plunge beneath the surface; the perpetually muddy currents of these great rivers discouraged this spectacular mode of fishing, widespread among terns. The Amazonian terns would fly down close to the water, pluck some small object from its surface by quickly bending down their sharp bills, then rise into the air again.

On the Lower Marañón we passed more human dwellings than on the upper river, and found more low, grassy shores. Here, as along the whole river at least as far up as the Pongo, many willow trees grew along the grassy banks. Their light, delicate sprays contrasted strangely with the coarse branches of the heavier vegetation.

At sunset on September 24, we passed the wide mouth of the Río Ucayali and entered the Amazon proper, which even here has the aspect of a broad lake rather than of a river. Early next morning we reached Iquitos, metropolis of eastern Peru.

The Napo and the Putumayo

A long flight of steps led up the high bank from the riverside to the terrace on which Iquitos stands. While we climbed upward, our baggage followed on a little car drawn by a cable along inclined rails. The town still bore many marks of those prosperous days, before the rubber plantations of the Far East made the tapping of wild trees unprofitable, when gold flowed through its streets as freely and was squandered as recklessly as in any mining camp where nuggets are gathered in the stream beds. The hotel was big, airy—and empty. It took us a while to find towels and soap in this grand establishment, and for our meals we were obliged to walk to a restaurant several blocks away.

From Iquitos we were to visit the Río Putumayo, the de facto boundary between Peru and Colombia, there to meet representatives of the Colombian government and explore lands north of the river. Since the Putumayo joins the Amazon far down in Brazil, the only easy way to reach Puerto Arturo, our point of rendezvous, was by air. The misinterpretation of a radiogram sent by the American Minister at Bogotá caused a further exchange of messages that delayed our departure for one day, with rather unfortunate consequences.

On the morning of September 28, we left Iquitos in a hydroplane of the Peruvian navy. Since we were to work in Colombian territory, the two Peruvian agronomists remained behind, and our party was reduced to the four North Americans, who, with the pilot and a mechanic, filled the airplane. At a point not far below Iquitos, the Río Napo comes close to the Amazon, then veers away and describes a long semicircle before it joins the mightier stream. Our route led down the Amazon, then across the narrow neck of land between the two rivers. As we flew over a military post that seemed lost amid the forests, the mechanic threw out a small bundle of newspapers and letters. Instead of falling to the ground, it lodged against a wing-strut, where it could not be reached from inside. The pilot continued to circle over the clearing, cutting a variety of queer aerial capers with his machine, in an effort to jog off the bundle. Finally, it fell to the ground, and we passengers breathed a sigh of relief. Then we followed up the muddy, winding Napo, shortening our course by flying over the narrow neck of many a long loop. In mid-morning we came down in the river opposite the military post at the mouth of the Río Curaray. Here our tanks were newly filled with gasoline, and we began to retrace our course down the Napo.

At a point, not far below the mouth of the Curaray, where the roughly parallel courses of the Napo and the Putumayo come closest together, possibly within thirty or forty miles, we turned left from the river and started across the forest. Soon we rose to an altitude of about 2,500 feet. From this height a vast expanse of territory was spread out beneath us; yet not one single mark of man's destroying hand could we detect amid all those many miles of forest. The land appeared to be everywhere perfectly flat; the distant horizon was a circle as regular and unbroken as one might ever see in mid-ocean. The impression we received of the vastness, the uniformity, and the solitude of these Amazonian forests was overwhelming and unforgettable.

Much of the land over which we flew was low and swampy. Often standing water glinted through the foliage. Large areas were covered with the crowded rosettes of the crowns of the noble Mauritia palm—the Aguaje of the Peruvians—which we had already, on our voyage along the rivers, learned to recognize as an indicator of marshy land. Some of the narrow forest waterways beneath us were so tortuous that they seemed to take ten miles to flow between points only a mile apart.

Now and again we overtook a flock of Blue-and-Yellow Macaws flying beneath us. How incredibly bright was their blue plumage when viewed from far above, with the sun shining full upon it and the dark verdure of the forest as a background! From our great height, these big, long-tailed birds appeared to be wholly blue. We could see nothing of their yellow under plumage, and their curiously marked white faces and thick black bills were indistinguishable. The raucous shouts that they rarely cease to utter as they fly failed to reach us above the motor's hum.

After about half an hour's flight we came in sight of the broad, muddy Putumayo serpentining through the forest. All these rivers looked much alike from the air, or even from their surface; they differed chiefly in breadth. Soon we came down in the river, in the midst of the wilderness. On one of my maps of Peru, Puerto Arturo fails to appear; on another, it is written large. Even making allowance for the cartographers' propensity to write almost anything on the wide empty spaces of their maps, I had expected to find at least a hamlet here. After the hydroplane had been moored to a stump, we jumped ashore and clambered up the steep bank to see Puerto Arturo—one solitary hut standing in a narrow clearing in the forest! It was inhabited by a couple of men and a boy who lived by hunting peccaries and other animals; in all Puerto Arturo there was not one person of the female sex. They were not so careful in disposing of their offal as they might have been. I took a single look around, a single whiff of the polluted air, and hurried back to the hydroplane—there was nowhere else to go. The rest of my sojourn on the Putumayo was spent seated on a stack of botanical driers on one of the pontoons, watching the river go by.

Now at last I made the acquaintance of the *piums*, of which explorers of Amazonia have so eloquently written. These minute biting flies were present in myriads along the shores of the Putumayo. The insect repellent that a kind friend in the Canal Zone had given me was effective against them for only about fifteen minutes; but since there was not much else we could do while we tried to decide upon our next move, I amused myself by continuing to anoint hands and face. This was the only time on our whole journey through eastern Peru when insects became unbearable, possibly because, if they became troublesome at night, we took refuge inside the screened gunboat.

And what of the Colombian party that we were to meet? We saw no trace of them. The hunters at the solitary hut told us that the Colombians had arrived by hydroplane the day before, which was the appointed date. While they bathed in the river, a sting ray pierced the foot of one of the men, making it imperative to take him to some point where he could be properly treated. Whether they ever returned to look for us, I never heard. We had come with only our clothes and scientific equipment reduced to a minimum to save weight in our hydroplane, for the Colombians were to have furnished food and bedding. Here in the midst of the wilderness, without food or shelter, it was obvious that our situation was untenable. When the afternoon was half gone without any sign of the Colombians, we climbed into the hydroplane and dodged thunderstorms on our way back to the Napo. At that moment our expedition to the Río Putumayo appeared a ridiculous failure; but, as I view it in retrospect after a long interval, I pronounce it a success—for otherwise I might never have looked down upon the unforgettable blue of the macaws or known the vast, monotonous flatness of the upper Amazon Valley as one can only know it from the air.

Back on the Napo, we landed at Santa Clotilde, an agricultural research station of the Peruvian government. The director, an Austrian who had served in the First World War, lived in a large, comfortable house overlooking the river. He had an apparently inexhaustible supply of beer, and he was most generous with it. After the rest of us had satisfied our thirst with a glass or two, our host continued to ply the pilot with bottle after bottle. We were amazed by this man's capacity, but even more by his boldness, for he was to return to Iquitos in a short while. The beer might not have been particularly strong, but in so much of it there was bound to be a good deal of alcohol. Finally, when he could hold no more, the pilot called his mechanic and the two men went down the boardwalk to the river. We stood to watch them take off, holding our breaths and thanking our stars that we were staying at Santa Clotilde. Somewhat to our surprise, the hydroplane rose into the air without mishap and soon vanished over the treetops. A few days later, we learned that it had arrived safely at Iquitos. A month afterward, while we were flying northward from Lima, one of my companions called attention to a brief paragraph in the newspaper. The jovial lieutenant who had piloted us had died in a crash while engaged in maneuvers with his hydroplane at Iquitos.

The two days that we passed at Santa Clotilde, waiting for the *Amazonas* to come around from Iquitos and pick us up, were a pleasant interlude in our almost constant traveling. On most of our short excursions ashore, we had marched through the forest—scientists, sailors, local guides, and camp followers, ten or a dozen strong—and scared away every living creature having feet or wings to bear it away. It was distressing to think about all the rare, little-known birds and other creatures that had fled at our approach and that I had not even glimpsed. But at Santa Clotilde I was free to wander through the forest alone and become acquainted with its inhabitants.

The high, well-drained land behind the small clearing supported a forest of medium density. As usual in lowland tropical forest, birds did not seem abundant and their voices rarely broke the prevailing sylvan silence. Yet I had no doubt that they were present in great variety, to be seen by one who had the patience to pick them out in the high treetops or glimpse them as they flitted through the dim undergrowth. The gem of all the feathered creatures that I met here was a Yellow-billed Jacamar, a slender, long-tailed, alert bird, about the size of an oriole, with a long, sharp beak. All his upper plumage was the most intense metallic green, with reflections of violet and gold. Below, he was a deep, rich chestnut, and his outer tail feathers were cinnamon. Doubtless his nest, like that of other jacamars, was hidden away in a burrow in some steep bank, or in a hard black termitary.

Here for the first time I met the White-bearded Manakin. More formal in attire than most of these little birds of the tropical American forests, he was impeccably clad in a black skullcap and coat, a broad and spotlessly white collar and shirt front, and a pearl-gray vest. In these evening clothes, he performed a solo dance above a small patch of bare ground amid the undergrowth

Yellow-billed Jacamar

that he had carefully cleaned of all fallen leaves and litter. As he leaped back and forth between the upright stems of saplings that grew around his little court, he produced startlingly loud snapping sounds by somehow knocking together the thickened shafts of his wing feathers—just as I have watched his more colorfully attired relatives in Central America do many times over. Others of his kind were performing the same odd antics above similar bare circles and ovals close by.

Even smaller than these White-bearded Manakins was the Golden-headed Manakin, a mite of a bird whose bright golden-yellow head belied his Greek scientific name *Pipra erythrocephala*. Elsewhere he was wholly black, with pale yellow eyes. But the manakin that most delighted me, because he was most different from any member of the family that I already knew, was the Striped Manakin. He was no bigger than the last, and the top of his head was bright red. Most of his upper plumage was olive-green; he wore a rufous-tawny band across his chest; and behind this his under plumage was finely streaked with pinkish chestnut and white. Pure white outer tail feathers completed this striking attire. Like most members of the manakin family, he was an accomplished acrobat. Bowing forward, he emitted a sharp buzzing sound from his widely opened mouth. Then, clinging to a slender horizontal twig, he pivoted rapidly around it, while a more plainly attired female of his kind looked on.

Antbirds, too, were numerous. The one occupied nest that I found on the Napo belonged to a blackish antshrike that I took to be a species of the large and often confusing genus *Thamnophilus*. The frail open cup, of the usual antbird type, was attached by its rim to the arms of a slender, horizontal, forked twig, five feet above the ground near a clear little rivulet running through the depths of the forest. The thin fabric was composed of coarse black fibers, covered on the outside with a little green moss. In all this, it resembled many another antbirds' nest I have seen; if its builders had stopped here, it would have been a quite inconspicuous structure. But, strangely enough, attached to the exterior were many pieces of a pure white, branched fungus, covered over thickly with little oblong tubercles. These hung far below the nest, making it glaringly white. Either the antbirds had lost all prudence when they built, or nature had tricked them cruelly. It appeared upon close examination that these white, branched objects were pieces of some dead inflorescence that had been overgrown by the fungus. Possibly this had occurred *after* the birds had added the pieces of inflorescence, brown and innocent enough, to their nest.

The male antshrike sat steadfast while I gazed at him with my eyes less than a foot from his own. It is not unlikely that I was the first human that he had ever seen, just as he was the first antshrike of his species that I had ever beheld. Of a sudden, he jumped to the ground and hopped and fluttered over it to the edge of the brook, twenty-five feet away. Here he recovered the use of his wings and flew up into a tangle of vines on the opposite side, where he repeated a complaining note many times over. Soon the answering call of his mate came from off in the forest. The two scolded and complained out of sight amid the undergrowth, not showing themselves near their nest while I watched from a distance. Finally, going to peep into the nest, I found one newly hatched nestling, pink-skinned, blind, with the newborn antbird's usual lack of any trace of down; and one white egg lightly scratched all over with brown, on the point of hatching.

Next morning I returned to the antbirds' nest, hoping to see more of the parents and write descriptions that would serve for eventual identification. But the nest was empty, probably having been raided by some slender snake! The dangers that beset birds' nests along the Napo seem no less numerous than in the forest beside my home in Costa Rica.

Among the birds at Santa Clotilde were many old friends. Oldest of these were wintering Barn Swallows, Bank Swallows, Spotted Sandpipers, and Solitary Sandpipers. Next were birds I had known for many years in Central America, including Southern House Wrens, Great Kiskadees, Gray-capped Flycatchers, Vermillion-crowned Flycatchers, little Wedge-billed Woodcreepers, and Blue Tanagers, which here had conspicuous white shoulders that northern races lack. Finally, I found many birds whose acquaintance I had made only the year before in the Oriente of Ecuador. Among these were Yellow-tufted Woodpeckers, black-and-white long-tailed Magpie-Tanagers like magpies in miniature, Silverbeaked Tanagers, Yellow-browed Sparrows, Green Oropéndolas,

Crested Oropéndolas, and the Giant Cowbirds that slip their eggs into the oropéndolas' long woven pouches.

I was sorry when the *Amazonas* arrived at ten o'clock on the morning of October 1. There were so many more things to be found in those forests about Santa Clotilde! We promptly embarked and returned upstream to the mouth of the Río Curaray, where, on our brief call in the hydroplane for gasoline, three days earlier, we had heard of rubber trees growing close to the military encampment. The soils expert and the botanist were sent across the river to hunt for rubber trees on the opposite shore, while the other members of the party went to see those that the soldiers had located near their camp.

We voyaged across the broad Napo in great style, in the ship's lifeboat driven by the outboard motor, flying the red-and-white banner of Peru, with an escort of sailors armed with rifles. We pushed in beneath the lush vegetation that fringed the opposite shore almost beneath a flock of strange, heronlike birds different from any I had ever seen. They were about the size of the Snowy Egret and like it nearly all white, yet not so purely, for they had black crowns and a slight yellowish tinge on the neck. Their bare faces were blue, and they had long, graceful plumes extending backward from their heads. I did not know what to call these odd birds until I found them figured in Goeldi's *Album* under the name *Pilherodius pileatus*, which seemed apposite.

These Capped Herons winged slowly off as we leaped ashore, to find that we had landed on low ground, subject to inundation at high water. With machetes we cut our way through the dense *matorral*, a rank and tangled growth of giant canes, heliconias and shell flowers with huge leaves, and interlacing vines, the whole shaded by scattered big trees. It seemed just the place to meet a huge, hungry anaconda or boa constrictor, and with our well-armed naval escort this seemed also a favorable time for the encounter. But neither here nor anywhere else in eastern Peru did we see any snakes much longer than our arms, and we noticed surprisingly few even of these small and mostly harmless ones. When, with much swinging of machetes, we had worked our way inland through this lush vegetation, we came to a backwater that blocked our way to the forest beyond. The afternoon was now so far advanced that we returned to our boat without having seen a single rubber tree, or any birds except the herons. But they were enough.

As we voyaged swiftly down the Napo, we saw flock after flock of parrots and macaws. Although these noisy birds were abundant along all the rivers, they were more numerous here than anywhere else. The macaws were of three kinds. The long-tailed Blue-and-Yellow Macaws, which were so enchantingly blue when we flew above them in the hydroplane, were mostly yellow as they flew above us in the ship. Somewhat less abundant was the Red-and-Green Macaw, a bird hardly less brilliant than the more familiar Scarlet Macaw, but lacking the yellow patches on the wings. The Chestnut-fronted Macaw, smaller and much plainer than the other two, was clad almost everywhere in parrot green, with a chestnut forehead and splashes of red on its wings. All these macaws were in great flocks among the Aguaje (Mauritia) palms that formed magnificent groves on swampy land beside the river, and they were doubtless feasting upon the queer, scale-covered palm fruits. With them were more parrots of lesser kinds than we could count or classify as the *Amazonas* glided rapidly past.

During much of our sojourn on the Napo, rain fell and the river steadily rose. In the middle of the afternnon of October 2, just as the sun was breaking through the clouds, we noticed hundreds of Wood Storks circling above the broad, muddy river. The big white birds were massed in three compact flocks. They gyrated around with long legs projecting behind and long necks stretched forward, their heads seeming to be weighted down by their massive bills. Their circulatory movement was evidently intended, like that of migrating hawks, to permit the birds to be borne upward on a local ascending current of air, without flapping their wings —an exercise in which most big birds never engage for long if they can avoid it. After gaining sufficient height, each flock in turn set off northward. The great storks now spread out until they flew side by side on a wide front, in a single long, sinuous rank. They advanced alternately flapping and soaring. Soon a fourth flock came into view over the treetops on the right bank and circled above the river, where evidently they found the strongest up-drafts. Our pilot explained that the Wood Storks were seeking other feeding grounds, since the Napo had risen over its lower banks, inundating the marshes, and covering most of the sand bars.

The Amazon and the Ucayali

Shortly before noon on October 3, we glided out of the mouth of the Napo into the league-wide Amazon. That afternoon we moored at Pebas, near the mouth of the Río Ampiyacu. We had intended to explore the neighboring forest the next morning, but the day dawned with a steady rain that gave no promise of stopping, so we continued downstream, leaving this locality to be visited on our return. On our way down the Amazon we met many islands, some quite large, dividing the river into narrower channels. Along the south shore were low hills that met the river in high banks. The forest along both shores was low and scrubby, possibly because the land had once been cleared for cultivation, but scattered through these woods stood large trees of Silk-cotton and of Capirona with attractive smooth brownish bark. At intervals we passed thatched huts in little clearings and rarely a more pretentious dwelling with a roof of corrugated iron. Many of these people lived far from their nearest neighbors. They seemed to have no way to leave their farms except by that universal highway, the river. High bars of silt newly formed along the shores were planted with rice and peanuts. In the midst of the rice fields we noticed tiny thatched shelters where, we were told, the owners stayed to frighten away grain-devouring birds while the rice was maturing.

That afternoon we went ashore at Caballococha, a big village beside a small southern tributary. Just enough of the day remained for a pleasant walk through shady pastures bordering the stream. Caciques and oropéndolas flew by in noisy flocks. The air was full of insects that attracted many flycatchers and other birds. Even one of the Large-billed Terns from the river flew about high in the air, catching insects like a swallow. A Yellow-headed Caracara likewise circled above the treetops, seizing insects now in its bill, now in its feet, as though this versatile forager had entered some intermediate stage in evolution, midway between a raptor and a flycatcher. As daylight faded, I watched a noisy family of Yellow-tufted Woodpeckers retire to sleep in a hole in a low stub standing in the pasture. This pretty black-and-crimson woodpecker is the member of the family that I most often saw at low altitudes in eastern Ecuador and Peru. As in the related Golden-naped Woodpecker of Costa Rica and Panama, families hold together for months after the young fly. On several occasions I watched a whole family of full-grown individuals enter a common bedroom at the day's end—once, in Ecuador, five together.

Leaving Caballococha the following afternoon, we continued downriver with Colombian territory on our left, Peruvian on our right. After dark a storm blew up; rain came down in torrents; lightning alternately illuminated the broad river and left it in utter darkness; the water became very rough. In this storm we reached Ramón Castilla, the easternmost settlement in Peruvian territory. Next morning, when we could see where we were, we found ourselves tied to a high bank, along which stood, in a single row, a handful of thatched cabins facing the river. The best of them was raised above ground on low posts and had walls of sawed boards neatly whitewashed. Above it, on a tall flagpole, fluttered the red-and-white flag of Peru. Close behind rose the forest.

After breakfast we continued a short distance downstream to the Río Yavarí, which separates Peru from Brazil. At its mouth, the territories of Brazil, Peru, and Colombia come together. A short run up the Yavarí brought us to Islandia (Iceland), named by someone whose sense of humor rose victorious over Amazonian heat. At this tiny settlement we found a small plantation of rubber trees, and many impressively large ones grew in the neighboring forest. While I examined one of the trees in the plantation, low, soft, musical murmurs drew my attention to a flock of small birds in the branches above me. Their bright orange bills, tapering from a thick base to a sharp point, provided the only touch of color on these drab birds, dull black above and dark gray below. Their eyes were large and dark; and I noticed that two of their toes were directed forward, two backward. Murmuring softly to each other, they twitched their black tails from side to side. These Black-fronted Nunbirds, members of the puffbird family, seemed so sociable, gentle, and confiding that I would have loved to remain in Islandia and learn more about them. Our tight schedule prohibited such diversions, and I have never again seen Black-fronted Nunbirds. But, many years later, amid the wet forests of northeastern Costa Rica, I studied a close relative, the White-fronted Nunbird, and confirmed my early surmise that nunbirds have exceptionally interesting habits. White-fronted Nunbirds nest in long burrows in the forest floor. The three nestlings are attended by three or four grown birds who all look much alike and are so fearless of man that we could watch them without concealment.

Across the river from Islandia was Brazil, a country that none of us had visited. It seemed a pity to come so close to this great nation yet fail to pay our respects to it. The *Amazonas* was not authorized to enter Brazilian territory, nor, apparently, could it send one of its boats to the other shore. So we four North Americans struck a bargain with a resident of Islandia to ferry us across the Yavarí in his dugout canoe for a few soles. Pushing in among the dense aquatic vegetation on the eastern side of the river, we jumped ashore and spent about ten minutes wandering through the forest. It was much like the forest on the other side of the river; yet it seemed to possess a different atmosphere, a distinct flavor—for was all this not Brazil? After this brief lark, we returned to the *Amazonas* and began the long voyage up the Amazon to Iquitos.

While pushing upstream close to the shore, we passed a pair of Jabirus resting in the top of a tall dead tree. These huge white storks, among the biggest and heaviest of flying birds, appeared to be rare along the rivers of Loreto. In addition to this pair, I saw only a few others along the Ucayali. Hoatzins were also rare along the Amazon; they preferred the narrower tributaries and the backwaters.

Arriving at Iquitos on the morning of October 9, we remained four days before we continued upriver to the Ucayali. In the town's central plaza I found an attractive little finch that flocked in the grassy spaces between the walks and flower beds. The male was largely gray on the upper parts, with black wings and tail. His throat, breast, and the center of his abdomen were bright rufous-chestnut. The female was brownish olive above, buffy below. Like other species of *Sporophila*, these Chestnut-bellied Seedeaters had short, thick bills and subsisted largely on the seeds of grasses. Although some of the seedeaters are gifted songsters, I heard from this one only an unmelodious chirping that recalled the notes of the House Sparrow and seemed in keeping with its urban setting. Yet it was by no means restricted to towns and villages; we met it in grassy clearings along the rivers and up into the foothills of the Andes to an altitude of nearly three thousand feet.

Where not swampy, the country around Iquitos was occupied by pastures, cultivated fields, or fields lying fallow and overgrown with bushes and weeds. The birds here were chiefly wide-ranging species that we had met elsewhere. One familiar with the birds of any region in the humid lowlands of the tropical American mainland may visit any other region, no matter how distant from the first, and find species that he already knows, or others closely similar, that he can name, and that make him feel at home. He will never again experience that feeling of utter strangeness and newness that was his if, instead of growing up somewhere in this vast area, he came to it from afar. Yet in every region that he visits, the bird watcher will find species that are excitingly new and different. This constant combination of the old and familiar with the new and strange makes travel in tropical America a delightful experience, on the one hand preventing bewilderment by a wholly unfamiliar avifauna, on the other hand dispelling monotony.

The situation is different in the more restricted arid parts of tropical America, for these are not as continuous as the humid areas, and their discontinuity has resulted in the evolution of avifaunas peculiar to each; yet even in the arid lands the bird watcher will find a few wide-ranging species that he first met far away. On the west coast of South America, I was impressed with the continuity of the avifauna of the humid regions of tropical America, the discontinuity of that of the dry regions. In the province of El Oro, Ecuador, where humid conditions prevailed, I found so many birds that I already knew in Central America far to the north that I felt quite at home; in semidesert areas fifty miles away, nearly all the birds were new to me.

At nightfall on October 12, we re-embarked upon the *Amazonas* and began the first stage of our long journey back to the coast. Next morning at breakfast, the captain told a tale that emphasized the vastness of the river on which we voyaged. After our return to Iquitos four days earlier, the two pilots who until then had guided our ship along the rivers had been transferred to another vessel, and we had set forth on this final stage of our explorations with less competent pilots. After proceeding a good way up the river in darkness, the *Amazonas* had somehow turned around in the wide expanses of open water and, all unknown to himself, our new pilot was taking it downstream again! He did not discover his mistake until the distant lights of Iquitos told him plainly that during the latter part of the night he had retraced his earlier course.

The next day we entered the Ucayali, a mighty river that flows nearly the whole length of Peru, in breadth comparable to the Marañón and, with its tributary the Apurimac, exceeding it in length. Along its lower reaches the shores are nearly everywhere even lower than those we had seen beside the other great streams of eastern Peru. We had not gone far up this river when our inexpert pilots ran the ship upon a submerged sandbar, causing minor damages that forced us to moor beside the bank for the night. Our first excursion ashore was at Requena, a village situated near the mouth of the Río Tapiche, where we visited a nunnery school and tramped over the neighboring hills examining their vegetation and soils. The most notable bird that I met here was a male Spangled Cotinga, a starling-sized bird of the treetops whose glossy turquoise-blue plumage was speckled with black on the crown and mantle and variegated with a patch of rich magenta-purple on the throat and chest. His wings and tail were black.

Not far above the Río Tapiche we entered the Canal de Puinahua, a side channel of the Ucayali somewhat straighter than the main river, yet with many a bend. Between this cutoff and the main channel lies a big island about seventy-five miles long. While we wound through this long canal I climbed up into the ship's crow's nest, the better to look over the surrounding forests and the narrow cultivated fields adjoining the waterway. Evening fell; the dusk deepened over the still, dark river; then the full moon floated up above the treetops, casting a gleaming pathway of light over the water, now ahead of the ship, now astern, as we twisted along the winding channel. The moonlight, glinting from the foliage of the treetops and reflected back from the somber water, made a scene of unforgettable enchantment. By moonlight we moored to a high bank beside a clearing called Gran Bretaña, where a big cabin stood beside a plantation of thriving bananas.

Next morning, in a small motor launch that had come up from Requena to meet us, we ascended the Río Pacaya, a narrow tributary of the Puinahua arm of the Ucayali. It flowed through wide grassy marshes, with a fringe of trees along its banks, or else through low, swampy woodlands. Bird life was more conspicuously abundant here than along any of the greater streams that we had navigated. The water through which we plowed was dark brown, almost free of sediment rather than laden with light brown or yellowish silt, like the big rivers that flowed down from eroding Andean heights. Here Hoatzins were so numerous that we met a flock of them every few hundred feet. Wattled Jacanas in maroon plumage flew along the shores and over the neighboring marshes, holding aloft their beautiful pale yellow wings each time they alighted. We saw Ringed and Amazon kingfishers, Neotropic Cormorants, Wood Storks, hawks of several kinds, and more small birds than I could identify as we glided rapidly along. Monkeys swung from the boughs of the riverside trees, and caymans showed their huge broad heads above the water, to be shot at by one of the Peruvian members of our party.

All of these birds and beasts I had known before, at one place or another. But scattered over the grassy marshlands, usually in pairs, were great, dark-colored fowls, looking as big and heavy as domestic geese, such as I had never seen anywhere outside of illustrated books on ornithology. When my binoculars picked out the long, slender filament standing up on the crown of each and the stout spur at the bend of each wing, there was no mistaking them—they were Horned Screamers! When alarmed by the passage of the boat, they flew up heavily and stood upon high, exposed branches of the riverside trees, from which one inferred that their natural enemies in the marshlands were flightless creatures without projectile weapons. Happily, our companion with the rifle reserved his shots for the caymans.

Some miles up the Pacaya we reached higher land covered with forest, where we went ashore to search for and measure rubber trees. Then we returned to the *Amazonas* and resumed our upward voyage. Next morning, after fourteen hours' running, we

Horned Screamer

emerged from the Canal de Puinahua upon the broad main channel of the Ucayali. Continuing up the river, we came next day to a
stretch with many exposed sandbanks, upon which rested multitudes of birds. Among them were Large-billed and Yellow-billed
terns, Great Egrets standing tall and white upon long black legs,
White-necked Herons, Neotropic Cormorants, three Jabirus that
dwarfed all the others, and Black Skimmers crouching low upon
the sands, all facing the same way. This was the only point where
we found skimmers in abundance. At Ramón Castilla, far down
the Amazon, I had watched two skimming over the river at sunset, plowing the water with the long, thin lower mandible of their
widely opened bills until they caught a small fish, which they ate
in flight. As they glided along only a few inches above the water,
they did not even dent its surface with the tips of their long
wings.

At dawn on October 18 we saw distant hills, the first elevation
high enough to break the uniform level monotony of the horizon
that we had glimpsed since leaving the Pongo de Manseriche
nearly a month earlier. Late in the afternoon we passed the village

of Orellana, situated among low hills, where there was a radio station. At sunset we glided by the end of a long, steep, wooded ridge that rose abruptly from the water's edge and from the surrounding flat lands to a height of perhaps a thousand feet. At the base of the precipitous end of this ridge, rocks lined the shore. After passing by so many hundreds of miles of muddy or clayey banks, with never a stone, they were a strange sight—we had seen nothing like them for weeks. Other mountains, seemingly higher, rose in the distant west. We were approaching the Andes, but they were still a long way off.

Next day we went ashore for the morning at Contamana, a big village on the right bank of the Ucayali. Remembering that it was his wife's birthday, the soils expert sent a greeting to her in Washington, to the great discomfiture of the local radio operator, who was not accustomed to transmitting messages in English. On October 20 we reached Pucallpa, the terminus of the still unfinished highway that the Peruvian government was building down from the Andes, by way of Tingo María. Here we regretfully took leave of the *Amazonas*, which for five weeks had been our floating home. From Pucallpa an airplane of the Peruvian government took us to San Ramón Chanchamayo in the Andean foothills—a two-hour flight over vast forests. Thence we returned by automobile, along narrow highways that skirted the brinks of unbelievable precipices, to Lima and the coast.

Long ago, talking to an old wanderer about the Amazon region, which was to him a recollection and to me still a dream, he told me that it was "the most monotonous country in the world." In a way, he was right. As the years roll by and my visit to Amazonia becomes a memory—and again a dream—those endless low shores of the Marañón, the Huallaga, the Napo, the Ucayali, and the Amazon melt into each other, making a single picture, one long tapestry across the mind, varied only as high forest, brakes of giant cane, or groves of stately Aguaje palms with tall columnar trunks and great fanlike fronds line the banks. But here and there in that long tapestry—as on a Chinese scroll-picture mounted on ivory rollers—are pricked out bright spots of color, wonderful new birds met for the first time at this or that point along the rivers, spots that serve to punctuate the interminable ribbon of verdure, to break it into units that the mind can grasp and retain.

CHAPTER 7

The Emerald Land

Torrent Duck

The assignment of our Rubber Survey Party was to explore eastern Peru and the Pacific littoral of Ecuador and Colombia. After our return to Lima from the Amazon and its tributaries, we made, literally and figuratively, a flying visit to extreme northwestern Peru, then embarked with all our baggage at Lima for the voyage up the coast to Guayaquil. From this city we flew to Quito, where Stakman and Blair remained, while Marion Striker, the soils expert, and I continued in the same airplane down to the port of Esmeraldas on the Pacific coast at the mouth of the river of the same name. We had been sent to search for lands suitable for rubber plantations in Ecuador's northwestern province, the verdant land of Esmeraldas.

A day and a half in the town of Esmeraldas sufficed to arrange for our canoe voyage up the river. November 22, 1940, the day set for our departure, dawned with a steady downpour. After waiting until mid-morning for the rain to stop, we embarked in our two big dugout canoes beneath it. One, manned by two stalwart black men, carried our luggage and provisions. The second, with a crew of three, held the members of our party: Colonel Julio E. Jáuregui, representative of the Ecuadorian government responsible for arranging the details of travel; Rodrigo Orellana, sent by the Banco Hipotecario of Guayaquil; Striker; and me. We were accompanied by Captain Simón Plata Torres, of Esmeraldas, who had surveyed the route of the proposed highway from Esmeraldas to Santo Domingo de Los Colorados, and who now generously offered to guide us to the best areas for planting rubber in the province that he knew so well and was eager to advance economically.

Our canoes hugged the shore, where the current was the weakest and the boatmen could most easily reach bottom with the long poles that pushed us upstream. For many miles above its mouth, the broad Río Esmeraldas winds among steep, level-topped ridges, rarely as much as a thousand feet high, between which lie narrow, level valleys. The forest covering these crowded ridges was verdant even now, toward the end of the drier half of the year. Even where we could detect no signs of logging, this woodland was surprisingly light and open, with fewer impressive trees than the lushness of the riverside vegetation had led us to expect. Probably the abruptness of the slopes and the sterility or impermeability of the heavy, plastic soil of yellowish clay were responsible for the meager forest growth.

Early in the afternoon we went ashore at San Mateo, a village of thatched cabins situated on a riverside terrace, seven or eight miles above Esmeraldas. This, we were told, was the first colony that the Spaniards planted in the province. Here, as we were to find at every hamlet we visited farther up the river, nearly every face we saw was black. In this typical riverside settlement, the houses, of one or several rooms, usually perched high above the ground on posts. Walls and even floors were made of the hollow stems of the giant bamboo that grows in huge clumps. The stems were simply split along one side and flattened out. The thatch was composed of palm fronds or the broad, fan-shaped leaves of the Paja Toquilla, or Panama-hat Plant, which when thickly overlapped would last for several years. These people had learned to make good use of what nature provided close at hand; only a minority of the buildings were made of sawed boards and roofed with corrugated sheet iron. With shoes on our feet and a load on our shoulders, it was not easy for us to climb the steep, ladderlike stairs that led up to bamboo floors which yielded alarmingly beneath our weight, although they never failed to uphold us.

Among the fruit trees that clustered around these picturesque riverside dwellings we recognized the orange, avocado, Nispero, Mammee, Zapote, Caimito, papaya, and mango. The many great-leafed Breadfruit trees seemed to be all of the seed-bearing variety, variously called breadnut and, in Central America, *castaña* (chestnut); the true seedless breadfruit appeared to be unknown along the river. Bananas and plantains were the principal cultivated crops, and we saw a few small patches of pineapples. Coconut palms grew abundantly all along the Río Esmeraldas, providing in their unripe fruits a clear, refreshing liquid that made it unnecessary for us to risk drinking river water. The few, mostly small pastures that we noticed were lushly green and supported healthy cattle and a few well-fed horses that seemed to work little, since travel and the transportation of produce were chiefly by water. Along this beautiful river nature was bountiful, enabling the inhabitants to lead their simple lives without great effort.

All along the river grew many Caucho trees, whose latex, although widely used, is less valuable than that of the Brazilian Rubber tree that most interested our party. Deep horizontal incisions encircling their trunks and lower branches at irregular intervals, up to a height of thirty feet or more, revealed that these trees were tapped, although we did not see this being done. We learned that in certain areas the stands of these Caucho trees had been improved by broadcasting their seeds in the forest, where sometimes the largest of the original trees were felled to make room for the new seedlings. Thus rude "plantations" were formed. Although the latex that oozes from Brazilian Rubber trees is commonly collected in a cup, the abundant white latex of the Caucho usually remains in the grooves until it hardens, which takes eight to ten days in dry weather and about two weeks in rainy weather. Then the long, thin strips of coagulated latex are pulled from the tree, rolled into balls, and carried downstream on rafts of Balsa logs or in canoes. At the port of Esmeraldas we were shown a heap of these heavy, dirty black balls lying in a rough warehouse, awaiting shipment to Hamburg. During the first half of 1939, the year preceding our visit, Esmeraldas had exported 312,000 pounds of this product of trees growing wild in its forests, the felling of which was prohibited by law.

In addition to the rubber that was exported, a small quantity was used locally for coating fabrics to make raincoats, ponchos, waterproof bags for carrying clothing, and similar articles. For this purpose, the latex of the Caucho trees was made to flow from the incisions into vessels and applied to the cloth in liquid form with a brush, after the addition of sulphur for vulcanizing, and whatever coloring was desired. The fabric, still on the frame on which it was stretched to be coated, was placed in the sun to dry the latex, which took only a few hours on a bright day. Six or eight applications of the latex were needed to prepare a raincoat or poncho of superior quality. Much latex was also shipped as a liquid to factories of rubber goods in high Andean towns. After adding ammonia to retard coagulation, the latex was sewed up tightly in burlap sacks for transportation. An Ecuadorian raincoat made as I have described served me well for several years in rainy Costa Rica.

After our first day of travel upstream, we from time to time came to low rapids, where our boatmen toiled strenuously to push the heavy canoes against the rushing water. While we struggled over these rapids, inch by inch, it was often doubtful whether we would win the contest with the strong current. Progress upstream was necessarily slow. Whenever practicable, we would leave the canoe, both to ease the boatmen's burden and to stretch legs cramped by long sitting on low benches improvised of blocks of Balsa wood. Then we would walk over the broad flats of exposed shingle: rounded stones of all sizes and many colors, from different geological formations, washed down from the mountains by flood waters and mixed together in the shallows. Or else, shaded by fruit trees and banana plants, we would follow narrow paths that led along the bank from hut to hut. But before long we would reach a point where a steep ridge came abruptly down to the water's edge, making us embark again.

Whenever our boatmen found it necessary to cross the river to avoid the swifter current on a concave shore, we would lose headway and be carried a short distance downstream. On the fourth day we passed the highest rapids in the Río Esmeraldas, called Corriente Grande, and watched two laden Balsa rafts rush over them, rocking wildly as they were borne swiftly through the broken water at the foot of the rapids. A short distance below the Corriente Grande, the channel was formerly partly blocked by a ledge of rock, on which many rafts were smashed to pieces; but this obstruction had been dynamited away a few years earlier by order of the government. At the time of our visit, the water was so low that motor-driven launches could not go upstream much beyond San Mateo. In the wet season, with more water in the channel, they could ascend considerably higher.

The rafts of Balsa were much the same as those that we had earlier seen on the Huallaga, Ucayali, and other tributaries of the Amazon; but, since they made much shorter voyages, they were not so well provided with living quarters in the form of a raised platform of poles covered by a thatched roof. Like the Amazonian rafts, they were steered, after a fashion, by a broad paddle attached to the end of a long, stout pole fixed at the stern. By much hard pulling on the pole, the helmsman obtained a sluggish response from the heavy, clumsy craft. These Esmeraldan rafts were used to carry bananas, rubber, and Tagua (vegetable ivory) downstream to the port. When the peeled Balsa logs of which they were made were sold to one of the several sawmills near the town, the proceeds not only covered the cost of transporting the cargo but often yielded a surplus.

The shores of the Río Esmeraldas are high and firm, never low and swampy. Through much of the river's length, the banks rise up steeply or even vertically to the edge of level terraces, which may be from ten to thirty feet above the water. More rarely, bold bluffs stand fifty to a hundred feet high. At many points, where the hills press close to the channel, steep slopes sweep up abruptly from the water's edge to lofty, palm-crowned summits. At low water, great expanses of shingle are exposed between the river bank and the shrunken current. At one spot along the shore, we found nearly naked black women washing gold in shallow wooden platters, and we noticed several places where the gravelly shores had been dug up by gold-washers.

The beautiful vegetation along these shores was perpetually

verdant. *Pithecolobium* trees with spreading, rounded, densely foliaged crowns and long, horizontal branches profusely laden with epiphytes carried my thoughts back to Central American streams, where I had so often rested beneath their deep shade, admiring the wealth of air plants they upheld. A shrubby related species, abundant on the rockier shores, was embellished by long clusters of stamens red at the tips and white at the bases. Precipitous slopes rising abruptly from the river's margin were green with a bewildering variety of bromeliads, great-leafed aroids, ferns, orchids, the Paja Toquilla, bushes, and creepers. Lower shores displayed a luxuriant growth of giant herbs, including Wild Plantains, Shellflowers, terrestrial aroids, and in places brakes of tall Wild Canes. Everywhere the vegetation, even now at the end of the drier season, gave evidence of abundant and constant humidity.

Along the lower reaches of the river, most of the level, or only slightly inclined land was, or had formerly been, cultivated or turned into pasture, and the remaining patches of woodland had not been exempt from exploitation. The first fairly undisturbed forest that we could examine was near La Delicia, forty-two miles above the town of Esmeraldas. The following morning, along the Río Sade, we again pushed into the forest back from the shore, following a lumbering road until we reached the point beyond which no trees had been cut. Here the land rose by three successive steep ascents, separated by broad, level terraces. On the highest of these terraces, undisturbed forest was dominated by massive, tall, well-spaced trees, between whose spreading crowns much sky was visible. One of the most abundant of these trees was a species of *Pourouma* that exceeded a hundred feet in height and had trunks over three feet thick. Its broad, palmately divided leaves have such rough upper surfaces that rural housewives use them to scour pots, pans, and unpainted woodwork. Among these trees many Pambil palms soared up grandly to equal heights. As is usual in moist tropical woodland with an open canopy, the dense undergrowth made walking difficult.

Toward noon on the fourth day of our voyage, we passed, on the right or eastern bank of the Río Esmeraldas, the long, steep ridge, possibly fifteen hundred feet high, that separates the Río Caninde from the Guaillabamba. Early in the afternoon, we reached the mouth of the latter, a stream laden with silt from the high Andes, almost as broad as that on which we traveled. As we continued to ascend the Esmeraldas above this affluent, low hills still rose on the western side, but they soon fell away to insignificant heights.

We slept that night on the floor of a cockroach-infested cabin in the black settlement of Malimpia. Early next morning we continued upstream, going most of the way on foot while the boatmen toiled valiantly with their poles to force the big canoes upward over many low rapids. The current had now become very swift; its might in times of flood was attested by great expanses of exposed blackish shingle and boulders along the shores. The banks had become higher, in many places rising up a hundred feet or more. Rivulets, leaping down into the main stream, formed many pretty cascades. Toward noon we reached the confluence of the Blanco and Quinindé, two rivers of nearly equal width whose waters join to form the Esmeraldas. We had reached a point about sixty miles above the river's mouth and were about one hundred and twenty feet above sea level, as we stood on the point of land where the parent streams mingled their currents.

The hamlet of Quinindé, known also as Rosa Zárate, the most important center of population in all this region, stood upon a high bluff between the Blanco and the Quinindé rivers. It contained a dozen rude houses, some of which were falling into ruin, two little shops that sold provisions and cheap wares, the *alcaldía*, or town hall, and the school. This last was a structure with walls and floor of split bamboo and a roof of corrugated sheet iron, all perched upon high posts. Since school was not in session, we occupied this building during our two nights in Quinindé.

On the morning after our arrival, we went by canoe for about two miles up the Río Blanco, between shores embellished by luxuriant vegetation that was, if possible, even more beautiful than that along the Río Esmeraldas. Near the mouth of a creek called the Estero San José, we scrambled up a low bank and entered the forest along a logging trail. Huge wild fig trees, standing well separated, dominated the rather open woodland, above an exuberant undergrowth of moisture-loving plants. Slender palms towered everywhere. Here we found the Sande, a species of *Brosimum* with such tall, straight, imposing trunks that the Esmeraldans called it *el rey de la montaña*—king of the forest. From incisions in the brown bark a white latex flows in such quantities that it is sometimes used as a nutritious drink, as Alexander von Humboldt recorded long ago of this or a similar species in Venezuela (Humboldt 1852, vol. 2, pp. 47–49). The fibrous bark of this and related members of the mulberry family can be beaten out to make a soft, thick tapa cloth, sometimes as big as a bed sheet. Each of our boatmen carried one of these bark mats folded up in his chest, to spread out at nightfall for his bed.

In the afternoon, after our return to Quinindé, the animals for our overland journey to Santo Domingo de los Colorados arrived over the trail. At San Mateo, our first stop along the river, Colonel Jáuregui had sent a message back to Esmeraldas, to be relayed by radio to Quito and thence by telegraph to Santo Domingo, requesting the horses and mules. We had been uncertain whether the message would reach its destination by this long, roundabout way, and were not a little relieved when the animals finally appeared, for without them it would have been impossible to transport our impedimenta to Santo Domingo. The troop, consisting of three horses and two mules with saddles for riding and two other mules with packsaddles for baggage, had come from Santo Domingo in two and a half days. On these tired animals we were forced to set forth next morning, for our schedule was tight.

The following morning we took leave of our boat crew and Captain Plata, to whom more than anyone else we owed the success of our excursion. By half past eight the pack animals were all loaded, the stirrups of our mounts were adjusted, and we started under a slight drizzle. The mule trail from Quinindé to Santo Domingo, a distance of fifty-three miles, followed the route of the proposed Quito-Esmeraldas highway. Over this trail the post between Quito and Esmeraldas traveled once a week; the mail bags were brought almost to Santo Domingo by automobile, then by pack animal to Quinindé, where they were loaded into a canoe for the voyage down the river. But the mails were usually light, and a short while before our visit the newly inaugurated airplane service between Quito, Esmeraldas, and Guayaquil had begun to carry much of the mail.

To judge by the condition of the trail, it could hardly have been used by anyone except the post-carrier and infrequent travelers like ourselves. A hundred yards beyond the outskirts of the village, we found the way nearly closed by bushes, giant herbs, and fallen trees. The colonel had engaged a man who for several hours walked at the head of our little caravan and opened the path with swinging blows of his machete. After this man turned back, we had to use our own machetes frequently to sever the branches and tangles of vines that blocked our way. For two whole days we struggled slowly along this neglected trail.

All day we rode through forest that was interrupted only at long intervals by small, mostly abandoned clearings. The way at first ran parallel to the Río Blanco, at times so near that we glimpsed the water through gaps in the foliage. Save for a few isolated huts along the shores, we saw no occupied dwellings. We passed not a single traveler on the long day's ride. For miles the trail was nearly level, except where it dipped to cross widely separated small streams; but in the afternoon, as we approached the Agua Colorada, we entered gently rolling country. Doubtless because it was trodden by so few feet, this path was not nearly as muddy as I have found many another forest trail, and we might have gone faster but for the undergrowth that persistently clung to us and held us back. We rode steadily through the day, without a pause for rest and refreshment; not until the afternoon did we realize that we had passed Thanksgiving Day with no dinner at all!

After riding seventeen miles, we halted in the evening beside the Agua Colorada, a small stream of clear, swiftly flowing water that fell into the Río Cócola a few hundred feet below our camp site. Here in the midst of the forest, close beside the trail, we found a low, crude shelter of palm leaves, too small to accommodate all our party, so that it was necessary to construct an additional shelter with our tarpaulins. Our difficulty in finding a few straight saplings to support the canvas confirmed our impression that the reproduction of trees in this forest was poor. After tucking the edges of our mosquito nets under our air mattresses all around, to keep out venomous snakes and spiders, we soon fell asleep, and passed a peaceful night in the midst of the vast forest.

At dawn we awoke to the deep-voiced roaring of a troupe of Howling Monkeys in distant treetops. These were the only fairly large mammals we heard on all our long journey through the forests; we saw none at all. Likewise, we heard very few birds, and saw even fewer. Parrots were the kind most in evidence. All this agrees with my experience on journeys through heavy lowland forests from Guatemala to Peru. The hurrying traveler sees little of their animal life, which reveals itself only to those who can pause and patiently court its acquaintance. In the more open woodlands of arid and elevated regions, birds and mammals often appear to the traveler to be more abundant, probably because less vegetation screens them from view.

As so often happened, the morning was half gone before we began to move onward from Agua Colorada. Our preparations for departure were aided by two black men who had built a tiny shelter of split bamboo and palm fronds beside the Río Cócola in this solitary spot and were collecting rubber from the Caucho trees that grew wild in the forest. They had already accumulated several hundred pounds of it, and when they had enough they would build a raft of Balsa logs and float their harvest down to the Río Blanco, then down the Esmeraldas to the town at its mouth.

Our way this morning was along a brush-choked trail such as we had followed on the preceding day. Early in the afternoon we reached the broad and carefully graded roadbed that extended halfway from Santo Domingo to Quinindé. Work on this road had been suspended several years earlier, and the unsurfaced road was now choked with weedy growths that here, in the broad corridor between the trees, sprang much more vigorously than under the shade of the neighboring forest. The passable portion of the road was only a narrow path through the weeds, kept open by the occasional passage of man or woodland animal. Here our progress became even more difficult than through the forest where no roadbed had been prepared. In the afternoon our muleteers killed a venomous *papagaya* snake, a green *Bothrops* only about a foot long, with an abruptly broad head. Men familiar with this part of Ecuador loved to dwell upon the number, variety, and horrendous character of the serpents that infested it; but this small snake, and another harmless to man, were the only ones we saw between the port of Esmeraldas and Santo Domingo.

The forest through which we now rode was much the same as that through which we had passed on the preceding day. Its outstanding characteristics were the scattered distribution of the big dicotyledonous trees and the abundance of tall palms. These palms, chiefly belonging to two species of similar aspect, both called Pambil, had slender, columnar trunks that often rose to a height of from a hundred to a hundred and fifty feet and upheld a narrow crown of big, pinnately divided fronds. They were supported at the base by spiny prop roots that extended well up the trunk, and they had well-developed green crown shafts. These towering palms lifted their heads above all but the tallest of the dicotyledonous trees and accounted for from 25 to 50 percent, and in spots even more, of the higher trees. But the widely spaced great dicotyledonous trees and the many narrow-crowned palms together formed a very broken and imperfect canopy, leaving half or more of the sky visible from the ground at points where the undergrowth did not interfere.

Perhaps the most abundant tree over considerable areas was a species of *Inga* that we did not see in flower. Very common also was another legume, a species of *Erythrina* that rose to a height of about 125 feet and displayed bright orange-red blossoms. But the biggest trees, and in places the most numerous, were wild figs (*Ficus*) and the related *Coussapoa*. The seeds of these trees germinate upon the trunks and branches of other trees, often high above the ground, where they are deposited in the droppings of birds that eat their fruits. The roots of the seedling creep down over the supporting trunk and eventually enter the soil. As the young tree grows, these roots increase in number and thickness, surround the trunk of the host tree, fuse together where they come in contact with one another, until at last they strangle the host and with their concrescent mass form the false trunk of the *Ficus* or the *Coussapoa*. Finally, all traces of the host tree decay away or are buried beneath successive layers of the wood of the parasite, whose massive trunk betrays its peculiar origin chiefly by its irregularly ridged and furrowed surface. As we approached Santo Domingo, the *Coussapoa* became increasingly abundant. We saw many of these trees on the trunks of tall palms, some barely started, others at various stages of strangulation.

Our way converged with the Río Toachi, whose deep wooded gorge we glimpsed through the trees. In the evening we passed a new clearing planted with maize—the first patch of cultivation we had seen since leaving the Río Blanco. The weed-choked trail had so retarded our weary animals that we were benighted in the woods. Under an overcast sky, the darkness beneath the trees soon became so intense that I rode with an arm in front of my face to shield it from projecting branches and warned those who followed me whenever I encountered such obstructions.

In a moment of inattention, I rode squarely into a fallen trunk that bridged the roadway where it passed through a cut. It struck my forehead hard enough to bring an inner vision of a bright constellation of stars. Had I been galloping or even trotting, I probably would not be writing this now, but fortunately we were riding slowly and I suffered no serious injury. This collision occurred about the time that we passed from the Northern to the Southern hemisphere, and I called out to my companions that I had struck my head against the Equator! After this, I thought it prudent to use a flashlight. Soon we reached La Cocha, where we found lodging in a large, solidly constructed building put up by the highway engineers. We covered twenty-three miles that day.

Rain was falling when we awoke next morning, and again it was nearly nine o'clock when we took to the road, which here was no longer weed-choked. The forest was still very light, with big trees even more widely scattered than in most of the region through which we had ridden. The undergrowth was dense and impenetrable; the epiphytic burden of the trees very heavy. Being less hurried, and enjoying a wider outlook, I saw more birds, including toucans, araçaris, oropéndolas, parrots, and honeycreepers. As we neared Santo Domingo, the clearings became more numerous and extensive. They were devoted to pastures where the grass was dense and lush, or to bananas and plantains. Some of the banana plantations were large; but without roads the planters could not sell their fruit, which was used only for home consumption and for fattening pigs. The new pastures were full of lofty Pambil palms, which the settlers did not take the trouble to fell because the hard outer shell of their trunks resists the axe and they cast little shade.

As we rode through the forest from Quinindé to Santo Domingo, my eyes were again and again drawn upward by great flaming red spheres of flowers high above me on a tall tree, which I recognized as a species of *Brownea*. As we approached Santo Domingo, where this leguminous tree became more abundant, we heard it called Clavelín. With a straight, clean trunk that may attain two feet in diameter, it grows to a height of a hundred feet or more. Its crown is usually high and narrow, and its close brown bark is thickly studded with small warts. When a spray of the big, pinnately compound leaves first elongates, it hangs limply and is often tinged with pink. Only after they are nearly full grown do the flaccid leaves harden and rise to a horizontal position. The brilliant red flowers are followed by flat brown pods that resemble those of the Honey Locust. The Clavelín was the most colorful tree that we saw. Other noteworthy plants were a hydrangea that climbed to the treetops, where it displayed flat inflorescences bordered by beautiful, pink, sterile flowers, and a tall, white-flowered begonia much like that which I had earlier found in the Pastaza Valley.

Late in the afternoon, we turned right from the unfinished main highway and followed a very muddy road to Santo Domingo, a distance of about two miles. The village was a group of palm-thatched buildings, unpainted and in various stages of decay, surrounding a grassy central square where pigs roamed and boys played soccer. Facing the plaza stood an elementary school, a ruinous church where services were held once or twice a year when a priest arrived, and several *pulperías*—little shops that sold a few poor articles of clothing, household wares, and provisions. This was the administrative and market center of a district with a population estimated at 2,500. It was noteworthy that in this slightly higher and cooler region, white and Indian elements, intermixed in all degrees, replaced the blacks who were almost the only inhabitants along the Río Esmeraldas.

The "hotel" was a dirty, paintless wooden building of two stories. Its bedsteads had solid wooden bottoms and filthy mattresses, which we threw aside in favor of our air mattresses. We had arrived on a Saturday evening, and our slumber that night was broken by the shouts and curses of drunken celebrants in the bar below our room. In an adjoining apartment lay the corpse of a girl who had died during the day, watched by relatives who, to speed her soul to a better world, swelled the volume of the uproar. The unbearable racket continued into the small hours of the morning. The next day a young North American naturalist, who had already resided in this hotel for four months, characterized the past night as "more than ordinarily peaceful." We admired the devotion that had kept him so long in this disorderly and unsavory place in order to explore the surrounding forests for orchids and other salable specimens.

The next morning, Sunday, we saw some of the Colorado Indians. The men went naked save for a neckerchief and a short skirt that covered their middles and thighs. All their exposed skin, including the face, was liberally smeared with a vermilion paste compounded of the seed coats of the Annatto and a vegetable fat obtained in the forest. Their straight black hair, worn with long bangs over the forehead and cut short behind, was so liberally plastered that at first I thought they wore close-fitting vermilion helmets. This brilliant ointment, we were told, was used by the Indians to protect themselves from the bites of woodland insects. Everyone was greatly amused by the resemblance to the Colorado Indians, painted as they were, of our rubicund, two-hundred-pound soils expert with flaming red hair.

On a road leading to Santo Domingo we met Alejandro, a local chief, going to the village dressed only in vermilion Annatto paste, a red neckerchief, an abbreviated red skirt, and heavy silver bracelets. Next day we hardly recognized the chief when we met him at the end of the completed part of the highway, waiting for a car to carry him up to Quito. He had washed all the vermilion paste from his black locks and at least the exposed parts of his body, and was now conventionally dressed in a bright blue shirt and khaki trousers. We reminded him that he would find Quito chilly without a jacket.

The land around Santo Domingo is rolling, broken by many watercourses that flow through deep, narrow, steep-sided channels. We were told of sinkholes that permit subterranean drainage. Where these were absent, the depressions were swampy. A many-voiced chorus of frogs sounded in our ears as we rode through this green, mist-veiled land. The abundant rain and prevalent cloudiness favored the growth of epiphytic plants that covered the trees in great masses. The palms, of which we had seen so many all along the way, were absent from the neighborhood of the village, where, we learned, all had been used for house construction.

After a day in Santo Domingo, we set forth for Quito in the middle of the morning, riding horses and mules to reach the part of the highway passable by motor vehicles. The unfinished road was bordered by pastures, beyond which rose the most impressive stand of timber that we saw between Esmeraldas and Quito. Tall dicotyledonous trees, standing close together, were heavily laden with mosses, ferns, and flowering epiphytes. It was noteworthy that not a single palm raised its head above the crowns of the branching trees. The whole aspect of the forest was strikingly different from that of the palm-dominated region between Quininé and Santo Domingo. Soon we passed from the rolling land into the steep foothills of the Andes, whose outlying lofty ridges rose up ahead. Here most of the slopes were too steep to support heavy forest, and on many of the ridges tall palms stood out prominently against the sky. The vegetation began to assume a subtropical aspect. Shrubby heaths (Thibaudieae) with bright red flowers, so typical of humid regions at middle elevations in tropical America, appeared among the epiphytes burdening the trees.

For some miles we rode past Indians toiling to widen the roadway, cutting it with pick and shovel into precipitous slopes and letting the loose stones and earth roll down into a mountain torrent. When, in the early afternoon, we reached the camp of the highway engineers, they gave us the most satisfying meal we had eaten since leaving the town of Esmeraldas ten days earlier. An hour later, we resumed our journey in a Ford *cazadora* (a small bus). As we wound slowly up into the high Andes over a narrow road cut into steep wooded slopes, the clouds closed around us, veiling the depths of the abysmal gorges that we skirted.

The owner of the car was a stout and genial Austrian who had resided many years in Ecuador; the driver, a young German refugee who had come to South America with his family two years earlier. Late in the afternoon, we stopped beside a tiny cottage of rough boards, set at the very edge of the highway, where there was barely enough level ground to support it at the brink of a precipice. Here amid the mists dwelt the youth's father, a dark, stalwart man whose nose had been partly shot away in the First World War, his gray, kindly-visaged mother, a younger brother, and a couple of the big dogs so dear to the Teutonic heart. They must have found life in this Andean solitude very different from that of the city of Düsseldorf which they had left—more repose and less excitement.

The evening gloom deepened as our overloaded car toiled up to greater heights. By the time we crossed the high divide into the watershed of the Río Saloya, the landscape was only vaguely visible; but, as far as we could discern, the steep mountainsides were still clothed with forest broken only by rare, narrow clearings. The few rough cabins were set close beside the road—those abrupt slopes offered scarcely any other sites for them. A tongue of soft, fresh earth, slipping down the declivity to our right, threatened to block the road. Our driver, who considered himself lucky to have squeezed past before it oozed farther, told us that the frequent landslides sometimes interrupted traffic for a day or two.

After it had become quite dark, we stopped for coffee and a bite of supper at a dingy roadside eating-house. Our weary driver's suggestion that we sleep on the floor there stirred up an argument won by those who, dismayed by the filth of the crowded building and the dearth of food, favored pushing forward despite the lateness of the hour. Presently we reached a stretch of narrow roadway so steep that the motor stalled and some of us had to get out and push the car. This happened at a point between a cliff and a precipice falling away into a profound abyss, where a misstep in the dark might have had dreadful consequences.

At eleven o'clock we crossed the cold summit at an elevation of about eleven thousand feet and started to coast downward into the inter-Andean valley known as the Hoya del Guaillabamba. Soon the myriad lights of Quito began to twinkle far below us, and shortly before midnight we rode into the capital city of Ecuador, 9,240 feet above the sea. After a day here, Striker and I took the train for Guayaquil, where we arrived after two long days of slow travel. Here we joined the other two members of our party, and on the following day we all embarked for a voyage up the coast to Buenaventura.

Thirty-four years elapsed before I again visited Ecuador, this time with a party of tourists whom I helped to find and identify birds. From Quito we traveled in a chartered bus, over a broad, well-paved highway, down to Santo Domingo de los Colorados, where we stayed in comfort at the Hotel Zaracay. Among the trees that shaded the grounds were many velvety black Yellow-rumped Tanagers, many of the widespread Bananaquits, and, to our great surprise, a number of House Sparrows. How these aliens arrived there we did not learn. On the following day, we continued down to Quinindé, stopping here and there to look for birds. As we passed rapidly through the center of Santo Domingo, I saw just enough to be assured that it had grown from the sleepy village that I knew to a large and busy commercial center, with much motor traffic and establishments for the sale and maintenance of agricultural machinery.

Instead of the narrow, brush-choked trail that we had traversed thirty-four years earlier, the same broad highway led all the way to Quinindé, and beyond. But all those miles of forest that we had seen had vanished and were replaced by great banana plantations, pastures, and rows and rows of African oil palms. Here and there a few of the tall native Pambil palms stood in lonely isolation, bringing to memory the multitudes that had once graced this region. As has happened all over tropical America, including the Costa Rican valley where I write, when the highways come the forest goes, leaving hardly a trace. Reaching Quinindé in the early afternoon, we found it transformed in the same way as Santo Domingo, on a smaller scale. An oleoduct spanning the Río Quinindé, carrying to the coast petroleum pumped across the high Andes from oilfields in Ecuador's Oriente, was another achievement of the "progress" that brings wealth to nations at so heavy a price to their flora and fauna.

Midway between the two towns we were given permission to enter a farm, where among scattered trees and bushy second growth we found no lack of birds, including Rufous-tailed Hummingbirds, Black-cheeked Woodpeckers, Golden-olive Woodpeckers, Lineated Woodpeckers, Streaked-headed Woodcreepers, Slaty Castlebuilders, Cinnamon Becards, Masked Tityras, Banded-backed Wrens, Bay-headed Tanagers, Buff-throated Saltators, and others familiar to me in Costa Rica. The bird that most delighted me was a lovely little honeycreeper, a Black-faced Dacnis, who permitted us to view his greenish blue, golden yellow, and black attire from every angle while he flitted about in a tree, with his plainly clad mate nearby. To most of the tourists, the most exciting event of our brief excursion into northwestern Ecuador was the discovery of a splendid male Torrent Duck, resting on a boulder amid the foaming current of the Río Toachi, then flying upstream low above the rushing water, toward the highlands to which we were returning.

CHAPTER 8

The Woodcreepers of Tropical America

Spotted-crowned Woodcreeper (left); Brown Creeper (right)

In the millions of years that birds have inhabited the earth, they have become adapted to occupy every habitat that can support warm-blooded, air-breathing vertebrates, and to exploit almost every source of food available to animals of their size and strength. Some, such as the penguins, spend almost their whole lives swimming and fishing in the sea, coming ashore only to nest and molt. Swifts pass their days catching insects high in the air.

Most birds are more closely associated with vegetation. Many of these subsist largely on fruits; and many others, including warblers and vireos, are well fitted to glean insects from foliage. Woodpeckers have many anatomical peculiarities that equip them to extract insects from deep in the wood of trees.

A special foraging niche that vegetation offers to birds is the bark of trees, in the crevices of which many insects and spiders live. The profitable exploitation of this food demands special capacities. Although numerous small birds of diverse families occasionally glean from bark, few birds make this their major occupation. In temperate North America, the chief bark foragers are the nuthatches, the Brown Creeper, and the Black-and-White Warbler, an aberrant member of its family. The nuthatches have short, rounded tails and can run over upright trunks in any direction, clamping themselves to the bark with their feet. The creeper has a relatively long, pointed tail which serves as a prop as it ascends tree trunks in an upright position, often spiraling around them, while with its slender, curved bill it extracts small invertebrates from the crevices.

In the Western Hemisphere, nuthatches extend southward only as far as Mexico, while the Brown Creeper reaches Nicaragua. In the tropical parts of their ranges, these birds of cooler regions mostly stay in the highlands. Thus they hardly begin to exploit the trunks of the countless millions of tropical trees. Throughout continental tropical America, the chief bark gleaners are the approximately fifty species of woodcreepers or woodhewers, a family that has failed to reach the West Indies or to spread much beyond the tropics. These birds superficially resemble the creepers of the family Certhiidae, a fact that impressed me in the highlands of Guatemala, where I sometimes watched a Spotted-crowned Woodcreeper and a Brown Creeper hunting over the same trunks in much the same fashion. But the creepers of the north and the woodcreepers of the tropics are not closely related. The former are true songbirds, whereas the latter belong to the branch of the passerine order that is considered more primitive because of its simpler vocal apparatus. Woodcreepers are related to such tropical families as the ovenbirds, antbirds, manakins, and cotingas.

In size, woodcreepers range from about five to thirteen inches, or from the length of a Brown Creeper to that of a flicker. Brilliant coloration is wholly lacking, all species being clad in shades of brown, olive, and buff, which are often brighter and richer, more chestnut or rufous, on the wings and tail than on the body. Many species are conspicuously streaked or spotted with lighter and darker shades, especially on the head, neck, shoulders, and breast. Bills range from short and wedge-shaped to very long, slender, and downcurved, as in the scythebills. These long bills are excellent instruments for probing among clusters of palm fruits or between twisted lianas. The feet have three toes directed forward and one backward, instead of two forward and two backward, as in woodpeckers. Especially noteworthy is the tail, consisting of twelve long, graduated feathers with stiff shafts whose sharp tips project beyond the vanes and are turned inward, the better to engage the bark and support the bird. Woodcreepers commonly maintain an upright position as they work up vertical trunks, although as one hunts outward along a drooping branch it may assume a horizontal or even a somewhat inverted posture. After following one trunk upward as far as hunting is profitable, the woodcreeper usually flies down to near the base of another and repeats the process.

Woodcreepers avoid fruits and other vegetable food and subsist largely on insects and spiders that they find in crevices in the bark or beneath tufts of moss or lichens, which they lift up or pull off to see what lurks beneath. They sometimes pry off loose flakes of bark, but only rarely do they dig noisily into soft, rotten wood for insects. They may vary their diet with small frogs and lizards, as is especially true of the short-billed dendrocinclas. These middle-sized woodcreepers frequently forage with army ants, along with a variety of other birds. They cling low on tree trunks while they watch for small creatures that the hunting ants drive into the open, then dart down or out to snatch up the fugitives. The big Barred Woodcreeper likewise accompanies army ants.

The calls or songs of woodcreepers are among the notable sounds of the tropical American forests. Some repeat loud, stirring cries, which exasperate the bird watcher because he thinks that a bird who makes so much sound should be easy to see, and he cranes his neck in vain for a glimpse of the brown bird clinging to a brown trunk amid screening foliage. Other woodcreepers have clear, melodious trills. The Brown-billed Scythebill's vocal performance never ceases to excite my wonder, for he seems to sing two songs simultaneously. To a fine, clear, ascending trill he adds a loud, ringing *tewe tewe tewe tewe tewe we we we we we we*; and how he can carry the second tune without dropping the first I fail to understand.

To the student of tropical birds, woodcreepers are a standing challenge. In the first place, the uniformity of coloration throughout the family makes many kinds difficult to identify; one must rely heavily on shape of bill, voice, size, and habitat to supplement plumage pattern as aids to identification. Second, woodcreepers' nests are exceedingly hard to find, usually also to reach if they have been discovered. Although sometimes these birds will deign to occupy an old woodpecker's hole with an obvious round doorway, they prefer a "natural" cavity in a tree; and the smaller and less conspicuous the entrance, the better they like it. Moreover, hammering on the trunk will not always make an incubating or brooding woodcreeper look out through its doorway and reveal that it has a nest.

About our house in Costa Rica, and among the shade trees of the coffee plantations, the most common woodcreeper is the Streaked-headed, a middle-sized species which, unlike many others, prefers light woods and clearings with scattered trees to heavy, unbroken forest. As they climb up the trunks of neighboring trees, the male and female, who remain mated throughout the year, often call to each other with long-drawn, clear trills, all at the same pitch. I can detect no difference in the responsive songs of the male and female, who wear the same streaked brown plumage, so that they provide no clue to their sex.

Woodcreepers become active very early in the morning and are among the last of the diurnal birds to retire at nightfall. Long after ease-loving woodpeckers have ensconced themselves in their neatly carved holes, the woodcreepers seek the irregular crannies where they sleep. The light is then so dim that it is often difficult to distinguish their dark forms from the dusky trunks up which they climb, but over the years I have traced many Streaked-headed Woodcreepers to their lodgings. The cavity chosen for roosting is usually well above the ground. Sometimes it is the end of a hollow stub with an upwardly directed opening that permits rain to enter. I have known woodcreepers to sleep in such roofless chambers in the wettest weather, despite the apparent availability of covered woodpecker holes nearby. Evidently concealment is more important than dryness. Like other species of woodcreepers on which I have information, the Streaked-headed always roosts alone. One evening, when one of these birds tried to join another, doubtless its mate, in the dormitory, both flew out. Then I thought I saw one return to the crevice, but the light was so dim that I may have been mistaken.

Early in March, Streaked-headed Woodcreepers begin to carry material into the high hole which, after much cautious exploration, they have chosen for their nest. Usually it is a "natural" cavity in a living or dead tree, but exceptionally it is an abandoned hole of the Golden-naped Woodpecker. The entrances to the occupied nests that I have seen ranged from about eighty to fifteen feet above the ground, but low sites are exceptional. The actual nest may be several yards below the orifice. The male and female share the work of building the nest, which is a loose accumulation of pieces of hard or corky bark, up to three inches in length and sometimes even larger. The woodcreepers pull these flakes from trunks and branches, often tugging vigorously to detach them. When working together, they call to each other with their pleasant trills, but one building alone is usually silent.

The few nests whose contents I could learn each contained two eggs or nestlings. As usual in the woodcreeper family, the eggs were pure white and the two ends about equally blunt. Some years ago, a Streaked-headed Woodcreeper with a conspicuous patch of whitish feathers on its nape frequented the trees around our house and nested in a tree that shaded the neighboring coffee grove. This abnormal bird was mated to a normal one with a brown nape. At last I had a pair of woodcreepers whose members were distinguishable, so that I could learn how much each contributed to rearing the brood. There remained the problem of learning which was the male and which the female. Since the normal bird occupied the nest by night, and among passerine birds this is as a rule the female's role, I concluded that White-nape was the male.

It soon became evident that the female was doing most of the incubation, even by day. In fifteen hours of watching, she took thirteen sessions on the eggs, ranging from 7 to over 72 minutes and averaging 37.5 minutes. White-nape sat only three times, for intervals of 15, 28, and 42 minutes. Often one partner flew away before the other came to relieve it, with the result that the eggs were left unattended for fourteen periods, ranging from 2 to 41 minutes and averaging 21.2 minutes.

In the following year, I failed to discover White-nape's nest; but two years later he again undertook to rear a family in the coffee plantation, close to his earlier nest. This time he was much more attentive to the eggs, in the course of a day sitting eight times, while his mate took eleven sessions. He was in the nest for a total of 138 minutes, she for 300 minutes, and the eggs were left alone for 288 minutes. Actual incubation was even less constant than these figures indicate, for the parent in the nest often climbed up to look out with its elfish head in the doorway, sometimes remaining there for as long as 10 minutes at a stretch.

The woodcreeper coming to take its turn at incubation often brought a flake of bark for the nest, and less frequently it carried a piece away when it flew off to forage. On one occasion, the female left with a flake as her mate arrived with another flake. Thus the materials of the nest were constantly changing; yet the accumulation grew, as more pieces were brought than were carried away. Such preoccupation with nest materials during incubation, rare in songbirds, is characteristic of woodcreepers and the related ovenbirds, as likewise of hummingbirds and certain cotingas.

I could not learn the incubation period at these inaccessible nests of White-nape and his mate. But some years earlier, a pair of Streaked-headed Woodcreepers and a female Tawny-winged Dendrocincla competed for a hollow palm stub as their nest site. The two kinds of birds built alternately, and finally two white eggs were laid. Then the lone dendrocincla, a belligerent bird, drove away the timid Streaked-headed Woodcreepers and proceeded to incubate the two eggs, one of which hatched after fifteen days. When the nestling, attended solely by the dendrocincla, was old enough to be identified by its plumage and voice, it became evident that the dendrocincla had hatched and reared her rivals' offspring! Incidentally, she provided me with my only determination of the incubation period of the Streaked-headed Woodcreeper. At an easily accessible nest of the Spotted-crowned

Woodcreeper, the highland counterpart of the Streaked-headed, the eggs took seventeen days to hatch. Probably the longer period was caused by the cooler temperature in the high mountains.

Newly hatched woodcreepers are typical passerine nestlings, with sparse down that fails to cover their pink skin and mouths that are yellow inside. White-nape's first mate gave more time to brooding the nestlings than he did, just as she had incubated more assiduously. But the two parents were about equally active in bringing food. Fifteen days after the eggs hatched, each parent came with food sixteen times during four hours of the morning, so that the two nestlings were fed at the rate of four times per capita per hour. On each visit, the parent brought a single insect, held conspicuously in its slender bill. Usually the insect's color was brown, suggesting that it had been plucked from bark rather than from foliage, and it had very long antennae. When the nestlings were quite young, the parents always entered the hole to feed them. After the nestlings were feathered and could look through the doorway, their meals were passed to them from outside.

Corresponding to these changes in the method of delivering food were changes in the attention devoted to sanitation of the nest. When the nestlings were newly hatched, I saw the parents carry out no waste and inferred that the droppings had been swallowed by them. Later, a parent often left the hole with a white sac in its bill. But after the adults no longer entered the nest to deliver meals, their housekeeping deteriorated. Apparently, the bottom of the chamber was becoming foul with droppings, but this probably did not incommode the nestlings, who spent much, if not all, of their time clinging to the walls of the chamber.

When the nestlings were about fifteen days old, I sometimes saw two streaked brown heads in the doorway. In their juvenal plumage, they closely resembled their parents. Now they often uttered, chiefly at mealtimes, a trill which resembled that of the adults but was weaker and less melodious. Eighteen days after I first noticed the parents taking food rather than bark into the hole, it was empty, the young having flown. Possibly they were in the nest at least a day longer, for nineteen days was the age of departure of the Streaked-headed Woodcreeper reared by the dendrocincla in the low nest into which I could look, and this was the nestling period of two broods of Spotted-crowned Woodcreepers. After the young woodcreepers flew, neither they nor their parents returned to sleep in the nest.

Two years later, when White-nape nested in the coffee grove for the second time, he vanished soon after the eggs hatched. A few days after his disappearance, a second, normally colored, adult arrived, and it seemed that the female had acquired a new mate who was helping to feed the young. But before I could confirm this, the cavity was torn open by some predator and the nestlings vanished.

In contrast to the Streaked-headed Woodcreeper, which prefers a high nest site, the diminutive Wedge-billed Woodcreeper often chooses a low one. The entrance may be only a foot above the ground, between the ridges of a massive, irregularly furrowed trunk of a forest tree. The nest itself, often well below the doorway, may be at ground level. Here two or, less often, three white eggs rest upon a mat of fine, fibrous material. A pair that I watched throughout a morning incubated much more diligently than the bigger Streaked-headed Woodcreepers. Sitting for eighteen to ninety minutes at a stretch, each remained at its post until relieved by its partner, with the result that the eggs were constantly attended. Each parent brought a billful of fibrous material when it came for a turn in the nest. The doorway was such a narrow slit, about three quarters of an inch wide, that the birds had to turn sideways to pass through it.

Although in choosing such low sites Wedgebills seem to expose their eggs and young to perils that they might avoid, high crannies may not be much safer from predation. The only nest more than a yard above the ground of which I know was twenty feet up in a crevice of the deeply furrowed trunk of a forest tree. I could not see what the deep hollow contained, but I spent hours watching the two parents carry in small insects that they held well back in their short bills rather than at the tips, usually one at a time. One morning the head of a large snake projected from the cranny. The nestlings were still too young to have flown. Thus this study, like so many others that I have begun in tropical forests, was prematurely terminated.

The small coffee grove where the Streaked-headed Woodcreepers nested was for several years the home of a Tawny-winged

Dendrocincla (not the one who years earlier had raised the Streaked-headed nestling). In three consecutive seasons she nested in old woodpecker holes in a dying avocado tree, and between breeding seasons she slept there. One of the most aggressive birds that I have known intimately, she could oust a woodpecker as large as herself that had already installed itself in a cavity in which she wished to roost.

In sharp contrast to the Streaked-headed Woodcreepers, this bird always built her nest, incubated her eggs, and raised her young quite alone, with never a mate in view—as I have seen also with other individuals of her species. Her nest was composed of strips of fibrous bark and whitish foliaceous lichens, and with these materials her two white eggs were often more or less covered while she took a recess from incubation. One year, when I was able to determine the incubation period quite accurately, it was between 20.5 and 21 days.

The young dendrocinclas remained in the nest for twenty-four days, or some five days longer than Streaked-headed Woodcreepers, although the two species are about the same size. Small lizards entered prominently into their diet; I saw a brood of two receive seven of these reptiles in the course of a morning, in addition to insects. Although through most of the day the nestlings' usually substantial meals were brought infrequently, the rate of feeding sometimes became very rapid in the evening twilight, after most birds had gone to rest. In the fading light, the parent caught flying insects on swift, graceful darts from the trunk to which she clung. One evening she gave her two nestlings thirteen insects and one lizard in little over half an hour. She kept the nest clean as long as the young remained in it. In contrast to the loquacious nestlings of the Streaked-headed Woodcreeper, the young dendrocinclas were always discreetly silent.

After the departure of one brood, one fledgling slept in the hollow decaying stem of a spiny Pejibaye palm in which White-crowned Parrots had earlier nested. Its sibling roosted in the hollow dead trunk of a neighboring Cecropia tree. Both of these tall trunks had broken-off tops that permitted rain to enter. After escorting her offspring to their dormitories and giving them supper in the waning light, their mother retired into her usual hole in the avocado tree. Each member of this family of three unsociable birds slept in its own hollow and would not permit another to join it.

In raising their families without a male's help, dendrocinclas are not unique in the woodcreeper family. In view from my study window a large clump of tall timber bamboos stands at the edge of an extensive tract of tropical rain forest. Several years ago, a Buff-throated Woodcreeper nested in one of the many thick, hollow bamboo stems, on the side of the clump toward the forest. I did not see the bird make the round doorway in the side of the decaying bamboo, but I have little doubt that she at least enlarged the opening. At a later nest, similarly situated, I watched a woodcreeper come with a piece of stiff bark, too long to pass through the orifice while she held it crosswise in her bill. Dropping the burden, the woodcreeper pecked at the edge of the doorway, making taps audible fifty feet away and detaching fragments of the rotting wood. On several occasions, after she had struggled vainly to enter with a particularly large piece of bark, she tried in similar fashion to widen the entrance, but she never continued for long.

The two nests in the clump (only the first of which was successful) were about twenty feet up in bamboos so far advanced in decay that we could not reach them amid the crowded stems without risking their destruction. Although the woodcreeper bore no distinguishing mark, not once in many hours of watching did we have any indication that a second individual was interested in the nest. For eighteen days after the parent began to spend long intervals in the cavity, revealing that incubation had begun, she took in a piece of bark on many of her returns from recesses. Then for twenty additional days she carried an insect, or less often a spider or small Anolis lizard—always one item at a time—when she entered. After leaving the nest at the age of about three weeks, the fledglings hid for hours in the dense bamboo clump, calling at intervals but remaining difficult to glimpse. Neither they nor their mother returned to sleep in the nest. Finally, when it appeared that the cavity was not to be used for a second brood, we opened the bamboo stem and found hundreds of pieces of stiff bark, from tiny fragments up to flakes over three inches long, filling the nest chamber to a depth of seven inches.

In mid-July, nearly two months after the young woodcreepers left the nest in the bamboo, I found a Buff-throated Woodcreeper, probably their mother, nesting fifty yards from the bamboo clump. A large strangling fig had thrown a network of thick anastomosing roots around the massive trunk of a Muñeco tree in the pasture. Between two of these roots an opening a foot high but barely an inch wide—too narrow to admit my hand—led into a fairly spacious chamber, where two white eggs lay on a bed of bark flakes. Without using a light or mirror, I could easily see them from a point in front of this nest only seven feet above the ground. At this nest, too, much watching failed to disclose that a second parent was attentive. For a month the solitary woodcreeper continued to incubate, then deserted her unhatchable eggs. With a large spoon, I extracted them through the fissure between the roots, measured, and then opened them, finding no trace of an embryo. Like birds of many other kinds, the woodcreeper had continued to incubate her eggs well beyond the date when they should have hatched.

The parent Buff-throated Woodcreeper was far from silent. Sometimes while out of sight in the nest, but more often while she looked out in preparation for leaving, or after she had flown into the neighboring forest, she repeated a loud, ringing *cheer cheer cheer*, occasionally continuing this for many minutes. Another note, that sounded like *chu chu chu*, was less melodious and seemed to express anxiety or irritation. From February to April, as the nesting season begins, Buff-throated Woodcreepers that are probably males cling high in trees while they call persistently, in clear, ringing voices, *doy doy doy doy* or *wic wic wic wic*. Doubtless they are advertising their availability to females with maturing eggs that require fertilization—females in whose domestic tasks they will not assist.

In many families of birds, from boobies to tanagers, the males of every species that has been adequately studied help with the nesting, at least to the extent of feeding the young. In certain other families, including hummingbirds and manakins, males are not known even to feed the young, except possibly as a rare abnormality. Woodcreepers and cotingas are exceptional in that males of some species faithfully attend the nest, while in other species they remain aloof from it.

CHAPTER 9

Bird Watching during a Revolution

Scarlet-rumped Black Tanager

Among the hazards that have long faced the naturalist in tropical America are political upheavals, which upset his plans, interrupt his studies, and may even jeopardize his life. After I had been on the margin of minor political disturbances in several other Central American republics, I decided to settle in Costa Rica, not only because of its rich avifauna, but also because it was one of the most stable and liberal democracies in Latin America, less afflicted than most by dictators and those abrupt changes of government, usually called "revolutions," that have plagued neighboring countries.

While it was easily accessible only by air, and its muddy or dusty, unpaved roads never revealed the tracks of a motorcar, I returned in 1941 to the Valley of El General in southern Costa Rica, where I had already lived for two and a half years, in borrowed or rented cabins. Now I bought a farm recently carved from the wilderness at Quizarrá. I called it Los Cusingos, and on it I built a house adequate for a bachelor accustomed to the simple life of the backwoods. I tried to earn a living by farming my stony, broken land, and, above all, set about to learn all I could about the birds that nested around my new home and in the large tract of unspoiled forest that adjoined my dooryard. In other books I have told about my life here at Los Cusingos and some of the animals and plants that surround me. In this chapter I wish to relate experiences that did not seem to fit into these other books, those that befell me while I tried to study birds during the most violent revolution that has shaken Costa Rica in the present century.

Gathering Clouds

I dwelt among illiterate or barely literate peasants who could talk about little except their crops and domestic animals, prices, and their ailments. It was pleasant to pass the first day of 1947 with my only highly educated and widely traveled neighbors, Roger and Doris Stone, who, after my arrival in the valley, had bought a farm a few miles away, along the same river, the Peña Blanca, that formed my eastern boundary. Here they came for weekends and holidays, when their children swam in the river and Doris Stone, a distinguished archaeologist, rode about the country seeking the petroglyphs which, long before, the Indians had carved on the huge rocks scattered through the valley.

On this particular New Year's Day, our conversation turned to the alarming increase of lawlessness since Teodoro Picado had won the presidency of Costa Rica through a coalition with the small Communist party and its astute leader, Manuel Mora. I recalled how my neighbors were saying that all the larger farms would soon be divided for distribution among the landless, that all cows in excess of two would be taken from the owners and

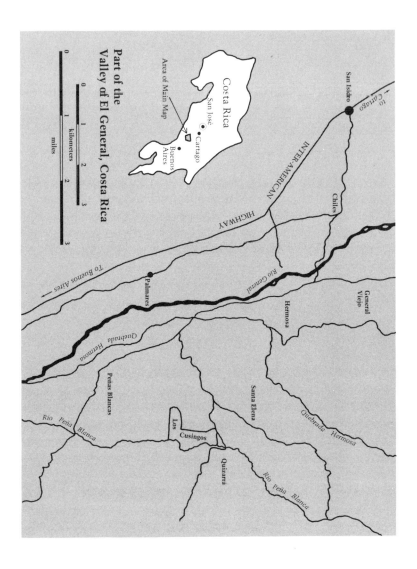

Part of the
Valley of El General, Costa Rica

given to the poor, and similar absurdities that revealed how little they knew about Communism.

From our seats on the porch of the Stones' cottage, we gazed across the sparkling river, far below, to a wide expanse of valley, which on our left swept up in long, wooded slopes to the rocky summits of the Cordillera de Talamanca. In the forest beyond the river, an absentee owner held a large tract of land, on which, for some weeks, a numerous party of men, led by Communist agitators, had been felling trees to make farms that they believed would become their personal property—an expectation hardly compatible with orthodox Communism. Some of those present at our New Year's Day party asserted that this seizure of land by those who needed it was right, since the absentee owner had claimed an excessive amount. I maintained that, if he held more than the law allowed, it should be taken from him by legal action, for only ill could come from mob violence. Police who had gone to order the "Communists" to vacate the land had been scoffed at, threatened, and driven away. Another farm, claimed by a hardworking pioneer while El General was still a remote wilderness, had been invaded in similar fashion. The ignorant and discontented were watching eagerly, ready to seize farms on a large scale if these first attempts proved successful.

In the afternoon we parted, wishing each other a New Year with more happiness and fewer troubles than in the one just ended. Fond hope! That very evening, after supper, I was visited by Emilio Ureña, one of the very few of my neighbors who knew the world beyond the confines of his own small country. A visit at this hour boded no good, for the roads were rough and people usually stayed at home after nightfall. He had come to warn me that "Communists" were planning to invade my farm on the morrow, thereby corroborating rumors that had earlier reached me. "*¡Pobre patria!*" he repeated over and over, "Poor fatherland, where such things come to pass!"

The invaders would probably come up from the south; so at daybreak I hurried down to the farm's southern boundary with two of my employees, old Pablo Garro and Manuel, his teen-age son. At sunrise a band of about twenty men and boys came marching in single file up through the pasture of my neighbor, Don Eloy, singing and waving their long machetes. To my surprise, Eloy accompanied them. As the leaders reached the fence that marked the boundary, I asked what they proposed to do. They replied that I had much uncultivated land, which they needed; accordingly, they would sow my fields and make them their own. To argue with them was useless.

Turning then to Don Eloy, who stood by in silence, I told him that I did not know how much he had to do with all this, but he should remember that he held his farm under a title similar to mine, and that, if my farm were treated in this fashion, his could hardly be immune from similar violation. He did not answer this, but, noticing the revolver at my hip, warned me not to shoot, for it would go badly with me. Having only five cartridges, old and possibly spoiled, to oppose to a score of long knives, I had no intention of committing such folly; I was prepared to shoot only if attacked. As, with shouts to raise their courage, the men began to pass through the barbed-wire fence into my land, I left with Pablo and Manuel, warning the invaders that, although they might sow my fields, I would reap them.

It was impossible to foresee where all this would end, and how much violence would ensue. I had just finished the manuscript of the first volume of *Life Histories of Central American Birds*, and it seemed wise to try to save at least this much from the general ruin, if such were in store for the farm and house. Hurriedly packing this work, I put it in my saddlebag and saddled my horse Bayon. We rode off toward San Isidro, the valley's administrative and commercial center eight miles away, while with machetes the invaders were slashing down the vegetation that covered resting fields at the southern end of my farm. I overtook the Stones just as their cavalcade was entering the village, on their way back to San José. They kindly offered to forward my manuscript to a prospective publisher in the United States and lent me a light rifle— my only weapon was a small revolver, for which I had been unable to procure fresh ammunition. We agreed that it would be better not to try to protect the farm with the firearm, but to defend the house even if it came to shooting—provided, of course, that I could return in time to do so.

Next, I went to report to the Jefe Político, or civil administrator, of the district what was happening. He informed me that a truckload of soldiers was coming from the capital, over the recently opened Inter-American Highway, to restore order, and suggested that I await their arrival and accompany them. So I passed the night in San Isidro, wondering what was happening at home. Next morning around nine o'clock the soldiers arrived. Horses had been found for them; and a number of local men with horses, including myself, were sworn in as deputy police and armed to accompany the troop. Toward noon we all set off down the valley.

As the troop trotted along the dusty road, I approached the commander to ask a question that I had no opportunity to ask before we started. After driving the invaders from the absentee owner's land, would he do the same for my farm? He replied that, since he had no orders to this effect, he could do nothing. If anyone were killed or injured in an affair not explicitly covered by his instructions, he would be answerable for it. Explaining that I had been acting under a misapprehension, I dropped out of the cavalcade, to return to San Isidro and take measures for the protection of my property. But just then I met a friend riding toward the village on a big mule. When he heard what was happening, he volunteered to arrange the matter for me, so that I could return to guard my house.

Without changing their dusty field clothes, the Stones went to President Picado as soon as they reached the capital, to request protection for my woodland. My friend on the mule sent a radiogram to the chief executive; and soon a message came, instructing the commander of the troop to clear my land of invaders. But when they learned that armed men were riding down the valley to evict them, the invaders fled from both properties without waiting for a confrontation. In two mornings they had slashed down the second-growth woods on five or six of my acres. Although their work was done carelessly, and too early in the season, it was not unusable. Not without a good deal of hard labor, Pablo, Manuel, and his brother Pastor prepared the drying brush to be burnt off before the rains began, so that we could plant maize. In August we reaped a heavy crop, thereby fulfilling my promise to the men who invaded my land on the second of January.

The aftermath of this episode revealed how, under the guise of helping them, selfish men use their less forceful fellows as tools to increase their own wealth or power. By his domineering conduct and sly scheming, Don Eloy antagonized his neighbors. Soon after the invasion, one who had reason to dislike him came to tell me that, from his own farm across the river, he had watched Eloy and his eldest son swinging machetes on my land, along with the other invaders. Eloy had been heard to say that he would gain possession of my farm and give it to his son. He had for some time been trying to make me sell it cheaply to him. When I put a fence along our common boundary, he cut the wire in many places.

My informant also said that, if I took legal action against the offender, he and others would bear witness to all this. Although I dislike litigation, I could not permit such flagrant abuses to go uncondemned, so I went to San Isidro and lodged a formal accusation against Eloy. According to Costa Rican procedure, plaintiff, defendant, and witnesses would not confront each other in court, but each would make a written deposition at the *alcaldía*. When weeks passed and I learned from my witnesses that they had not been summoned, I inquired the reason for this neglect. The documents in this case and a dozen others had mysteriously vanished! A lawyer whom I then consulted regarded it as a waste of time, money, and paper to renew the legal process in the present condition of the country. I dropped the matter.

The Storm Breaks

Invasion of farms and purloining of legal documents were only a small sample of the abuses that were occurring throughout the country, and perhaps not the most flagrant. People hoped for relief when the Opposition candidate, Otilio Ulate, a newspaper publisher, won the presidential election in February of the following year. But, when a subservient congress nullified his election, some people could stand no more. Among them was José Figueres, an engineer who had studied in the United States and married an American. He had been exiled for too freely criticizing the government, and now he returned to lead the Opposition in an armed rebellion. Little San Isidro, tucked away in its mountain fastness and hitherto unknown to history, was chosen to play a leading role in the events that now rapidly unfolded. The population of the valley contained a high proportion of landowners who were unsympathetic to Communism and intolerant of bureaucratic corruption. They wanted to see roads, bridges, law enforcement, and honest administration in return for the hard-earned money they paid as taxes. I had watched the abutments being prepared and the girders assembled for a new bridge over the Río General, of first importance to our side of the valley. Then I had noticed the disappearance of all the movable parts of this bridge, after the valley had supported the Opposition candidates at the polls. Now the local population was in a mood to aid the revolution.

To hold the single long mountain road that linked the valley to the center of the country would not be difficult for determined men. The airstrip in San Isidro could then be used to bring in arms and equipment from Guatemala, in commercial airplanes seized from a local airline; the Government had no regular air force to oppose this traffic. After their forces had been consolidated and equipped, the Opposition would advance over the Inter-American Highway that they held to attack the capital. Such, in brief, was the strategy of the revolution in the southern part of the country.

This was before the days when every dwelling, no matter how humble, contains a transistor radio. With the outbreak of hostilities, I lost contact with the world beyond our narrow lateral valley. In San Isidro the post office and shops were closed, cutting us off for weeks from mail and supplies. Accordingly, I had no motive beyond curiosity to take me to the village, where bullets now began to fly—and I was not sufficiently curious. As an isolated foreign resident, I had not been informed of the secret preparations for the political explosion; and, until the turmoil was over and people moved and talked freely again, I had no clear idea of what was happening. Such news as I had of the revolution reached me through the atmosphere, or in the confused accounts of the people closest around me, who themselves had little understanding of events in the larger world. But in early March, 1948, I began to hear the sounds of volleys of shots coming from the west, where San Isidro lay, and the explosions of bombs dropped from airplanes whose motors hummed in the distance. Although all remained quiet and peaceful on the farm, I lived within hearing of a besieged village.

On Wednesday, March 17, Pablo and Manuel were cleaning the pasture on the hilltop behind my house, when above the next ridge to the west we saw an airplane, circling low, and soon afterward heard the *pop pop pop* of distant gunfire. Before the middle of the morning, Pablo dropped his work, went to his cabin for early lunch, then dressed to go to San Isidro. I tried to dissuade him, as did his family, but in vain. He argued that it would be better for him to die for his country than for his sons to die; if he went now to offer his services to the Opposition, perhaps they would not come to take his boys to fight. This sounded very heroic, coming from an old man of seventy with a crooked right forearm, broken when a log fell upon it and never properly set. I remembered that Pablo always had a weakness for going to the village and staying a day or two, when he should have been attending to his work and his family. So he set forth alone, in spite of all remonstrances. Before long, he was back again; along the road he had met somebody coming from San Isidro who could tell him what he wished to know.

But exciting sounds and news continued to arrive from the direction of the village, and old Pablo could no longer be restrained. On Sunday morning, disregarding the counsel of his wife and others, he dressed in his son's newest shirt and his own best trousers, hung his machete by his side and his woven saddlebags over his shoulder, and set off on his bare feet over the stony road to San Isidro. Juana, his wife, charged him to return promptly with soap, kerosene, and other household supplies that were urgently needed.

Monday and Tuesday passed without bringing news of Pablo. I decided to spend Wednesday morning watching my first, long-sought nest of the Turquoise Cotinga. The slight, open structure was situated on a trifurcation of the horizontal lowest branch of a Muñeco tree, about thirty feet above the little-used path that led down to our lower riverside pasture. By standing on the top of my longest ladder and raising a mirror attached to a long pole, I could see two buffy eggs spotted all over with brown. As she had built alone, so the grayish, speckled female incubated alone, often sitting continuously for two or more hours, then remaining away for from half an hour to well over an hour. The only sound I ever heard from her, even when my presence near her nest might have elicited a vocal protest, was the low whistling of her wings in flight. This silence did not surprise me, for I had never heard any other sound from the males, who are clad in glossy plumage of a lovely shade of blue, with patches of deep purple on the throat and breast. I did not once see a male Turquoise Cotinga near this nest; just as, in an earlier year, I had failed to see a male Lovely Cotinga take any interest in a nestling. A female Blue Cotinga, watched in Panama by Frank M. Chapman (1929), likewise attended her young without male assistance.

While I sat watching the Turquoise Cotinga's nest in the middle of Wednesday morning, Juana came running down the path, breathless, her gray hair streaming, tears in her eyes. "Where is Manuel?" she gasped. Only ten minutes earlier her son had come down that same pathway, returning to his work from the lunch that she had served to him. "Where is Manuel? Pablo has been shot!" I suggested that she return to her house, and went myself to call the boy, who was chopping down the weeds in the cow pasture with his machete. On reaching the cabin, he was sent to see a neighbor who had just returned with his rifle from the fighting in San Isidro. The man told Manuel what he hesitated to tell to the old woman. His father was dead and buried.

Later, returning neighbors brought more details. On reaching San Isidro, Pablo had gone to help in one of the kitchens that fed the troops of the Opposition. In the small hours of Tuesday morning, he was drinking a cup of coffee when the Nicaraguan mercenaries that the Government had sent against the Opposition made a foray into the village. Apparently, he crouched behind a wall when the shooting began; but a ball penetrated the thin board and passed quite through his body. Next day he was buried in the same trench with another old man. His family wondered what had been done with his big, old-fashioned gold watch, his machete, and his clothes, including Manuel's best shirt.

Pastor, the elder of the two Garro boys, was then working at the Río Sonador, six hours away by horse. Juana wanted to send Manuel with news of his father's death; but I saw nothing to be gained, and much to be lost, by sending the boy on a long journey over roads that had become dangerous. Pastor remained for several weeks in happy ignorance of what had befallen his family, while the Garros proceeded to perform the rites for their dead in his absence. In the *sala*, or front room, of their house, they built a small booth of palm fronds and black cloth. In this was a table with a picture of the Virgin, before which candles flickered. For nine days the family held a novena to speed the departed's soul to heaven. The farm was full of people coming and going and prying about my house, until I was ready to cry for mercy. Food was consumed in great quantities. In the evenings I heard, issuing from the cabin, the sounds of earnest prayer by a smooth-tongued, not-too-honest neighbor who was paid for his words. At night the cottage was packed with family and friends, who could not all have crowded into the single bed and could hardly have found space to stretch out on the floor. On the ninth day the novena was concluded with the biggest feast this farm has ever seen. Breathing a sigh of relief, I hoped that all these prayers and festivities had forwarded poor Pablo's soul on its long way.

I missed old Pablo Garro. Despite the stormy disputes that from time to time arose between us, I did not dislike him. He never knew his father; he could neither write nor read. In a little wooden chest with a tiny lock, he kept a thin roll of soiled, crumpled, almost illegibly written promissory notes for money he had loaned at interest, or for land he had sold. At intervals he brought these documents to me, to read the names they bore and the date when each payment was due. He would then lay them out, repeating, "This is from Don José, this from Don Pedro, and this . . ." Then he would roll them up, promptly forget which paper corresponded to which debtor—and, after an interval, bring them back to be identified once more. Although no more literate than their father, his boys had quicker, more flexible minds, and more readily understood what I wanted done on the farm. The old man was sometimes hurt when I turned to the lads to explain something that perplexed him; but at times this was the only way to get the work done properly. Hard and grasping, he levied contributions on the wages of his children, and would stigmatize his daughter María as *sucia* (dirty) if she refused to relinquish what he considered to be an adequate share of her small salary as my cook.

After Pablo's disappearance, a malicious tongue came to tell his widow that neither patriotism nor desire to save his sons, but infatuation with a woman, had lured him to San Isidro when the bullets began to fly. Well, he was not the first whom Eros had led to a hero's death to the glory of Mars. Now I understood why Pablo used to go so often to San Isidro, and to my great exasperation delay there a day or two, even at times when we had crops to be harvested or other urgent work to do. They said that he gave his paramour a good deal of money, which his wife said was more than he ever did for her moncy which, at least in part, was earned for him by his children. But he left a modest patrimony for his family's support: a small farm back in the hills, with a sprouting field of maize that he had sown just before he died, a yoke of young oxen, a heifer, a mare with a colt, grains enough to support them until his new cornfield matured, and the roll of soiled promissory notes locked in the little wooden box. Then, after the revolution, his widow received a pension from the new government, whose cause the old man was presumably serving when he was shot. For a while, the old woman seemed gayer than I had known her to be.

A Reign of Terror

With the country all in a turmoil, I tried to preserve our mental equipoise by carrying on our customary routine, keeping Manuel busy on the farm, María occupied in the kitchen, and myself immersed in the studies of nesting birds that usually engaged me at this season. In an Annatto bush right in front of the house, a pair of Blue Ground-Doves built their frail nest, and I devoted many hours to watching them hatch their two white eggs and feed their nestlings. The blue male incubated for five or six hours in the middle of each day, his brown mate all the rest of the time. They took about equal shares caring for the young. While I sat watching their nest at noon on Easter Sunday, I heard the droning of an airplane motor in the direction of San Isidro, then the loud detonations of three bombs. "Easter eggs for San Isidro!" I thought.

It was difficult to preserve the calm tenor of life in a terror-stricken countryside. In early April the days were bright and warm, the air heavy with the fragrance of orange blossoms and charged with fear and unrest. Unable to enlist enough loyal Costa Ricans to support their cause, the faction led by Ex-President

Calderón and President Picado, which controlled the government, went to the great banana plantations on the southern Pacific coast to recruit the many Nicaraguan laborers employed there. Some of these men had fled their own country after committing crimes of violence. On the whole, they were a rough, hot-tempered crew, lured into the service of the Costa Rican government with the promise—so it was reported—of a wage of ten colones per day and freedom to loot and rape *ad libitum* if they captured San Isidro, that rebellious community hated by the party in power. Other Nicaraguans were forced into the service by their reckless compatriots. I cannot vouch for the accuracy of the report that these men were lured with promises of loot and rape, but I do know that the "Nicas" or "Mariaches," as those cutthroat mercenaries were called by the Costa Ricans, acted as though it were true.

One evening, as I was falling asleep, I was aroused by María coming to tell me that she had just heard that a party of Nicas was advancing up the valley and already in Volcán, a day's march away. All next day we received conflicting rumors. Some said that a troop of sixty men of the Opposition had marched from San Isidro to oppose the party of mercenaries; that Núñez, the commercial pilot who became a hero of the revolution, had gone in an airplane to bomb them. Late in the morning, while an airplane motor droned in the distance, I heard the deep report of exploding bombs; but the sound seemed to come from San Isidro rather than from any point nearer Volcán. Meanwhile, the people who lived around us were deserting their homes and going off to sleep in the bush, carrying off their household goods, hiding things, burying things, shifting things back and forth, in a frenzy of fear and desperation. By evening we received rumors that the Nicas had reached Peñas Blancas, three miles away.

Since Quizarrá lay several miles above the main road up the Térraba Valley, we hoped that the invaders would pass it by. Since my house was screened from the Quizarrá road by groves and thickets, there was a possibility that, even if the mercenaries came this way, they would overlook it. Some of the neighbors had found fault with the secluded site of my dwelling, saying that they would have built close to the public road. Now, at last, they saw an advantage in my seclusion. A neighbor who lived beside the road brought clothing, sacks of beans, buckets, utensils, and two new straw hats, thinking they would be safer with me; but I could not guarantee to safeguard his possessions—or my own.

I was apprehensive chiefly for the safety of the horses and cattle, and of my notes and manuscripts, mostly still unpublished, the harvest of two decades of work in politically unstable countries, in which I now feared that I had lingered too long. Many of these records were in a small iron safe, where I also kept a few legal documents of importance and a small sum of cash for the year's expenses. Surmising that, if I fell into the clutches of the Nicas, they might attempt to force me by torture to reveal the combination of the safe, I removed and buried the bank notes. I doubted that their thirst for knowledge was strong enough to induce them to carry away the manuscripts, even if they could lay hands on them.

Later, when we heard that the Nicas were blowing open safes with their automatic guns, four of us carried the iron box with all its contents into the forest, laid it face downward, and covered it with brush. With loose boards, we built a small shelter in one of the densest and most secluded nooks in the woods, as a cache for saddles, blankets, records that had overflowed the safe, and other articles of value. The roof of boards would also serve as a refuge for ourselves, if the house were invaded or destroyed.

The reports that the Nicas were so near us were exaggerated. When we heard that they were at Peñas Blancas, they were still at Buenos Aires, far down the valley. But they came, although not so swiftly as rumor, spurred by fear, advanced them. After the Opposition had consolidated its forces and was ready to march toward the capital, San Isidro was left without a garrison; and the Nicas moved in without meeting resistance. Then they spread over the valley, to begin a reign of terror and brutality that lasted several weeks. In the tense, fear-laden atmosphere that we breathed during this anxious time, I could not avoid thinking bitter thoughts about the president and ex-president who, unable to find enough of their compatriots to support their cause, had enlisted foreigners to plunder and kill their fellow citizens. To this pass had the "model democracy" of Central America fallen; to this we had come in a republic that boasted of having more school teachers than soldiers!

I also thought much about how I should behave if the Mariaches suddenly burst in upon us. Should I bolt into the neighboring woods, or hold my ground? To flee from a bunch of ignorant
cutthroats seemed lacking in dignity; to stay and have one's
throat cut, when no cause save that of pride could be advanced
thereby, seemed stubborn and foolish. Had not Spinoza declared
that the free man, who has dominated his passions and acts ra-
tionally, gives equal proof of his courage by facing danger or
avoiding it, according to the circumstances? Nevertheless, I determined not to run from the Nicas. How one who had never
faced gunfire would have reacted if the villains had suddenly advanced upon the house discharging their automatic guns at random, as happened to some friends of mine, I suppose that only
the actual experience can decide. But at least I slept in my own
bed every night during the revolution, even when everyone else
on the farm had fled into the forest, where they cut down a number of my beautiful palm trees to make a shelter.

After reading over Milton's sonnet:

> Captain, or colonel, or knight in arms,
> Whose chance on these defenseless doors may seize,[1]

I decided that it would not impress a horde of Nicaraguan black-
guards. So, instead of copying this out and posting it on my door,
I printed some signs in bold letters, stating in Spanish that the
owner of the farm was a citizen of the United States of America
who did not meddle in Costa Rican politics, and that he was protected by the power of the United States. I added this last clause
for what it might be worth, but without conviction. It seemed to
me that my country, with its conciliatory "Good Neighbor" poli-
cy, had lost ground in this respect since the day when Charles
Dickens could write that it was "honourably remarkable for protecting its subjects, wherever they may travel, with a dignity and
a determination which is a model for England."[2] I posted these
signs conspicuously about my house and on the Garros' dwelling.

1. John Milton, "When the Assault Was Intended to the City."
2. Charles Dickens, *A Child's History of England*, last page.

At seven o'clock on the morning of April 14, Manuel and another boy suddenly returned with their tools from their work in the fields. Going direct to the Garros' cabin, they brought out a chest containing clothes and other valuables and fell to work digging a hole to bury it. Had they done all their work with the same energy that they put into digging that hole, my farm would have become one of the most productive in the country! This big wooden box retired underground whenever rumors became particularly alarming, to emerge when fears were allayed and something was needed. This was the second interment of the restless chest. I could watch its inhumation from where I sat quietly in the garden, watching a Black-striped Sparrow's nest.

Black-striped Sparrows are attractive birds, with olive-green upper plumage, pale gray under parts, and four narrow longitudinal stripes on their gray heads. Over the years I had found a number of their bulky, roofed nests, built amid the low, bushy growth that they prefer; but their mistrust of my blind consistently thwarted my efforts to study them as intimately as I desired. Although always wary, a pair that lived in the garden and ate bananas on the feeding shelf lost so much of their shyness that, when the female built a nest among the big yellow trumpets of an Allamanda bush in front of the house, I could sit in my brown wigwam and look right through the round, sideward-facing doorway at the bird warming her two white eggs. She and her mate could not be distinguished by their plumage; but he often revealed his sex by his clear, melodious song, consisting of soft whistles that were delivered at first haltingly, then with gradually accelerated tempo until they formed an ascending trill. Although he never took a turn at incubation, at long intervals he brought food to his sitting partner, and later he did his full share in feeding the nestlings.

Because earlier attempts to take full advantage of this unique opportunity to study the nesting of Black-striped Sparrows had been interrupted by alarms that proved to be false, I had given strict orders that I was not in any circumstances to be disturbed while watching these birds. But when the frenzied excitement continued in the cabin a hundred yards away, and I heard three shots that sounded very near, I could no longer remain quiet, and emerged from my blind to learn what it was all about. Somebody had seen a troop of Nicas marching up the Quizarrá road, intent upon plunder and murder!

I ran down to the lowest pasture, where the animals were kept during these troubled times because it was farthest from the road, caught the three horses, and led them to the secluded spot in the woods that I had earlier selected for just this emergency. Then, with the boys, I carried back to the secret shelter in the forest the valuable articles that during this period became accustomed to traveling back and forth. If they stayed too long in the woodland, they would be injured by the dampness, for the wet season was now beginning; or they might be found and stolen by some marauding neighbor. If they remained in the house, the Nicas might destroy them or carry them off. It was in such a state of perpetual unrest that we lived.

Even a revolution and reign of terror is not without amusing incidents and compensations. For safekeeping, I hastily threw a pair of new shoes into a dense Thunbergia bush on the bank in front of the house. Soon after I hid them there, my attention was drawn by a great commotion among the Scarlet-rumped Black Tanagers who frequented this bush and ate bananas on the neighboring shelf. The brilliant birds were flitting around and complaining loudly, and their cries had drawn as interested spectators a colorful assemblage of small birds of other kinds. Expecting to find a snake, or at least a big, bedraggled moth such as sometimes caused great excitement among these temperamental tanagers, I searched and searched, but the only thing unusual I could find in the Thunbergia was—a pair of new shoes!

While hiding some kitchen utensils in the woods south of the house, María saw a small, brown bird emerge from a burrow that went obliquely into a steep slope. Looking in with the aid of a small electric bulb attached by a long cord to my flashlight, I found three blind nestlings, with pinfeathers just sprouting through their downless pink skin, reposing on a bed of dead leaves in the enlargement at the end of the short tunnel. It was my second nest of the White-whiskered Softwing, a chubby brown puffbird that I wished much to study. Even a revolution may advance our knowledge, of birds or of men!

Tied up in the woods for safety, the horses passed a hungry day, as we an anxious one. But, except for a single additional shot, heard in the distance, the hours passed quietly enough. Investigation failed to confirm the report that the Nicas had visited Quizarrá; either it was a downright lie, spread by a malicious tongue, or the hallucination of a too-fevered imagination. The horses were returned to the pasture, and we went about our occupations with freer minds. The orange blossoms always seemed more fragrant after these alarms proved to be unfounded!

In the evening I sallied forth from the farm to search for news. All the dwellings on our side of the Río Peña Blanca were deserted; my house and the Garros' were the only ones from which smoke arose. The pastures were as abandoned as the habitations; the people had driven their horses, cattle, and pigs higher into the hills. Those who had boasted most loudly of how valiantly they would behave if the Nicas came were among the first to flee when danger seemed imminent.

Crossing the river by the covered wooden bridge, I found the people on the eastern side living and working more or less normally, although hardly less exposed to danger than those who had fled. In Don Odilio's little store a number of men were discussing the rumors, the atrocities committed by the Mariaches, and their pospects of escaping similar treatment. I heard that the mercenaries had sacked Don Belisario's house, midway between Quizarrá and San Isidro. When they tried to knock open a wardrobe with the butt of a gun, it went off with the shock, causing great confusion among the Nicas. Those outside the house thought they were being fired upon from within. The women of the family took advantage of this turmoil to flee into the bush. I was also told of civilians, including some that I knew, who had been lined up and shot in cold blood by the mercenaries.

After hearing these alarming reports, I suggested to the assembled citizens that we organize an expedition, burn the wooden bridge over the Río General, and fell trees along the Quizarrá road, where it passed through forest, to block the way with an abatis. Although this project for making ourselves less accessible to the enemy seemed to be sound military tactics, it found no favor with those present.

Our situation was grave and disquieting enough, but not quite as terrible as those about me made it by recounting over and over, always with horrendous amplifications, the rumors that they had heard at second hand. This constant debilitating talk threw into high relief the amount of spite, ill will, and mutual distrust that existed in a backwoods community, and what malicious liars some of the people were. In several instances, men led the mercenaries to attack and plunder those against whom they bore grudges. *Pueblo pequeño, infierno grande* (little village, big hell), runs a Costa Rican proverb. I was nauseated with the whole situation, from the presidential candidate who could not accept defeat at the polls and brought in foreign brigands to terrify his own people, down to the peasants with their sloppy, suspicious minds, unable to stand together in the face of a peril that menaced all alike. For the moment, I was sick of democracy. Monarchy seemed to me the most decent form of government, and I should have shouted huzzas for an Augustus Caesar. But on mature reflection, I became convinced that all forms of government are equally provisional and unsatisfactory, as long as men are unable to govern themselves individually, to keep their appetites and passions under control. And if enough people could achieve this dominion over themselves, perhaps any of the traditional arrangements for the government of the state would be tolerable.

Troubles rarely come singly. The dry season had been prolonged and severe; and now toward its end we had scarcely anything green to eat, amid all the persisting verdure of the forest, and no fruit. With the farm's stored grains, cassava and other starchy roots, eggs and milk, we were far from starving. But our supply of milk was irregular. Manuel was convinced that if the Mariaches came and found the calves tied in the yard, they would butcher them; so, when danger seemed most imminent, we left them overnight with their mothers in the most secluded pastures, with the result that the cows had been sucked dry before we could catch them next morning. San Isidro, where at this season I often bought a few vegetables, and Palmares, where oranges were often available even in March and April, were overrun by the mercenaries. With neither fruits nor green vegetables, I felt disordered and perpetually hungry, no matter how much I ate. And I missed my breakfast cocoa.

At about this time, I broke the skin of a finger while cutting down a small tree in the pasture. Although the injury was inconsiderable, it developed an infection that spread, until my legs were full of ugly, painful, dry sores—an ailment common enough in the locality, which never attacked me while better nourished. In spite of all the confusion, we managed to plant an acre or two of maize. When the plants sprouted, I would go down to the cornfield, sit upon a rock, and eat the softer tissues at the growing points of the stout young shoots, which I surmised were full of vitamins. After the pharmacist, who had fled at the outset of the revolution, returned to San Isidro at its conclusion, he gave me an ointment and sulfa tablets for a streptococcus infection. With these medicaments, and the better diet we enjoyed after the rains returned and the new crops grew, I was soon completely cured of the nasty sores, which have never returned.

In the midst of these troubles, I wrote in my journal: "I have been under the impression that our life here this last month has been somewhat abnormal; but, upon second thought, it occurs to me that since the revolution broke out we have been living the life that has become normal and usual for people of the twentieth century, as it was for people of the tenth; a life of warfare and violence and civil strife and insecurity of life and property. No matter where one dwells, he can hardly escape it these days. These are signs of the decline of Western civilization—of a civilization based upon technical skill that outruns moral competence, and the enfranchisement of great masses of people so deficient in education that they cannot understand the basic issues of their times, and are plastic in the hands of demagogues."

After the Revolution

For six weeks we were without mail, or news from friends, or fresh supplies. Finally, toward the end of April, the Opposition, having won secure control of the capital and principal towns of the Central Plateau, returned to drive the hated Nicas from San Isidro, birthplace of the victorious revolution. After a sharp encounter, the mercenaries fled the village, to be hunted down and killed where they sought to hide in the surrounding country. On

April 28, I saddled Bayon for the first time in nearly two months, and set out for San Isidro. Along the way, I noticed the remains of a house and a store that had been burnt by the Nicas.

As I looked down on San Isidro from the last elevation on the hilly road, the cluster of low buildings, surrounded by green fields, appeared much as I remembered it. But on the outskirts of the village were the blackened sites of three or four dwellings that had been burnt. Although most of the buildings still stood, many had suffered damages in the form of broken windows, holes in the roof, boards wrenched from the walls, missing doors. Only on peering into them did I become aware of the full extent of the destruction wrought by the invaders, who had systematically ransacked the community, smashing what they could not carry off, so that many people had lost everything except the clothes they wore. In front of each of a number of the small shops stood an iron safe, its combination lock destroyed by bullets. One might have understood so much wanton destruction if wrought by an afflicted people against their brutal oppressors; but, done by men who had not been wronged by the local inhabitants, such behavior was almost incomprehensible. It revealed one of the darker sides of human nature.

Trenches ran along two sides of San Isidro's central plaza, as one can see depicted on a postage stamp issued by the new government to commemorate the War of Liberation. These, as the engraving shows, were not straight but laid out with many angles, so that an enemy who managed to enter at one point could not rake the whole length with gunfire. When I remarked that these trenches must have been planned by someone familiar with trench warfare, I was told that Padre León, the old German priest who during the First World War had served in von Hindenburg's army and bore a scar on his face, had directed the work, and even helped with pick and shovel. I was also told how, when a Government airplane flew overhead bombing or machine-gunning the village, the younger of the two German padres had snatched a rifle from a soldier whose marksmanship was poor and shot at the plane. After the Opposition withdrew its forces for the march on Cartago and the Nicas came in, they treated the church as they did the rest of the village, destroying all the saints and images, damaging the edifice itself, and removing all the contents from the adjoining priests' house. This happened before San Isidro, having grown from a village to a town, became the seat of a bishop and replaced the old church with an impressive cathedral in the modern style.

At the edge of the airfield lay a badly wrecked bimotored airplane. This was the machine in which the intrepid Núñez attacked the president's house in San José. In order to place his homemade bomb where it would be effective, he had flown so low that his plane was struck by rifle bullets or, as others said, torn by the explosion of the bomb he dropped. He was barely able to remain airborne long enough to regain his base at San Isidro. When the Opposition evacuated the village, they could not remove the damaged machine, which was utterly demolished by the invading Nicas.

Of the two or three dozen shops in the village, I found all but two or three closed and boarded up. All the merchandise that the proprietors had not carried off and hidden had been stolen or destroyed by the invaders. The two *pulperías* that were doing business had very little to offer; but I managed to buy a broom that we greatly needed, mine having worn out during the revolution. Morning and afternoon, a long queue of people gathered in front of the *jefatura* (administrative headquarters), waiting to receive food that had been sent from other parts of the country. No other town, it was claimed, had suffered so much as this.

The village was full of soldiers carrying rifles, but dressed like everyone else, except for their blue trench caps with white bands. There were still no civil authorities, and military law prevailed. The aviation company had resumed its services and brought in that day the first mail pouch to reach San Isidro in six or seven weeks. I received the first news from the outside world and my parents in the States in all this interval, and left letters for the first outgoing post. The young postmaster, who had fled when the Nicas came in, had saved the registered mail by carrying it with him and burying it, along with the registry book, which he proudly showed me, all stained by moisture during its long sojourn under ground.

I looked in vain for a number of acquaintances who had been murdered by the mercenaries. I was told that, had the Opposition delayed only one day longer its victorious return to San Isidro, my home would have met the same unhappy fate as so many others. Someone had informed the Nicas that I had a safe containing money, and had agreed to lead them to me. If they had not found enough cash to satisfy their avarice, they would, if possible, have captured and threatened to kill me unless I paid a ransom. Such, at least, was their custom, and in some instances, when their captives resisted, they carried out their threat. This marauding expedition to Los Cusingos had been scheduled for the very day on which the mercenaries were driven from San Isidro. I cannot vouch for the accuracy of this account of my narrow escape from an unwelcome visit, but it intensified my conviction that I had been exceedingly fortunate to have passed through such a harassing interval with nothing worse than minor infections that soon vanished.

Now, at last, I could watch the birds with better health and fewer interruptions. For the first time that year, I heard the song of a migrating Olive-backed Thrush. In other years their musical spirals of sound rose freely in our woods and thickets from late March until early May; but in the year of the revolution they were strangely silent, whether because of the severe drought or some other reason, I cannot tell. In the Allamanda bush in front of the house, the Black-striped Sparrows raised both of their nestlings, who spontaneously hopped out of their covered nest before sunrise on their twelfth day. Their parents led them over the lawn to safe retreats in neighboring shrubbery, boldly fluttering into the faces of some pullets that were attracted by the excitement, and driving these relatively huge fowls away. Then a pair of Gray-headed Tanagers nested for the second year in our small coffee plantation. To reach the forest where they foraged, three or four hundred yards from their nest, they flew through our shady dooryard instead of taking the slightly shorter route across the open pasture. Sometimes the male paused in a tree to sing. Of all the tanagers' songs that I have heard, his was one of the best.

A memorable event of the quieter days following the revolution was my second meeting with a Pheasant Cuckoo. As I walked through tall second-growth woods with dense undergrowth, the long-tailed, grayish bird flew ahead of me to alight on a thin horizontal branch, where it fanned out its great tail and fluttered its half-opened wings. Then it turned to face me and sat almost motionless, holding its wings and tail half spread. It maintained this inexplicable attitude until I took a step forward, when it flew to a more distant perch and assumed the same posture, with its back distinctly humped. As I continued to approach, the cuckoo retired to successive perches, on each of which it displayed as before, always without uttering a sound. Finally, a flycatcher darted at the strange bird and chased it beyond view.

This cuckoo appeared to be giving a distraction display, on perches four or five yards up, rather than on the ground, where the first that I saw performed in similar fashion. But why should a parasitic bird that foists its eggs on others give a distraction display, when no egg or helpless young could be found? The habits of this bird, as of so many others in tropical America, are little known; and I was thankful that, in a country that had become peaceful and abolished its army, I could resume my efforts to learn more about them.

CHAPTER 10

The Most Hospitable Tree

Cecropia tree; Chestnut-mandibled Toucan

While still an undergraduate in college, I was familiar with that remarkable work, *Botanische Mittheilungen aus den Tropen*. In the nine slender volumes of this beautifully illustrated series of monographs, edited and in part written by the famous plant geographer A. F. W. Schimper and published during the years 1888 to 1901, I became acquainted with some of the most fascinating phenomena of tropical botany: the adaptations of epiphytic plants, the strange modes of secondary thickening in the stems of woody vines, the complex relations between ants and the plants that provide shelter for them, the fungus gardens of leaf-cutting ants. Perhaps no other single work so strongly influenced my determination to devote some years to the first-hand study of tropical nature—years that have stretched on and on to half a century.

To a young student of nature in the first exhilaration of his studies, no John Mandeville or Marco Polo had filled his pages with more wonder stories than were to be found in these records of sober scientific investigation. And perhaps the most marvelous of all the volumes, both in the patent drama of the situation described and in the agelong series of delicate adjustments and readjustments between organisms implied in the relationship, was the monograph by Schimper himself on the Cecropia tree and its garrison of Azteca ants. Widely traveled, enthusiastic, keen-sighted, endowed in no small measure with the capacity for "the scientific use of the imagination," the author pointed out the unusual features that made the tree an exceptionally favorable abode for the ants, providing them not only with commodious lodgings but also with a special and delicate food. In return for food and housing, the hordes of little biting ants defended the tree against its enemies. Such, in brief, was Schimper's thesis, which, during many years of rsidence and travel in widely separated parts of the range of the Cecropia tree, I have had constantly at the back of my mind, so that observations, made deliberately or by chance, were classified according to whether they confirmed or refuted it. Would this story, which stirred the imagination of the young student, stand the test of a much longer familiarity with the Cecropia tree than its author himself enjoyed?

When finally I reached the tropics, I was not long in recognizing the tree whose remarkable history I knew so well. Indeed, the genus *Cecropia*, of the mulberry family, contains the most distinctive trees of the New World tropics. It comprises forty to fifty species, distributed not only over the whole length and breadth of the intertropical areas of the American continents, but in the Antilles and other outlying islands as well. Were a wizard to drop a naturalist at random, blindfolded, somewhere within the vast sweep of the earth's central zone, no other single group of trees would so help him to decide, by its presence or absence, whether he had been set down in the Western or the Eastern hemisphere. For over its great range, there is hardly a district with heavy or moderate rainfall where it is not abundant. It is absent only from desert and semidesert areas and high mountains subject to nocturnal frosts. Yet in the equatorial Andes it grows freely up to an altitude of at least 8,500 feet, and in Central America to no less than 6,000 feet. Most common in clearings and light second-growth woodland, where frequently it is the dominant tree, it is by no means absent from primeval forest, where it often springs up in the narrow, light-flooded opening left by the fall of a forest giant. Almost everywhere it is recognized and named by the country people. Throughout Central America it is called *guarumo*; in the Montaña of Peru, *setico*; in the former British West Indies, trumpet tree, apparently because certain of the aborigines made trumpets from its hollow branches.

Not only wide range and abundance but also the ease with which the veriest novice in the forest can recognize them, entitles the Cecropias to be considered the most characteristic trees of tropical America. In tropical forests, trees of many species tend to have leaves with rather similar outlines, without the great variety of indentations that help us to identify the oaks, maples, beeches, and chestnuts of northern woods. Flowers are usually high out of reach, often inconspicuous, and available only at certain seasons and to the most adept climber; color and texture of bark sometimes lead the practiced eye to a correct identification, but they are not always to be relied upon. Familiarity with the trees of a tropical forest is to be gained only by long and arduous collecting, patient research, and much taxonomic skill. Very few botanists can correctly name at sight even half the species of trees in an acre of well-developed primary forest anywhere in the tropical lowlands of the American continents. How refreshing, then, to find a tree so different from all its neighbors, in foliage, bark, form, and half a dozen well-marked characters, that it can hardly be confused with anything else! Any intelligent lad from some far northern land, sent with only a written description to a tropical forest and told to bring back a specimen of a Cecropia tree, should be able to pick it out unaided. I know no other tree of the tropical American forests for which I would hazard the same statement.

The Cecropias are small, middle-sized, or rarely (for the tropics) tall trees, never attaining the height of the giants of the forest, nor ever remotely approaching them in the girth of their slender, graceful trunks. These are covered by a smooth bark, light gray, whitish, or greenish in color, and prominently ringed, at intervals of a few inches, with narrow ridges—scars left by the fallen bud sheaths. This smooth, light-colored, strongly ringed trunk alone serves to distinguish the Cecropia from nearly all its neighbors. At the very base, where it nears the ground, the trunk becomes slenderer instead of thicker; and the deficiency in girth and strength is compensated by the presence of numerous prop roots, sometimes springing from the bole as high as four or five feet above the earth, and descending obliquely until they enter the soil and ramify through it. Prop roots are not peculiar to the Cecropia—many other dicotyledonous trees, many palms, the pandanus, and even the maize plant have them—yet they will distinguish it from the majority of the trees among which it grows. The boughs of the Cecropia are coarse, stiff, and few in number. The lowest usually spring from the trunk well above the ground. These branches are distributed in loose clusters or false whorls of three to six together, with long stretches of branchless trunk between successive clusters. Like the trunk, the obliquely ascending boughs diminish little in thickness from base to tip, and they bear few branchlets of the second order. Accordingly, the tree has a very open crown.

If the leaves were small, such a branch system would produce a stiff and awkward tree; but on a well-developed Cecropia, stiffness is avoided by the generous breadth and grace of carriage of the foliage. The ample leaves, which on vigorous young trees are sometimes a yard in diameter, are held more or less horizontally, at the ends of long, rounded petioles. They are peltate, roundish in outline, divided by deep and narrow indentations into long radiating lobes, and in some species silvery on the lower side, giving them a pleasing and characteristic aspect when tossed up by the wind. Rarely, as in *Cecropia araliaefolia* of the eastern foothills of the Andes, the lobing has been carried to the point where the leaves are divided into distinct, stalked leaflets, all radiating from the end of the long common stalk, like those of the horse-chestnut tree.

The flowers, minute and individually inconspicuous, seem unworthy of a tree with such pronounced and individual characters. Yet in their arrangement they, too, are sufficiently distinctive. They are closely packed in fingerlike spikes, in some species short and stubby, in others long and slender, sometimes twisted. These fingers are borne, in clusters of four or more, at the end of a common stalk or peduncle which may be short and stiff or long and pendulous. Male and female spikes are produced on separate trees, the former whitish and soon falling, the latter green and persistent, scarcely altering their appearance as their myriad florets swell into tiny one-seeded fruits. Each cluster of spikes develops within a close-fitting sheath, white within and often an attractive shade of pink or red on the outside. This sheath splits along one side and drops when the flowers are ready to shed, or to receive, their pollen. It is the most colorful part of the tree.

A few words about the ecology of the Cecropia will help us to understand some of its peculiarities of form, especially its system of branching. It is a tree pre-eminently adapted for the colonization of denuded lands, whether these be new clearings in the forest, abandoned patches of cultivation, flood plains along the shifting course of a great river, or the long, narrow strips of raw earth streaked upon a mountainside by landslides. In such areas, tropical vegetation wears its most lush, most riotous and undisciplined aspect. Competition among the colonizing plants is exceedingly keen; the slow-growing seedling, although of the noblest lineage of the forest, has slight chance of success; victory—immediate victory, at least—belongs to the plant that can keep its "head and shoulders" above its rivals, and so enjoy full exposure to the strength-giving sunlight.

A wide-spreading, many-branched plant is likely to be smothered over and crushed down by a tangled mat of vines and creepers, which by their excessive growth greatly retard the reforestation of cleared lands in the humid tropics. The successful tree must not only grow rapidly in height; it must also be sparing in the matter of breadth, hugging itself together, so to speak, lest it waste much-needed energy in horizontal expansion and give the eager, grasping vines a firm hold on itself. Such a tree is the Cecropia. Seemingly intent only upon outreaching its competitors, in crowded tangles it may attain a height of twenty or thirty feet, or even more, before it ventures to extend a single branch. Its ample leaves, each of which appears capable of the photosynthetic work of a whole spray of the smaller leaves of a northern plant, fall when their activity is taken over by younger leaves above them, thereby giving the creepers no permanent grasp upon the tree. So great is the sunward impulse of the vigorous young Cecropia that its slender stem is commonly dilated upward and, like scarcely any other tree, is thickest at the top, in the succulent green portion just below the apex. The inverted taper of the trunk is corrected in later life, when the tree has won the victory and spread its branches proudly above the rival vegetation, in part by secondary thickening, in part by the development of the stout prop roots at the base.

Such, then, is the appearance and mode of growth of the most highly individualistic tree of tropical America. We have already noticed, in its very lineaments and most obvious outward vesture, enough idiosyncracies for any one tree. Yet we have scarcely begun to explore its peculiarities. Shake the branches of a Cecropia, and a host of small brown or blackish ants come swarming out through narrow, symmetrically situated orifices. They run hastily over bark and leaves, and on to any object touching them, each biting with all its small might if it meets the skin of an animal. Cut through the young stem or branch with a single sharp stroke of the machete, and the severed end reveals a central hollow, left by the almost total breakdown of the pith, wider than in any other young woody stem that I know except the timber bamboos.

Stand quietly contemplating one of the ant-inhabited species. A keen eye will soon notice that each of the long leaf stalks is swollen at the base, where it joins the stem, on the lower side, into an angular, knee-like protrusion, which is densely covered with brown hairs. After years of collecting tropical plants, handling thousands of species, I can recall no other tree with just such a leaf base. It would be remarkable enough without the little white bodies, each about the size and shape of a small ant's pupa, that stud it over, like little white-headed pins stuck up to the head in a brown velvet pincushion. Watching patiently, one may be fortunate enough to see an ant crawl over the cushion, touching with its antennae one after another of the little white beads, until it finds one that is ripe, plucks it off, and carries it into the

Cecropia stem with protein bodies; Bananaquit

hollow center of the branch through one of the small apertures. These are the protein bodies, the special food of the ants, often called Müllerian corpuscles after their discoverer.

In harboring a colony of ants within its living tissues, the Cecropia is not unique in the vegetable kingdom. It belongs in a heterogeneous group known as the myrmecophilous or "ant-loving" plants.[1] Like so many other things, the Cecropia can be best understood by considering it in relation to the class of objects to which it belongs.

The myrmecophilous plants, also known as myrmecophytes, have only a single feature in common: the habitual occurrence of colonies of ants in hollow living organs which, in many instances, appear to have been specially developed for the accommodation of the insects. All or nearly all are of tropical distribution. As a rule, a particular species of ant is found in each true myrmecophilous plant, and sometimes the ant is restricted to this peculiar habitat, suggesting that the myrmecophilous habit was evolved in relation to this particular kind of guest, and the plant has not merely happened to form a hollow organ open to tenancy by the first small insect that finds it. The myrmecophilous plants are scattered sparingly through a considerable number of unrelated families, including the Piperaceae, Moraceae, Polygonaceae, Mimosaceae, Boraginaceae, Verbenaceae, Melastomaceae, Rubiaceae, and even the ferns, in a manner that indicates that they are not genetically related but that the habit has developed independently in a number of distinct groups.

The nature of the organs in which the insects are accommodated is as diverse as the families in which the myrmecophilous plants are classified. Perhaps the most common abode of the ant colony is in a stem left hollow by the breakdown of the central pith. Such ant-filled stems are found, in addition to the Cecropia, in the beautiful Palo Santo and in certain arborescent species of *Piper*. In *Cordia alliodora* the insects find shelter in gall-like hollow nodes, situated at the point where several branches depart together from the end of a thicker twig. In certain melastomes of

1. Some writers have objected to the term *myrmecophilous*. The plants, they insist, do not actually love their ants. However, we need not take the word too literally.

the genus *Tococa*, the ants dwell in paired hollow lobes at the base of the leaf blade, each with a narrow orifice on the lower side of the leaf. In certain American species of *Piper*, they establish themselves in the long, narrow hollow formed between the incurved, closely appressed thin edges of each petiole, and from this space they make their way into the stem by removing the pith.

In the bull's-horn acacias, the ant colonies occupy the great paired, hornlike hollow thorns from which the curious little trees take their name. The hollows of the paired thorns intercommunicate at the base, and one thorn in each pair is provided by the ants with a small round aperture for going in and out. Perhaps the strangest of the myrmecophilous plants are two epiphytic genera of the madder or coffee family, *Hydnophytum* and *Myrmecodia*, natives of the Indo-Malaysian region, whose curiously swollen stems are penetrated by a labyrinth of winding galleries in which the ants dwell. In eastern Costa Rica, I found a species of polypody fern whose slender stems, creeping over the mossy branches of trees, bear numerous brown, gall-like bodies, about an inch in diameter, each with a doorway leading into a central cavity infested by tiny, stinging ants.

As a rule, the host plant makes no special provision for the board of its lodgers. But in some, the ants attend aphids that suck the juices of the plant, which thus indirectly provides for the support of its guests. Among the most hospitable of all these myrmecophytes are our Cecropia and the bull's-horn acacias, which set before their guests a special food in the form of tiny white protein corpuscles. In the Cecropia, these minute, many-celled bodies are, as we have seen, liberally produced, in successive crops, on the cushionlike base of each leaf stalk. In the acacias, a single elongate white food particle terminates each of the many small leaflets of the twice-compound leaf, and once it has been removed by the ants that dwell in the hollow thorns at the base of the leaf, it is not renewed. The food bodies of the acacia are sometimes called Beltian corpuscles, in honor of Thomas Belt, who first made them known to naturalists, just as Fritz Müller first described those of the Cecropia. In the myrmecophilous species of *Piper*, the surface surrounding the tubular hollow along the upper side of each petiole bears innumerable minute white corpuscles that nourish the tiny ants who live there.

Of the ants regularly associated with these myrmecophilous plants, some are fiercely aggressive; but others are among the smallest, weakest, most defenseless and sluggish of their kind. They rarely, if ever, devour the foliage of their host plant, nor do they indiscriminately attack its living tissues. Some naturalists believe that these ants benefit the plants that shelter them by driving away foliage-eating insects, browsing mammals, and other enemies of vegetation. If this view is correct, the association between ant and plant is one of mutual benefit: the plant provides lodging and sometimes also food for the insect; the latter in turn protects its host from attack. How true this is in the case of the Cecropia we shall now examine.

The Cecropia appears to be one of the most highly specialized of myrmecophytes. It seems to have made a greater effort to attract its ant guests than most other "ant-loving" plants. Three unique features make it an unusually favorable abode for ants:

1. A remarkably wide central hollow in the stem. Hollow stems appear to be more common among herbaceous than among woody plants; but, except the bamboos, no other plant that I know has, in sound young shoots, a central cavity as wide as that of the Cecropia. Vigorous stems often have a cavity fully two inches in diameter, surrounded by walls only about one-sixteenth of an inch thick, at a point only a few inches below the growing tip of the shoot. With age, the tissues immediately surrounding the cavity become hard and resistant. When old, fallen trunks decay, this is the last part of them to disappear. The hollow internodes, with their enclosing walls and transverse partitions, remain lying on the ground like a chain of whitish, elongated, cylindrical boxes, or the bleaching vertebrae of some huge ribless serpent.

2. The presence, in the wall surrounding the hollow that occupies each internode, of a pit where the ants find it particularly easy to open a doorway. At the upper end of each of the short internodes, directly above the point of insertion of the leaf next below, is the small, slightly elongated depression. The tissues separating the bottom of this pit from the central hollow are even thinner than the wall elsewhere, and they are composed wholly

of soft, thin-walled cells. Vascular bundles are absent here. The ants readily gnaw through the bottoms of these pits; in a tree inhabited by a flourishing colony, each one becomes the site of a doorway through which the insects pass in and out. Schimper laid great stress upon these pits, pointing out that they were present in species of Cecropia habitually infested by ants, but absent from species that had not developed the myrmecophilous habit. Similar pits are said to occur in the walls of hollow-stemmed plants of other genera not inhabited by ants, but they are so rare that I have been unable to find any.

3. The protein grains at the bases of the petioles. Although such corpuscles, which appear to be modified hairs or glands, occur on other plants, some of which are not myrmecophytes, such plants are rare. The only other plants on which I have seen similar corpuscles are the bull's-horn acacias and the above-mentioned species of *Piper*. In the tropics of the Eastern Hemisphere they are reported to be present on *Pterospermum javanicum*, where they are produced in tiny pitchers at the bases of the leaves, and on the long shoots of climbing species of *Gnetum*, which apparently do not attract ants.

Here, associated in the same tree, are three features—exceptionally wide central hollow, pits, and protein bodies—that, although not unknown in plants not myrmecophilous, are so rare that one might botanize through the tropics for months or even years without finding any one of them singly, apart from the Cecropias. What, then, are the chances for a *random* association of the three in the same species? Of about the same order, I would suggest, as those for finding, while wandering through an uninhabited wilderness, an inn whose loosely closed door opened at a tap, giving access to a table excellently spread, and a bed prepared for the weary traveler. It is easier to believe that the Cecropia has developed these three rare features not by chance—in the sense that they are not causally related—but rather through natural selection, because they make it an attractive abode for the ants that help it to flourish by protecting it from its enemies. Such was Schimper's view. Now let us see how effective in guarding the tree these ants really are.

We may as well begin by considering the effectiveness of these Azteca ants in guarding their home tree against the animal most destructive to vegetation—with shame I write it—man himself. As one of the abundant plants in the tall second-growth thickets that in the tropics are cut and burned to make fields for maize, rice, and other crops, the Cecropia is subject to attack by the axe or long machete of the agricultural laborer. The garrison of ants serves not at all to protect the tree—and themselves—from destruction by his swinging blade: Cecropia trees are leveled indiscriminately with all the lush growth of giant herbs, bushes, vines, and other trees among which they are so conspicuous an element. The sweating laborer is indeed often bitten by the Azteca ants; but they are among the less formidable of the hosts of ants of many kinds and habitats whose bites and stings, along with those of a variety of other insects, are an inseparable accompaniment of his toil.

For the Aztecas can only *bite* with their mandibles, without injecting any venom into the victim. Ants capable of inflicting really severe punishment *sting*, like honeybees, with the end of the abdomen, injecting a drop or so of formic acid or some other irritant into the wound. Neither biting ants nor biting bees, of which tropical America contains many kinds, command the same respect as their stinging relations. I would rather endure the gnawings of a dozen of the Cecropia's ants than one fierce sting of the long, slender ants that dwell in the bull's-horn acacia, or of the tiny brown fire ants so annoyingly abundant about houses and lawns in tropical America. The Aztecas, weak and not very agile, are seriously incommoded by hair no denser than that on the back of a man's wrist. A few of them biting away at the tough skin of a man's hands are of no great consequence. Only on the tender skin of the neck and parts of the body habitually clothed do they cause much discomfort.

Cecropia trees are, as a rule, left unmolested by man, except when clearing land for sowing and other purposes, largely because they are of little use to him. Sometimes a segment is removed from a felled trunk, exposing the central hollow, which then serves as a gutter for conducting water, and is perhaps the best substitute for a pipe in forest communities remote from both factories and native bamboos. The tough fiber in the bark is sometimes twisted into rope or used for making hammocks; but where the Burío or the Juco are available, the Cecropia is rarely disturbed for this purpose, not because of its ants but because these other trees yield superior fibers. Yet the botanist will admit that Cecropia trees are unpleasant to collect; if individually the ants are not formidable, their very abundance is troublesome.

One has only to watch an Azteca ant struggling among the hairs on one's forearm to suspect that on the body of a furry animal the insect would be as incapable of rapid and effective action as a man amid the debris of a newly felled forest. Mammals of several kinds consume large quantities of Cecropia leaves. Howling Monkeys, agile browsers of the treetops, are fond of the great leaves and tender catkins; in regions where these primates abound, their vociferous bands are often seen among the boughs of Cecropia trees.

When first, in Panama, I studied nature in the common range of the Cecropia and the Howling Monkey, I was reluctant to believe that the particular trees in which the monkeys foraged were in fact infested by ants. To one influenced by the writings of Schimper, it seemed more probable that they had somehow escaped colonization by the Aztecas. I recall vividly how, years ago, I cut into the trunk of a tall Cecropia, whose growth in girth had wholly obliterated the lowest of the ants' perforations for ingress and egress, while the howlers who had been feasting among its lofty branches shouted down their protests. But when I reached the hollow center, the little Aztecas swarmed out; and I knew then that they were ineffective in guarding the tree against the depredations of the monkeys. To be sure, these animals spend much time scratching themselves, as do Spider Monkeys and others; but the amount of this activity bears no relation to the kind of tree in which they happen to be. Probably the irritation is caused by their own parasites rather than by the Azteca ants.

Another treetop browser very fond of the Cecropia foliage is the Three-toed Sloth. These phlegmatic creatures, whose life appears so nearly vegetative, do not eat all kinds of leaves indiscriminately. In Central America, they appear to prefer the Cecropia to other trees; just as, in the highlands of Costa Rica, the Two-toed Sloth is found eating the compound leaves of the tall, weedy Capulín tree too often for this to be attributed to chance. Of five Three-toed Sloths that I saw in one day, while paddling along a lagoon in western Panama, four were in Cecropia trees.

One of them, a female carrying a baby on her breast, was descending the trunk of a Cecropia that had been defoliated to the last leaf. In eating, as in other activities, the sloth is quite as slow and deliberate as its name implies; a single large Cecropia leaf may engage its attention for a half hour or more; and a denuded tree indicates long and persistent activity by the browser. One might suppose that a Cecropia would produce leaves faster than a sloth could consume them.

Like the monkeys, the sloth devotes a large share of its waking hours to scratching, with a steady, deliberate, almost mechanical movement. In this case, too, the source of the irritation appears to be other than the Azteca ants, which can hardly find their way through the animal's coarse, dense pelage. When sated by its meal of foliage and finished with its scratching, the sluggish creature seeks the base of a stout limb, bends its head forward until its short, dull face is hidden between its forearms, and sleeps while sitting upright in the angle between branch and trunk, a featureless mass of gray hair, oblivious of the ants that crawl over the boughs around it.

Birds of many kinds visit the Cecropia tree, whether to rest among its branches, where the ants appear not to molest them, or for more special purposes. The thick, green fruiting spikes, although dry and insipid to us, are a food attractive to frugivorous birds as diverse as pigeons, parrots, trogons, toucans, barbets, woodpeckers, cotingas, certain flycatchers, thrushes, honeycreepers, oropéndolas, tanagers, and finches, all of which evidently help to scatter the tiny seeds far and wide and are responsible for the far-flung distribution of the tree. In the dry season when other kinds of fruits often become scarce, these catkins are an important source of nourishment for many birds, who begin at the tip of each spike and denude it toward the base. Other birds, from big Squirrel Cuckoos to little wintering wood warblers, seek the varied insects that thrive upon the foliage.

Although the coarse, open branch system makes the Cecropia a poor site for nests, a few kinds of feathered creatures build their homes upon it and appear to raise their families without molestation by the ants, just as birds of more numerous kinds place their nests in the bull's-horn acacias, taking advantage of the protection afforded by the fiercely stinging ants that dwell in the thorns.

The bulky, domed nests of the Vermilion-crowned Flycatcher are sometimes built in a crotch of a Cecropia tree.

Most of the feathered visitors to the Cecropia tree benefit it, either by disseminating its seeds or by removing harmful insects. The theory that the Azteca ants protect the tree does not require that they keep these birds away. But one bird that habitually frequents the Cecropia, and certainly does it much more harm than good, is attracted by the ants themselves. The big Lineated Woodpecker, a black bird with a flamboyant scarlet crest, pierces young trunks and the more slender branches with its powerful chisel-bill, to extract the ants and their pupae from the hollow center, now and again pausing in its work of perforation and extraction to pick off great numbers of the unfortunate Aztecas that swarm over the bark. In widely scattered parts of its range, I have often watched this myrmecophagous woodpecker at its feast. These ants are an important constituent of the bird's diet. Like those other ant-eating members of the family, the flickers, the Lineated Woodpecker feeds its nestlings by regurgitation, although woodpeckers that nourish their young with fruits and larger insects carry these items visibly in their bills.

The holes that Lineated Woodpeckers make in the branches and young trunks of the Cecropia are closed by wound tissues that eventually form great tumorous protuberances; but many young trees break at the point where they have been pierced low in the stem. Trees that have received much attention from the woodpeckers are less flourishing than their undisturbed neighbors, and their ant colonies are greatly depopulated. In regions where these woodpeckers are abundant, it is hard to believe that the ants help the tree enough to compensate for the tremendous injury that their presence brings upon it.

To the Lineated Woodpecker, the Cecropia is alluring in proportion to the number of ants it shelters. To a number of other birds of quite different tastes, it is most attractive when the Aztecas are few or absent. For only in the absence of the ants do the little white protein corpuscles become abundant and prominent on the furry cushions at the bases of the petioles. When this occurs, they offer a dainty food to a variety of small birds. I have watched at least a dozen species take advantage of this food. The little yellow-breasted Bananaquit is fond of these tidbits, which may make a not unimportant contribution to its diet. In parts of its vast range as widely separated as Costa Rica and Ecuador, I have repeatedly seen the small bird pluck off the minute white grains with the sharp tip of its strongly curved black bill. The Tropical Parula Warbler feasts upon these dainties, while such wintering members of the family as Wilson's Warbler, the Tennessee Warbler, the Chestnut-sided Warbler, and even the thicket-haunting Mourning Warbler have discovered them. Among finches, the Yellow-faced Grassquit and seedeaters sometimes consume them; among tanagers, the euphonias and the Bay-headed Tanager; while in the Costa Rican highlands the queer little ovenbird known as the Red-faced Spinetail devours them in numbers. In this same region dwells the biggest bird that I have seen eat the protein bodies, the Yellow-thighed Finch, as large as a towhee.

In excessively wet mountains where the spinetail and this finch dwell, the hollow stems of the Cecropia are often flooded with water, with the result that they contain no ants to share the protein grains with the birds. The visits of all these small birds are of no importance to the tree, nor do they help us to decide whether or not the Azteca ants are an effective guard; yet their presence is further proof of the multiform bounty of the Cecropia.

It was not in defending their home tree against birds and four-footed animals, so much as against the depredations of other insects, that early observers supposed the garrison of Azteca ants to be of greatest service. Nevertheless, one frequently sees a Cecropia with its foliage more or less damaged by leaf-eating insects. Sometimes the softer tissues of the great leaves are all but consumed by a budworm, even on trees with a thriving colony of ants. My own observations, made largely north of the equator, are in full accord with those of Karl Fiebrig (1909), who years ago, from studies made in Paraguay near the southern limit of the Cecropia's vast range, concluded that the ants were ineffectual in protecting the trees from a variety of adult and larval insects.

In the tropics perhaps no category of insects is more injurious to vegetation than ants themselves. Abundant as these creatures are in the temperate zones, one who has not lived in the tropics can hardly conceive their numbers and variety in regions of perpetual warmth. From crevices in soil and rocks to the topmost branches of great forest trees, they swarm everywhere in unbelievable variety and abundance. At times one's house is invaded by a horde of Eciton or army ants, which flow like a stream through every nook and cranny, seeking the small creatures of many kinds on which they prey. These carnivorous legions perform their generally beneficial work of reducing the number of insect pests and pass on; but ants of other kinds are nearly always present, attacking not only food but the very beams and boards of the house, where they are often more injurious, and more difficult to control, than the more notorious termites.

The nests of these tropical ants are of the most astonishing variety. Some are situated underground; some hang like great stalactites from lofty boughs of trees; some occupy hollow dead branches; some are woven of finest silk secreted by the larval ants, among living foliage skillfully attached to the walls. It is not surprising that the hollow living organs of many species of plants have been discovered and occupied by ants, which in the course of ages have become specially adapted to life in these snug retreats and in turn have gradually produced changes in the structure of the host, thereby developing the curious phenomenon of myrmecophily.

The agriculturist in the tropics wages a never-ending war against the battalions of the ants. They devour seeds if germination is slow; they bite the tender young tissues of plants, enlarge crevices in the bark of fruit trees for their nests, damage young sprouts by covering them with earth, spread mealy aphids over sugar cane. Since I began to farm in the tropics I have become sceptical of Schimper's view that the extrafloral nectaries common on the plants of warm regions help them by attracting beneficial species of ants. I have never known a husbandman in tropical America who had a good word to say for the ants.

In the Orient, however, the situation may be somewhat different. In Java, the people of certain districts collect, in the forest and among the trees along the seacoast, nests of a kind of large and fierce red ant, which they hang in their mango trees. Here the ants protect the developing fruits by devouring the larvae of the beetle *Cryptorhynchus mangifera*, which are capable of causing great damage. The Javanese are said to attend these red ants with care, providing flesh to suit their carnivorous tastes, destroying other kinds of ants that are hostile to them, and joining the mango trees together by bridges of bamboo to facilitate the insects' visits to all parts of the grove. In ancient times, Chinese orchardists collected and propagated ants, which they placed in their orange and tangerine trees to keep them free of caterpillars. A special class of laborers attended to this.

These husbandmen of the Far East never had to contend with the leaf-cutting Attas, which of all ants in tropical America do most conspicuous injury to vegetation. The subterranean nest of these brown, spiny ants becomes with time a far-flung labyrinth of chambers and intercommunicating tunnels, beneath the wide bare mound of soil thrown out in the course of their excavations. From the mound as center, narrow, well-defined pathways, kept clean and bare of vegetation by the ants, extend far and wide over the neighboring terrain. Along these myrmecine highways a stream of ants is constantly flowing. Those hurrying outward from the nest go unburdened; but in the returning stream a large proportion of the middle-sized workers bear in their jaws pieces of green leaf larger than themselves, rising above their backs like irregular standards or sunshades. Hence comes the name, parasol ants, sometimes applied to them.

Each bit of leaf is cut by the scissorlike mandibles of a worker ant from the foliage of a growing plant, a tree, shrub, or herb. As it is borne along by the worker toward the nest, another smaller ant, or sometimes two or three together, may often be seen clinging to the already huge burden and being carried toward the mound. Doubtless these riders are trying to bear the burden themselves; but the strongest of those attached to the bit of leaf lifts the would-be helpers into the air and marches off with both cargo and assistants. After reaching the nest, the pieces of leaves are carried into the subterranean chambers and cut by the jaws of the ants into fine bits, which form a sort of compost heap, upon which a special kind of fungus is grown. The ants eat, not the leaves, but the fungus, which produces a profusion of minute, knoblike bodies in white, flocculent masses. It is supposed that the duty of the smallest workers is to weed the fungus gardens, removing all kinds of fungus growths save that upon which the population subsists. When they have served their purpose, the discolored bits of leaf, far from being eaten, are thrown out upon midden heaps near the entrances to the burrows.

Although these ants use the foliage of a great variety of plants native to tropical America, the only kinds available to them during a long age before Europeans brought the products of the Old World to the New, some writers have detected a special fondness for the leaves of cultivated species introduced from the Eastern Hemisphere. Possibly many native plants have, for their own protection, become distasteful to the ants that attacked them. Or this seeming preference for exotics may result from the circumstance that in plantations, where little variety is within their reach, the Attas concentrate upon the dominant plant. A colony established in a lawn may defoliate the nearest ornamentals; while in the forest, with many plants of many kinds available, they show slight preference for particular species, and their injury to the vegetation is less evident. But it is true that in some regions one cannot profitably grow certain crops, or enjoy beautiful shrubbery and flowers around one's dwelling, without combatting the leaf-cutters. Great coffee plantations keep men busy destroying their colonies, now usually with poisons, but formerly often by digging them out, leaving great holes in the ground. The thoughtful farmer may feel a bond of sympathy with these laborious fellow agriculturists even as he reluctantly proceeds to destroy them; but if they become too abundant they may seriously reduce the productivity of his farm.

Are the Azteca ants of the Cecropia tree an efficient guard against the destructive leaf-cutting Attas? Examine a hundred Cecropias, even where leaf-cutting ants abound, and few, if any, will show severe injury by them. But the same would be true of almost any other kind of tree, native or introduced, except in plantations and dooryards where the bare soil invites the establishment of Atta colonies and they have little variety of vegetation to choose from. Rarely the Atta ants make great inroads upon the foliage of a Cecropia, cutting away the great leaves until only the principal veins remain, each margined by a narrow strip of tissue with semicircular indentations that reveal the ants' method of work. I have seen such depredations on Cecropias that supported flourishing colonies of Aztecas.

To supplement casual observations made in other regions with a more thorough study of Atta-Azteca interactions, for several months I searched for a Cecropia that gave evidence of the Attas' work, but without success. This might be construed to favor the theory of mutual protection; but I also failed to see the leaf-cutting ants at work upon a Burío, a soft-wooded, swift-growing tree of the same habitat as the Cecropia and no less abundant, but with solid stems that offer no accommodation to ants. The Attas were happily not very abundant on our farm, except in the cane field.

Finally, in order to witness what would happen when Atta and Azteca came face to face, I captured a few of the former and placed them upon the stem of a young Cecropia tree. The occupants were mostly indoors; and the unintentional trespassers wandered aimlessly about without meeting them; so I shook the sapling to bring the Aztecas out. The little ants came pouring through their narrow doorways and raced about over stem and leaves, as though seeking the cause of the disturbance. Many of them passed close by the Attas; often they ran beneath the longer-legged brown ants, without paying any attention to them. This might happen a number of times, and the interlopers remain for several minutes unchallenged in the midst of the swarming Aztecas.

Sooner or later, however, an Azteca would seize an Atta by a leg, or more rarely the body, and then one of several things might happen. Sometimes, in a manner difficult to understand, the tiny Azteca would throw the big Atta from the tree, retaining its own hold. Far more often, the tussle would continue until the unequal adversaries fell, clutched together, to the ground. Or, if the struggle was long-drawn-out, other Aztecas, bumping into the contestants, would join the fray. Although many of the smaller ants might brush against an undisturbed Atta and pass on, every one that came within touching distance of an ant already attacked would immediately seize it. Soon the unfortunate leaf-cutter would be in the midst of half a dozen angry little Aztecas, pulling its long legs this way and that, biting its hard brown body, until at length the whole writhing mass fell from the tree. Some of the Attas, especially the larger workers, easily repelled each attacking Azteca with a single nip of their powerful mandibles, and went wandering around until they reached the ground.

The same was true of some large black ants with golden abdomens that I found on Cecropia trees: The Aztecas were helpless against their strong jaws. I have no doubt that the Cecropia tree's garrison of ants attempts to repulse invading ants, in many instances with success. But if the defenders are not stirred up, as in my experiments, a foreign ant might wander far over the tree without meeting one of them; and the Azteca often fails to attack when at last it encounters the stranger. The Attas that I placed, one by one, upon the Cecropia were lost, aimless, far outnumbered. From what I saw, it was not difficult to imagine a whole organized column of them mounting the trunk of an otherwise undisturbed Cecropia and cutting the leaves, without meeting real resistance from the supposed garrison. But resistance or no resistance, they are quite capable of carrying off the foliage of a well-populated tree when they want it.

Monkeys, sloths, woodpeckers, tanagers and many other birds, Azteca ants, leaf-eating insects, at times even Atta ants—are they not all in the same category, guests that come to enjoy the bounty spread for them by the most hospitable tree of tropical America? Some harm it by stripping it of foliage or drilling holes in its trunk; others, including the small birds that eat the protein grains, and apparently also the Azteca ants themselves, seem to be neither beneficial nor directly harmful; only the fruit-eating birds that scatter its seeds far and wide and the insectivorous species that remove caterpillars from the leaves are an undoubted positive benefit. The Aztecas, instead of being a formidable guard to repel all intruders from an inhospitable tree, may be simply the foremost beneficiaries of a bountiful one. They cannot compare with the *Pseudomyrmex* ants of the bull's-horn acacias, of which I tell in other chapters, as an effective garrison for the host plant.[2]

The admission that the most distinctive tree of tropical America is also the most hospitable tree forces us to concede to it still a third superlative. For to deny that the ants are of positive benefit to the tree is to refute the only plausible explanation that has been advanced for the evolution of its three outstanding structural peculiarities: the exceptionally wide central hollow of the stem, the furry protruding leaf bases with their protein corpuscles, and the pits that facilitate the perforation of the wall surrounding the hollow internode. Without some single end to

2. Daniel H. Janzen has demonstrated the great services rendered by the *Pseudomyrmex* ants to the bull's-horn acacias that they inhabit. See Janzen (1969) and references there cited.

which all three contribute, how can we account for the presence in a single species of features that would be surprising enough as random developments in three different families of plants? The mystery continues to challenge us. The Cecropia is the most enigmatic tree of tropical America.

CHAPTER 11

Birds on a Venezuelan Farm

Crested Bobwhite

It was nearly midnight on March 11, 1966, when the huge air-plane from Panama set my wife, Pamela, and me down at Mai-quetía Airport, beside the Caribbean Sea. Midnight had passed be-fore we cleared immigration and customs and were free to enter Venezuela. Knowing by sight not a single person in the country, we hardly expected to be met at this inconvenient hour; but as we passed out the gate of the airport building we were greeted by a tall, bespectacled man in field clothes. Evidently he recognized me by the binoculars slung over my shoulder, and I knew at once that he was Paul Schwartz. Years earlier he had come to Venezuela as a representative of a North American manufacturer of refrigeration and air-conditioning machinery. Falling under the spell of the country's marvelously rich bird life, he had already spent about two decades studying Venezuelan birds, photographing them, and recording their voices. Through correspondence while we were still in Costa Rica, he had most kindly offered to find us a place to live and study birds for several months.

In Paul's Volkswagen laden with camping equipment and sound-recording apparatus, we joined the stream of cars climbing the Coastal Range toward Venezuela's capital, which lies in a mountain-rimmed valley about 3,500 feet above sea level. Through long, brilliantly lighted tunnels, the broad concrete highway pierced abrupt mountain barriers that at the beginning of the nineteenth century had made the journey from the coast to the city a strenuous undertaking that Alexander von Humboldt (1852–1853, vol. 1, pp. 386–389) compared to crossing the Swiss Alps. After threading a seemingly endless maze of the streets of Caracas, we reached our hotel in the small hours of the morning.

To one who had dwelt for decades in a remote tropical valley, with only widely spaced visits to Costa Rica's small capital, huge, bustling Caracas was a revelation of modernity. So many tall apartment houses; such wide avenues, with four or six lanes of rushing traffic crossing each other at two or even three levels; so much noise and confusion! Amid such obvious signs of wealth and prosperity, we had only to raise our eyes to survey countless mean shacks huddled together on the steep surrounding slopes— the city's "belt of misery." The contrast was, to say the least, disquieting, and we were not sorry when Paul suggested that we go that same afternoon to the Parque Nacional Henri Pittier.

Parque Nacional Henri Pittier

The superhighway from Caracas wound in wide curves through steep mountains covered with low, scrubby woods, which became sparser as we sped westward, until the slopes bore little

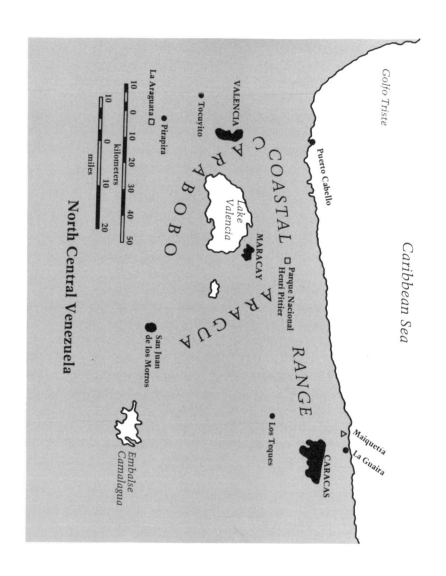

more than grass and low weeds, dry and brown now at the height of the rainless season. As though these steep slopes were not already desolate enough, they were scorched by many recent fires deliberately or carelessly set, which left a thin layer of black ash over the exposed rocks and sterile soil. We were told that when Marcos Pérez Jiménez was dictator, he authorized the police to impress men to fight such fires, if necessary calling them out of the theaters to extinguish the flames that lit up the night on surrounding hills.

Passing by a tunnel through a rocky ridge, we entered the Valley of Aragua, where the road traversed great level fields, planted with sugar cane and citrus fruits. These flat, fertile lands were once the bottom of Lake Valencia, which in historic times has been steadily shrinking, joining islands to the mainland and leaving around its margins marshes that finally become good farmland. At the beginning of the nineteenth century, when the lake was at least one-half more than its present length of about twenty miles, Humboldt (1852–1853, vol. 2, pp. 2–22) attributed its retreat to the destruction of the natural vegetation on the surrounding plains and hills. He learned that, fifty years before his visit, the steep slopes of the Coastal Range north of the lake, now so scorched and barren, had been clothed in forest.

After a pause for refreshments at Maracay, we turned northward toward these mountains. As we wound upward along a paved highway, grass-covered slopes gave way to scrubby woods, which soon merged into heavy forest. Presently, in the midst of this forest, we rounded a curve and came in view of a huge pile of steel and concrete, set on a shelf dug into the steep mountainside. Called facetiously Rancho Grande—a name that has stuck—this monstrous building was begun over thirty years earlier by the dictator Juan Vicente Gómez to serve as a hotel or private resort for himself and friends, but it was still unfinished when he died in 1935. Only a minority of its many high-ceilinged rooms had, over the years, been made habitable, to serve as living and working quarters for scientists and the staff that administers the park. One of its great halls held a natural history museum.

Early next morning, Paul led me along a narrow trail cut into the heavily wooded slope behind the building. The mellow, trisyllabic call of a White-tipped Quetzal floated down from the trees, and by imitating these notes my guide drew a male into plain view. Although undeniably a splendid bird, with glittering metallic upper plumage and a rich crimson belly, he lacked a prominent crest, and his green upper tail coverts extended but little beyond the white tips of his tail; he could not compete in magnificence with the Central American Quetzal, perhaps the only legitimate bearer of this name. Groove-billed Toucanets, grass green with blue cheeks, were abundant in this forest and announced their presence by croaking notes. A pair of Blue-winged Mountain-Tanagers gave us a too-fleeting view of their loveliness.

Around the great somber pile of Rancho Grande lived many beautiful little Swallow-Tanagers, who nested in burrows and crannies in the walls, and in this very spot had been carefully studied by Ernst Schaefer (1953), a former superintendent of the Rancho Grande Biological Station. More familiar to me were the Blue-and-White Swallows that filled the air and nested in crevices of the building. Flying around with the swallows, exhibiting much white on their blue-black bodies, were a number of Lesser Swallow-tailed Swifts. They drew attention to themselves by the rapidly repeated, sharp, clicking notes that they constantly emitted as they wheeled and looped in the air. Paul told me that they nested in vertical tubular apertures in the concrete roofs, evidently intended for drain pipes. Here they avoided the labor of constructing their usual long, tubular sleeve of felted down glued together with saliva, and attached the shelf for their eggs directly to the concrete.

The Parque Nacional Henri Pittier is named for the Swiss scientist who, after making important contributions to the geography and botany of Costa Rica, dedicated the remaining years of his long and laborious life to studying the flora of Venezuela. The park's 200,000 or more acres straddle the abrupt Coastal Range of northern Venezuela. From the barren, burnt-over foothills on the northern rim of the Valley of Aragua it rises to cloud-forested ridges and peaks that attain 7,870 feet, then falls precipitously, through humid subtropical and then tropical forests, to the semi-arid Caribbean coast. In its higher parts the park is still a vast wilderness, difficult to explore.

A short distance above the building, the highway by which we arrived crossed the continental divide by a pass known as El Portachuelo, then wound steeply down to several small settlements and a naval base along the coast. As we followed this road in the afternoon, beneath splendid, tall, epiphyte-laden trees whose branches interlocked above us, it was heartening to see, in this age when such forests are rapidly shrinking before man's devastating inroads, so little evidence of human disturbance, even beside this fairly busy highway. This park should serve as an example of what other tropical countries might do to preserve representative areas of natural vegetation, with their flora and fauna all intact. Its diversity of life zones, from semiarid to very wet, makes it especially interesting to naturalists.

North of the park, we reached a spot where steep hills rose abruptly from the sea. Amid the low trees, thorny shrubs, and cacti that grew on them, a flock of Rufous-vented Chachalacas were shouting loudly together in the twilight. Their deep, raucous voices were not unlike those of the Plain Chachalacas of the north, but they seemed to be trying to repeat their name with full mouths. Venezuelans call this long-tailed, gray bird *guacharaca*, which is a good rendition of its call.

Continuing along a road cut through the hills high above the surf, we came to a point whence we could look down into a charming little cove with a wide, curving sandy beach, bordered by a grove of coconut palms. Daylight was already fading when we turned back.

Paul is a diligent student of the voices of wild creatures, including those of the night. On our way up the mountain, he parked his car beside the road and the three of us dismounted to hear owls. While we stood in the darkness, intently listening, two jeeps pulled up behind us, and in a moment we were surrounded by soldiers with rifles at the ready. A stern voice demanded to know what we were doing there, so near a naval base. Venezuela had been sorely troubled by terrorists supported by Castro's Cuba, and doubtless we were suspected of spying for the Communists. The officer in charge was understandably skeptical when we said we were listening for birds; but when Paul showed certain papers from the Ministry of Agriculture, which employed him, the tension relaxed. Soon the soldiers were asking Pamela and me about Costa Rica. Then they shook hands all around and vanished into the night.

Higher up the winding road, we stopped again to examine two little mossy pockets, opening downward, attached to the vertical, stony side of a highway cut. They resembled a nest with two white eggs of the Spotted Barbtail that I had discovered fastened to a log that had fallen across a rivulet in a Costa Rican mountain forest. These nests were less massive and had no eggs. Paul had found one of these retiring brown birds of the ovenbird family sleeping in each of these pockets, one of them over an interval of many months, and we hoped to see them there. But our flashlight revealed that the barbtails were not at home.

La Araguata

Paul had arranged for us to study birds on a cattle farm belonging to the Venezuelan artist-naturalist Walter Arp, situated near Pirapira, about fifteen miles south of Valencia. On the following day, our third in Venezuela, we visited the Arps at their town house in Valencia, and in the afternoon we all rode out to La Araguata, as the farm was called. As for mile after mile we speeded, trailed by clouds of dust, through unattractive flat country with sparse vegetation and few houses, my anticipations withered in the afternoon heat. But after a while we descended a rough road into a wide hollow among the first of the hills that border the valley of Valencia on the south and entered a less denuded region, where multitudes of yagua palms held their feathery crowns above the thickets on the slopes. At last we came to a gate with a sign reading "La Araguata," from which a stony road, cut into the hillside, led steeply down to the farmhouse.

Long, low, and spacious, of modern construction, the house stood in a garden beside a rivulet, amid lightly wooded slopes, beyond which spread wide, nearly treeless pastures. In the fully furnished house were more modern conveniences than we had at home: electricity from the farm's own diesel-powered generator, water piped in from a small reservoir in a neighboring ravine, a gas stove for cooking. Even in the heat of a March afternoon, the voices of birds filled the air; and Walter pointed out three nearby nests of the Rufous-fronted Thornbird, the species I most wanted to study. With such a commodious dwelling, pleasant surroundings, and an amiable host, the situation boded well for our work.

We returned to Rancho Grande for our luggage. The following afternoon we shopped in Maracay while Paul patiently waited. Then he took us to La Araguata, where we arrived long after nightfall, to begin a sojourn of more than four months. During this long interval the only permanent residents on the 1,500-acre farm, beside Pamela and me, were the caretaker's wife and two little girls, who lived on the other side of the brook. The caretaker himself, whose name, Selvaleón, suggested the wild character that he was, preferred to sleep off the farm with another woman. On most weeks Walter came in his car, obligingly bringing our provisions, and stayed a few days while, always to the sound of his radio, he painted lovely pictures of birds. Before our departure, a collection of his earlier bird portraits, many of which had been waiting for a decade, was published by the Banco Central de Venezuela in a large and sumptuous volume titled *Avifauna Venezolana*, of which he gave us an autographed copy. On many weekends and holidays, Walter brought his wife, Elena, and their three children, and often guests as well, along with much food, for a festive day or two.

When we arrived at La Araguata in mid-March, the countryside was parched after long months with little rain. The midday heat was oppressive, but nights were pleasantly cool. In the evenings after supper, we sometimes sat on the lawn, watching the artificial satellites speed across the sky like swiftly moving stars. We happened to be situated below a frequented satellite route, and Walter took a special interest in them. The jaragua grass in his pastures was over head-high, as he had only about thirty cows grazing over hundreds of acres. These overgrown pastures harbored few ticks, probably because the pests were desiccated; but whenever I incautiously ventured into the lush herbage along the streams, I emerged a few minutes later covered with tiny, crawling seed ticks. In the low second-growth woods, trees were not only shedding their foliage but also covering themselves with fresh green leaves, in spite of the drought. The most colorful small tree scattered through the pastures and in the woodland on less sterile slopes was the Cañafistula, one of the golden sprays that in March still bore long clusters of deep yellow flowers.

Voices of Venezuelan Birds

The avifauna at La Araguata was not rich; in over four months I identified only 150 species. Lacking old forests, the region was without trogons and toucans, and I found only four kinds of antbirds. Nearly half the birds were of wide-ranging species that live on our farm in southern Costa Rica, 1,200 miles to the west at the same latitude.

In late March many of the birds had started to sing, just as they do at that time in Costa Rica, and it was interesting to compare the voices of sedentary populations that probably had been isolated from each other for many thousands of years. On the whole, their notes were quite similar. At dawn the Streaked Flycatchers at La Araguata sang the same calmly beautiful song that I had heard from them in Costa Rica and Panama. Before sunrise, the Vermilion-crowned Flycatchers enunciated *chipsacheery*, over and over, as clearly as those about our house in the Valley of El General. Neither in the dawn song, a harshly asseverated, endlessly reiterated *WE-DO*, nor in their garbled duet, did I notice any difference between Venezuelan and Central American Yellow-bellied Elaenias. High in a tree, Boat-billed Flycatchers repeated at daybreak the same clear, ringing notes that I had heard in Costa Rica; but I failed to notice the slurred *bo-oy* that the Costa Rican flycatchers from time to time interject into their dawn song. The clear flute notes that issued from Little Tinamous lurking unseen beneath dry thickets at La Araguata sounded no different from those of the Little Tinamous in much lusher vegetation on our Costa Rican farm. The prolonged duets of Gray-necked Wood-Rails—*chirincoco-co-co-co-co*—were just the same here as there. Rufous-browed Peppershrikes repeated much the same far-carrying, ringing phrases, that seemed to invite translation into human words, as I had often heard in Central America.

The song of the abundant Blue Tanagers at La Araguata began much like that of the Costa Rican population but ran into high, wiry notes that I had not previously heard. This finale was so similar to the Bay-headed Tanager's song that I looked for the latter, without ever finding it at La Araguata. Most surprisingly different were the songs of the Black-striped Sparrows, which I did not hear until late April, when the wet season was about to begin. I never heard from these finches that lurked in dense thickets the accelerated "locomotive" song so familiar in southern Central America. They had such a varied repertoire of clear, cheerful phrases, delivered in a full, rich voice, that I considered them the best songsters in the region.

On certain April mornings when the air was clear, cool, and springlike, weedy fields and hillsides overgrown with light woods rang with the crisp *bob bob white* of the Crested Bobwhite. Although these notes reminded me strongly of the Common Bobwhite's call that I knew in my boyhood, and of that of the Spotted-bellied Bobwhite of Central America, these Venezuelan birds were more ornate. One day a flock of eleven ran across the pasture in front of us, heads held high rather than stretched forward. Their tall, upstanding crests, chestnut faces, and plumage of deep, rich shades of brown variegated with prominent white spots on the underparts made them exceptionally handsome quails.

As nearly everywhere in the Americas, the thrushes here were among the most tireless songsters. The Bare-eyed Thrush, a large olive-brown bird with eyes set amid bare yellow skin, was most abundant around the house and in the clearings. The Pale-breasted Thrush preferred light woodland, but the two species often intermingled. The Bare-eyed Thrush's flowing, liquid song resembled that of Gray's Thrush of Central America; its *tock tock* and querulous *queo* when its nest was disturbed were also similar; but its deep, throaty *trabahar trabahar*, uttered while the bird perched unseen amid foliage, was unlike any thrush's note that I had ever heard, and it took me long to trace it to its source. The Pale-breasted Thrush tended to group its musical phrases in two's, as does the White-throated Thrush of Central America. The calls of these two species were also rather similar.

No bird's voice delighted me more than that of the Lance-tailed Manakin, a tiny black bird with a brilliant red crown, pale blue back and shoulders, and protruding, pointed central tail feathers. Females are olive-green with orange legs, like those of the adult males. While still in this greenish plumage, young males reveal their sex by their bright red caps. Like their cousins, the Long-tailed Manakins of the more arid parts of Central America, these handsome birds are much easier to hear than to see. One April morning, on a steep hillside covered with light second-growth woods, I followed their notes until I spied one, who promptly vanished amid small trees and crowded young saplings. Apparently it was his continued calls that drew others of his kind, until a number of them, including adults and at least one red-crowned greenish male, were flitting through the tangled growth, permitting only exasperatingly fleeting glimpses of their elegance.

Although what I saw was most unsatisfactory, what I heard was charming. Most of the sounds that continued to issue from the thicket in amazing variety were melodious, some surpassingly beautiful. I heard full, mellow notes uttered singly in different keys; a soft, clear quaver or trill; a trisyllabic musical whistle, *toe-e-ho*, the second *e* very short; a somewhat similar triplet, *toe-weee-do*, with the prolonged second note high and clear, the third lower in pitch. From no other manakin have I heard such a variety of musical utterances. Contrasting with all these liquid notes was a grating, nasal mew or buzz that from time to time interrupted them. A similar sound accompanies the elaborate "dance" in which two males of the related Long-tailed Manakins engage; but, to my great chagrin, the density of the vegetation prevented a view of whatever these Lance-tails were doing. Hopefully, I revisited the spot, without finding a single manakin.

The other manakin at La Araguata, the Wire-tailed, was no less handsome, with its brilliant red crown, hindneck, and upper back giving way abruptly to the black of the remaining upper plumage; bright yellow forehead, cheeks, and under parts; and black tail feathers ending in long, curving, filamentous tips. Although it was more abundant, or less elusive, than the Lance-tailed species, I learned nothing of its voice and courtship. In early May, I watched a solitary olive-green female building at eye level in a horizontal fork of a slender twig, far up on a dry hillside covered with light second growth. Although she finished her slight, shallow hammock of small dry leaves, bound together and fastened to the arms of the fork with cobweb and a few dark fibrous strands, she never laid an egg in it. Another nest that, in late June, a female built a dozen feet above a stream flowing through a deep, wooded ravine, also remained empty.

Of all the avian voices at La Araguata, the most powerful was that of the Rufous-vented Chachalacas. From the time of our arrival, we heard their chorus at intervals through the day, and even on moonlit nights. Soon after daybreak on April 13, I sat eating my breakfast of sandwiches on a rock amid a light growth of small trees and yagua palms. The rain that had fallen slowly through the night had left the ground and foliage wetter than it had been for the last month, and a slight drizzle came intermittently from the heavily overcast sky. The chachalacas all around me made the dim, dripping woodland resound with their harsh, spirited cries. The long-tailed birds seemed to be jubilantly greeting this forecast of wetter weather and more abundant food.

Now on this side, now on that, now strongly close at hand, now subdued by distance, the loud *guacharaca guacharaca* surged back and forth over the hills, reminding me of the many-voiced choruses of Plain Chachalacas that, long ago, had deeply impressed me amid second-growth thickets in the distant Motagua Valley of Guatemala. It was as stirring an expression of the spontaneous exuberance of feathered creatures as I had heard in many a year—for, strangely enough, the quieter Gray-headed Chachalacas amid which I live in Costa Rica never perform in the manner of closely related species on either side of them. These Rufous-vented Chachalacas were participating by pairs in the general vociferation. I repeatedly noticed that, of two voices that seemed to come from the same point, one was much deeper than the other. Undoubtedly the stronger voice belonged to the male, whose elongated trachea or windpipe forms a great loop between the skin and body before it enters the thorax. The female lacks this arrangement that amplifies the voice.

Early in May I found my only nest of this chachalaca, four feet up between the clustered spiny stems of a low palm growing in the thicket that covered a slope above a stream. The broad, shallow bowl was composed chiefly of coarse pieces from disintegrating fronds of the palm that held it, along with fragments of stout jaragua grass from the neighboring pasture. It contained only two of the rough-shelled, whitish eggs typical of chachalacas, although sometimes this species lays as many as four, in a nest that is occasionally placed on the ground and may be high in a tree. Aware of the many perils that beset chachalacas' nests, I was careful not to disturb this one. Even after an egg vanished, the female continued to incubate the remaining one, which likewise disappeared a few days later, doubtless eaten by the predator that tore the nest apart.

Monstrous Spider Webs

Close by a rivulet in a sheltered vale, amid the woods where I listened to the chachalacas and the manakins, were the most monstrous spider webs that I had ever seen. The base of each web was a closely woven sheet of silk, five feet across in the larger examples, and usually spread over the herbage within a foot of the ground, although smaller webs of the same spider were as much as eight feet up in shrubbery. In places this basal sheet was reinforced by a second, smaller sheet over it. Above this unbroken cloth the spiders had stretched a tangled maze of single strands that crossed each other in all directions and sometimes extended as much as three yards above the sheet. This maze, which became more open upward, was attached by guy lines to surrounding shrubs and trees.

The basal sheet caught and held everything that fell upon it, until it was heavily laden with dead leaves, withered flowers, twigs, and the remains of insects that the spiders had sucked dry. In all this decaying trash dwelt a teeming multitude of spiders, probably numbering thousands in the larger webs. The biggest individuals had reddish brown bodies about a quarter of an inch long and blackish legs. From this size they ranged downward to tiny spiderlings, as the young broods grow up among the adults.

The careless butterfly, beetle, grasshopper, or other insect that blundered into the crisscrossing strands above the nest was confused. Trying to escape, it often dropped lower and lower until, entangled in the silk it had torn from the maze, it fell among the spiders that lurked in the debris. Soon the unfortunate creature was covered by a seething, ravenous mass of spiders of all sizes, which promptly sucked it dry. The gregariousness of these peculiar spiders was displayed not only in the huge number in a single nest, but in the concentration of numerous nests in a single spot, a few yards apart. All that I found were in this one small area.

Tanagers, Finches, and Doves

Of the eight species of tanagers at La Araguata, the most abundant and songful was the wide-ranging Silver-beak. The male's velvety plumage, in some lights appearing almost wholly black, suddenly becomes the richest crimson as he shifts into a more favorable position. The female of this race is nearly everywhere dull red, of a shade less changeable than the male's crimson, so that often she appears brighter than he, and than the female Silver-beaks that I saw in eastern Ecuador. Birds of semiopen country, lush thickets, and light woodland rather than dense forests, they wandered in loose, straggling flocks over most of the farm, avoiding only broad, treeless pastures and the denser groves.

In late March the males became increasingly vocal, often singing fluently in rather weak and squeaky voices from high perches, sometimes a treetop. Their songs resembled those of the Scarlet-rumped Black Tanagers that visit our feeder in southern Costa Rica but were less clear and forceful. One morning at the end of April, while passing through a deep ravine with lightly wooded sides, I heard a finchlike song that puzzled me. The long-continued flow of slight, varied, musical notes led me to expect a seed-eater, goldfinch, or some other small member of the family. To my immense surprise, I traced this pleasing medley to a splendid male Silver-beak, perching at the edge of a tangle of bamboo. For several minutes he continued to pour forth his animated song, the most musical that I heard from his kind. Only once again did I hear a Silver-beak singing in this manner, as he went to roost in the evening. Such whisper singing is rare, or at least seldom noticed, in the tanager family.

The five Silver-beaks' nests that I discovered in April and May were substantial open cups, composed of rootlets, slender vines, strips of leaves, and similar materials. The highest was seven feet up in a *Nothopanax* shrub growing beside the front porch; the lowest, in a tangle of green vines that hung over the bank of a small stream, was a foot below the top of the bank and four feet above the water. Only four of these nests contained eggs, two in each. They were bright blue, marked with tiny spots, roundish blotches, and thin scrawls of black, along with finer flecks of brown and pale lilac, all chiefly on the thicker end.

In the *Nothopanax* shrub beside the porch was a lower nest only a yard from the first. Although both were occupied at the same time, the two females were never seen to pay the least attention to each other—they were not territorial. Possibly both had the same mate, but he was most inattentive, remaining aloof from the nests and failing to help feed the nestlings. Because adult males were much less numerous than birds in female plumage, some breeding females could not find a full-time partner and were obliged to form irregular attachments to the father of their nestlings, as happens also among Scarlet-rumped Black Tanagers. This situation is unusual in the great tanager family, in which nearly all the species that have been studied are monogamous, with the male helping to feed the young and often also to build the nest, but never incubating or brooding.

Another abundant bird was the tiny Blue-black Grassquit, which in the dry season lurked unseen in pastures and weedy fields, to fly up, singly or in loose flocks, as I walked along. In March and early April, none of the numerous individuals that I saw wore the full, glossy blue-black plumage of breeding males. Many of the males could hardly be distinguished from the brownish females except by their black wing and tail feathers. It was evident that after the breeding season male grassquits go into "eclipse," changing their shining attire for plumage more like that of the females. From observations in Guatemala and Costa Rica, I had long suspected this, and Helmut Sick (1967) has found it to be true of this species in Brazil. Such pronounced seasonal changes in coloration are rare among the passerines and other land birds of tropical America, where even the most brilliant males wear their nuptial garb throughout the year. The only other exception to this rule known to me is the Blue Honeycreeper, the males of which lose their azure, blue, and black plumage after the breeding season, becoming for a few months much like the greenish females, except for their black wing and tail feathers.

In mid-April I noticed one male grassquit whose body was largely blue-black, with white patches at the elbows, although his head and neck were still brownish, as in females. At this date most males were much less advanced in the acquisition of their nuptial plumage. I did not see one in full, shining breeding plumage, with no trace of brown, until July 1. By mid-July such males were common, although others were still in transitional plumage late in the month. It was the middle of July before I noticed a male Blue-black Grassquit jumping straight upward a foot or two in the air and uttering a plaintive, squeaky note as he fell back upon the same low perch. He repeated this simple act tirelessly over and over, in a nuptial display that can be seen in bushy fields and hedgerows over much of tropical America, from Mexico to northern Chile and Argentina. Sometimes the grassquits begin to display before they have acquired their full nuptial attire.

In the pastures and weedy fields where the Blue-black Grassquits foraged, ground-doves were also abundant. They hunted over the ground, hidden beneath the herbage, their presence unsuspected until they flew up suddenly when I was a few yards away. In March and April, when the drying weeds were freely shedding seeds, Common Ground-Doves were by far the most abundant members of the pigeon family on the farm. By late June, when frequent rains had covered the fields with lush verdure, they had quite vanished from La Araguata, although they were still present at Tocuyito, the nearest town. Ruddy Ground-Doves, which earlier had foraged with the Common Ground-Doves, remained in considerable numbers after the latter's departure; in many parts of their wide range they inhabit country too humid for the related species. White-fronted Doves were equally abundant from March to July. Pale-vented Pigeons were numerous for a while in May, but by July they had become almost as rare as they had been in March. The only other member of the family that I saw here was the beautiful Blue Ground-Dove, and that but seldom.

Anis and Other Cuckoos

Two species of anis, the Smooth-billed and the Groove-billed, were present at La Araguata. As in other regions where I have found both of these long-tailed black cuckoos together, the more aggressive Smooth-bills were the more conspicuously abundant, spreading over the open fields, pastures, orchards, and roadsides. The Groove-bills lived chiefly in dense canebrakes and thickets along streams. From these retreats they ventured into neighbor-

ing pastures, to hurry back to the sheltering streamside vegetation when alarmed. Not only was the Groove-bill more restricted
in habitat than in the extensive areas of Central America and
Mexico where its slightly larger congener is absent; it also impressed me as being a much quieter, more subdued bird. The *tuc
tuc* that Central American Groove-bills voice in flight was here
reduced to a slightly audible *tick*, and the soft, high-pitched *pihuy*
that characteristically follows the *tuc*'s was represented by a
slight, shrinking splutter or sibilant note, or, at loudest, a wheezy
pitchu. Probably the low profile that these Groove-bills kept was
the secret of their ability to coexist with the Smooth-bills. In the
Valley of El General in Costa Rica, where the latter species is a
recent arrival, it has almost displaced the Groove-bill.

Although the two kinds of anis usually keep their distance, on
two afternoons I watched both foraging with the same large
swarm of army ants, near a stream. They tended to remain in
separate flocks, but sometimes they intermingled; and I watched
Groove-bills foraging unmolested amid Smooth-bills. In these
mixed parties the Smooth-bills made most of the noise, but the
Groove-bills quietly took their share of the booty. Both species
rested on low perches, or else stood on the ground near the ants,
and when they spied a suitable insect or spider trying to escape
from the hunters, they dived into the midst of the horde, seized
their victim, and as quickly retired. As the anis jumped wildly
about in pursuit of prey, they made a scene of great animation.
They were employing the ants as they more commonly use grazing cattle, to drive hidden insects into the open.

The two species of anis do not fraternize, and once I watched
three Smooth-bills persistently repulse, over an interval of six
weeks, a lonely Groove-bill that had become separated from
others of his kind, in a district where they were rare, and tried
hard to join his nearest relations for company. I suspect that, if
only he could have stilled his so-different voice, the solitary one
might have been accepted by the others that he so closely resembled; but perhaps the ridges on his bill would have betrayed his
identity.

Among their own kind, however, both species of anis are among
the most sociable, and I believe we may truly say "affectionate,"
of birds. They roost lined up on a horizontal branch at no great

height, pressed closely side by side, all facing the same way. Once, in Costa Rica, I found eleven Groove-bills sleeping so in the midst of a lemon tree—a pretty sight in the beam of my flashlight. At La Araguata a flock of Smooth-bills roosted in vine-draped bushes at the edge of a copse, beside an open pasture. Warier than the Groove-bills, they always dashed into the thicket the moment my light fell upon them; although I saw that all perched close together, heads toward the copse into which they fled, I never succeeded in counting them.

In the daytime, too, anis rest in compact rows. One day, at La Araguata, I found fifteen Groove-bills perching at the edge of a lush riverside thicket, so crowded together that they were hard to count, while ten more rested nearby. When a bird at an end of the long row wished to move to the opposite end, it walked over the backs of its companions. Another, flying up from a distance, alighted upon the massed anis. Two perching nearby nibbled each other's feathers, as anis frequently do. Their communal nests, in which several pairs lay their eggs in a single heap and rear their nestlings with no distinction of mine and thine, have frequently been described.

Two other species of cuckoos were also present at La Araguata, and here, again, the larger species was the more widespread. Although the Little Cuckoo is very much smaller than the Squirrel Cuckoo—eleven instead of sixteen inches in length—it resembles the latter so closely that sometimes, without a yardstick, I was puzzled to distinguish them, until I noticed that the Little Cuckoo has a narrow ring of bare red skin around each red eye, while the Squirrel Cuckoo has a large area of bare yellowish green skin surrounding each red eye. Although the Squirrel Cuckoo might be found among scattered trees almost anywhere on the farm, I saw Little Cuckoos only in the denser vegetation along or near streams, usually in pairs. The note I most often heard from them was a slight, sharp, squeaky *pfut*, rather like a chicken's sneeze. Less commonly they called *huc rarr*, seeming to imitate, with weak, undeveloped voices, the *eee-kah* or *hícaro* call of their larger cousin.

Conspicuous Nests and Their Builders

Of the two birds at La Araguata that built nests so large and exposed that the most unobservant could hardly avoid noticing them, one was no less conspicuous than its nest, the other exceedingly inconspicuous. The conspicuous builder of conspicuous nests was the Crested Oropéndola, a big, blackish, blue-eyed bird, with a chestnut rump and tail coverts and bright yellow outer tail feathers. Its sharply pointed bill is whitish. The crow-sized male has a crest of narrow, elongated black feathers that often passes unnoticed because it is laid flat. The considerably smaller female wears the same colors, but her crest is rudimentary.

The female oropéndolas built without help from the less numerous, polygamous males. Their nests, skillfully woven of thin green vines, long strips from palm fronds or banana leaves, and other fibrous materials, were slender, pear-shaped pouches, up to four or five feet long, that hung like gigantic gourds from the ends of thin branches of tall, isolated trees, always far above my reach. Others have reported that each nest contains one or two pale green or gray eggs, spotted and streaked with black, which rest upon a loose bed of leaf fragments that may keep them from knocking together and breaking when a strong wind blows. Although, like other oropéndolas, the Crested Oropéndola breeds in colonies, at La Araguata, where the species was abundant, I found no more than seven occupied nests in a tree. In Trinidad the colonies contain about a dozen nests, and rarely as many as forty, some of which may be vacant; but even this is only half the size of colonies of the Montezuma Oropéndola that I have seen in Central America.

While the females built and incubated without his help, an idle male often displayed amid the pouches. Bowing forward until his body was inverted, his bill pointing earthward and his tail lifted toward the sky, he raised his wings above his back and at the same time made a sharp, rattling sound, followed by a liquid, soprano, far-carrying *whoo-oo*, often with a rippling or quavering effect. Then, while resuming his normal stance, he vigorously shook his wings, audibly striking the relaxed primary feathers together.

When we arrived in mid-March, some of the oropéndolas had

already completed their pouches. By late June, all but a few be-lated hens had finished nesting, and the birds had begun to flock. Many with ragged plumage were molting. The flocks, which were obviously composed of oropéndolas from a number of the small nesting colonies, continued to grow until, in July, I sometimes counted a hundred oropéndolas together, flying with measured wing beats high above the fields in long, straggling columns. Their flight was accompanied by clucking sounds that were some-times dry but often pleasantly melodious, especially when soft-ened by distance. The abundant mango trees, great domes of dark green foliage standing singly or a few together amid the pastures, were now ripening their luscious fruits in such quantities that people, birds, domestic animals, and White-tailed Deer from the thickets hardly sufficed to consume them all. Oropéndolas shared the feast, sometimes alighting on the ground to peck into fallen mangos. They also ate the small yellow fruits of the *Cordia bi-color* trees so abundant in this region, and they laboriously pecked open hard green pods of Inga trees, to reach the sweetish white pulp that surrounded the smooth green seeds.

Well-grown juveniles traveling with the flock continued to re-ceive food from their mothers. I watched a female attending a young male larger than herself. Flapping his big wings, he uttered raucous, groaning-moaning cries while she fed him; then he clumsily helped himself to *Cordia* fruits. Other female oropén-dolas fed clamorous young Giant Cowbirds, whose bills were al-most as pale as those of their foster parents, rather than black, as in the adult cowbirds. I wondered whether this was an adaptation to make the oropéndolas respond more readily to their pleas for food. One morning I watched a female cowbird cling successively to the sides of three neighboring oropéndola nests, from each of which an oropéndola promptly emerged, chased the intruder away, then re-entered before the cowbird could slip in and leave an unwanted egg. The eyes of adult Giant Cowbirds were yellow, not red as in Middle American populations of the same species.

The inconspicuous builder of conspicuous nests was the Ru-fous-fronted Thornbird, a brownish, wrenlike member of the hornero or ovenbird family that hunted its insect food on or near the ground, sometimes disappearing beneath loose accumula-tions of fallen leaves. So retiring was this bird that one would hardly suspect its great abundance in northern Venezuela if its nests did not so often attract attention. This was the bird that I had come to study, for I had read brief reports of its habits that whetted my appetite.

Even while speeding along the superhighway toward Valencia, we noticed the thornbirds' nests, in trees or less often on utility poles. Nearly always they hung upright on thin, drooping twigs or vines, for, although they were sometimes started on a more or less horizontal limb, their weight bent it down. Occasionally a thornbirds' nest hung among the very different nests of Crested Oropéndolas or, as we saw on the llanos, of Yellow-rumped Caciques. In height they ranged from seven to about seventy-five feet above the ground. Aside from the lining, these nests were built wholly of stiff interlaced twigs, often two or three times as long as the six-inch bird who laboriously carried them up from the ground, or more rarely broke them from a tree.

Probably no avian family in the world builds a greater variety of nests than the 215 species of castlebuilders, spinetails, horneros, earthcreepers, and foliage-gleaners comprising the family Furnariidae of tropical America and the temperate zone of South America. They dig burrows in the ground, carve holes in trunks, fashion oven-shaped nests of clay, hang globes of moss high in trees, or erect great castles of sticks. The peculiarity of the Rufous-fronted Thornbird's nest is that it contains several chambers, nearly always one above the other, rarely two side by side. The smallest finished nests (if a thornbird's nest can ever be said to be finished) contained two chambers and were about sixteen inches high and a dozen inches in diameter. The tallest that we saw, but could not reach, was attached to a long, dangling vine that seemed to invite the birds to build up and up, until the nest was about seven feet high and appeared to contain eight or nine rooms.

The several chambers in a nest do not communicate internally, but each has its own entrance from the outside. Usually all these inconspicuous openings amid the twigs face the same way. The globular rooms, each about five inches in diameter, are lined on the bottom with anything soft or flexible that the builders can find. Away from the habitations of men these materials are usually strips of fibrous bark, pieces of decaying grasses and weeds, and fragments of shed snakeskin. Near human houses the nests are

Rufous-fronted Thornbird and nest

often lined with an amazing assortment of trash, including fragments of plastic bags, scraps of cellophane, brightly colored candy
wrappers, tinfoil, paper, and chicken feathers. On this rest the
thornbird's three pure white eggs, nearly always in the lowest,
and accordingly oldest, compartment, which would be the last
that a predator approaching along the supporting branch would
reach.

Since one often sees a number of thornbirds at a single nest
and three or four may build together, it was natural to assume
that these large structures were avian apartment houses, occupied by several families, like the even bulkier nests of Palm-Chats
on the island of Hispaniola, Sociable Weavers in Africa, and Monk
Parakeets in Argentina and the eastern United States, where they
were recently introduced. Yet I watched more than twenty occupied thornbirds' nests without finding more than one breeding
pair in any of them. These birds are strongly territorial and probably would not tolerate a second breeding pair, no matter how
many empty rooms the nest contained. The size and complexity
of these nests is not a provision for communal life so much as an
outstanding expression of that strong impulse to build, widespread in the ovenbird family, that impels many species to bring
more and more material to elaborate nests that appear to be completed and may already contain eggs or even nestlings. The hanging branch or vine around which the thornbirds' nest is constructed often seems to stimulate them irresistibly to extend it ever upward. Perhaps the plurality of chambers makes it more difficult
for predators to find the eggs in the one least accessible to flightless animals, yet many of their nests are plundered. Lacking the
thatched roof that castlebuilders (*Synallaxis*) arrange over their
egg chamber, the thornbirds' nest appears to be poorly designed to
keep its occupants dry during the heavy downpours of the wet
season when they breed.

But if the big nest is not an apartment house, it is a family residence. After about sixteen days of incubation, by the two sexes alternately, and a nestling period of three weeks, the young leave
the nest, already able to fly well. In the evening, the parents lead
them back to sleep in the nest, which continues to be their nightly lodging for months. While the parents raise a second brood,
their older children may sleep in an upper room. Each of three

nests that I watched was occupied by six grown thornbirds, apparently the parents with the surviving young of two broods of the preceding season. After the return of the two fledglings of the current season, one of these nests sheltered eight sleepers—the largest number that I found. Soon after this, two birds, probably the oldest of the breeding pair's offspring, disappeared, doubtless having gone off to establish homes of their own. The number of lodgers in this nest was again reduced to six before the parents started the year's second brood.

The thornbirds' song, a series of rapidly repeated, similar notes that sounds bright and joyous and at its best is beautiful, suggests a cheerful nature. Often, while I stood below a nest in the earliest dawn, to count them as they flew out, I would hear this song issuing through the twigs. Sometimes it was replaced by a low, long-continued twittering from, I surmised, a pair or family cosily cuddling together. Later in the day, perching side by side or facing each other on their hanging mass of twigs, a pair would lift up their heads and pour out their clear notes in a ringing duet. Their day ended as it began, with song and twittering floating down from their nests in the dusk.

Although their large houses often contained empty rooms, thornbirds did not welcome guests. Nevertheless, unmated birds or mated pairs who had suddenly lost their own nests frequently sought hospitality with neighbors and were not easily turned away. These interlopers forced their way in when the light had become dim, long after the resident family had retired; and no matter how long they continued to intrude, they seemed never to become integrated with their unwilling hosts.

One evening, by the light of a full moon, I watched a thornbird, whose nest had just fallen when the supporting branch broke, try to join a single pair in a nearby smaller nest. After being repeatedly repulsed, it adopted a maneuver that I had not seen before. After each ineffectual attempt to enter, it turned around and stood with its tail in the doorway, doubtless receiving on this insensitive extremity the pecks or bites of the resident pair. Finally, at the unusually late hour of half past seven, the persistent intruder forced its way in, at least far enough to be no longer silhouetted against the starry sky, and there it stayed.

Homeless individuals of their own kind are not the only birds that seek admission to the thornbirds' many-chambered nests. Most parts of the world contain birds that prefer to nest in holes or closed constructions but cannot prepare them for themselves. Venezuela has many such species, and no ready-made residence attracts them more strongly than thornbirds' nests. Blue Tanagers, usually content to build their neat open cup amid the foliage of tree or shrub, sometimes place it in an old chamber of a thornbirds' nest; and on the llanos we watched a pair of Sayaca Tanagers building in an unfinished, apparently abandoned structure of the same kind. Cattle Tyrants, large flycatchers that like to ride on the backs of horses, cows, donkeys, and pigs, then jump down and walk along catching the insects that these animals stir up, also exploit the thornbirds by appropriating their nests for their own broods. Still another claimant of the thornbirds' structures is the pretty Saffron Finch.

In their relations with Piratic Flycatchers, thornbirds enjoy an advantage not given to other victims of these pesky little thieves. As far as we know, these wide-ranging flycatchers never build their own nests, but steal those made by other birds, always choosing one that is roofed, including the domed or pensile nests of a variety of flycatchers, the great enclosed globes of becards, the woven pouches of orioles and caciques, or the cavity that Violaceous Trogons have dug in a high, papery wasps' nest. Instead of fighting the builders, the Pirates persistently worry them until, at an opportune moment, they slip in and throw out the eggs, or more rarely the nestlings, thereby causing the owners to abandon the despoiled nest. Then the thieves carry in a few small leaves and lay their own eggs. Unlike all the other nests that I have seen these flycatchers take, those of the thornbirds can accommodate both the intruders and the rightful owners. In June I watched a pair of Piratic Flycatchers and a pair of thornbirds simultaneously incubating in adjacent chambers of a high, inaccessible nest, and later each pair fed nestlings without much interference by the other.

More serious threats to the thornbirds' homes are the melodious Troupials, orange, black, and white orioles with bright blue bare skin around each yellow eye. Although most orioles skillfully weave their own nests, Troupials apparently never do so in regions where they coexist with thornbirds. Instead, they capture a thornbirds' nest, expelling the little builders, sometimes chasing them mercilessly. They alter the stolen nest by pulling out sticks from the middle until it has the shape of an hourglass and enlarging the doorway of a chamber below the constriction. After lining the floor of the chosen room more softly than the thornbirds did, the female lays three dull white eggs that are irregularly speckled, blotched, and scrawled with brown and pale lilac. Before, during, and after rearing their family, the male and female Troupials sleep in the same thornbirds' nest or neighboring ones, but always in separate rooms; a male was repulsed whenever he tried to join his mate in the chamber where she later laid. To provide themselves with bedrooms and a nursery for their young, the single pair of Troupials that I found nesting at La Araguata captured two nests built successively by one family of thornbirds and one nest of a neighboring family, destroying one set of the thornbirds' eggs and one brood of nestlings.

With piratic habits, bare facial skin, and pointed neck feathers, the Troupial is hardly typical of the genus of brilliant, songful orioles to which it belongs. Because it is such a thief, some Venezuelans deem it unworthy to be their country's national bird; they would prefer either the Andean or the Guianan Cock-of-the-Rock, which live on opposite sides of the republic. However, the raptorial birds and ravenous beasts that other nations have chosen as their emblems likewise represent predatory power rather than more admirable qualities. Among the world's nations, Guatemala is somewhat unique in having as its emblem a bird that is both lovely and irreproachably peaceable—the Resplendent Quetzal.[1]

Jacamars

The narrow, unpaved road that bordered La Araguata on the west led far back into the denuded hills of the state of Carabobo. At one point it ran along the edge of an abrupt slope that fell away into a lightly wooded ravine, through which flowed a small brook.

1. A more detailed account of the thornbird and the invaders of its nests appeared in Skutch (1969). Accounts of certain other birds at La Araguata are given in Skutch (1968).

Standing beside the little-used road, I could look over the treetops and watch the birds that flitted through them. As I stood there on a sunny morning in early May, a small bird new to me alighted on a high branch, holding a butterfly. By the long, thin bill that grasped the insect and the slender body, I knew that the bird was a jacamar, although its plumage lacked the brilliance of other members of this small, delightful family of tropical American birds. Its head and neck were pale grayish brown; a faint gloss of purple and blue on its dull blackish upper parts called to mind the glittering iridescence of its more colorful relatives; its richest color was a broad band of chestnut across its breast, interrupting the dull white and dark brown of its ventral plumage. It was my first Pale-headed Jacamar.

While I watched this sprightly little bird, it was joined by a second, no more brilliant than the first, whose black bill was soiled with brown earth, an almost certain sign that it was nesting in a burrow. It did not take me long to find the tunnel in a bare, vertical bank of clay, a yard above the base of the cliff below the road. The mouth of the horizontal shaft was only one and a quarter inches high by one and five-eighths inches wide. Cutting a slender, flexible vine, I pushed it inward to measure the burrow's length, which was thirty-one inches. Then, illuminating the tunnel with an electric bulb attached by a flexible cord to a flashlight, I peered in and saw four nearly feathered nestlings, huddled together with their long bills all pointing toward me.

In the preceding month I had found at La Araguata three nests of the slightly larger and far more brilliant Rufous-tailed Jacamar. Two were in tunnels that these birds had dug horizontally into hard, blackish termitaries that rose above the ground like low domes. The third was in an earthen bank beside a rivulet in a deep, shady ravine. The tunnels in the termitaries were a foot long, that in the stream bank only a trifle longer. The longest of the dozen or so Rufous-tailed Jacamars' burrows in earthen banks and steep slopes that I and others have measured, in localities ranging from Guatemala to Trinidad, was only nineteen and a half inches, and most were little over a foot in length. Why had these Pale-headed Jacamars dug, with delicately slender bills that seemed made for probing flowers, a burrow more than twice as long as that commonly used by their larger cousins?

The steep side of the ravine offered no site for a blind, so to watch the Pale-headed Jacamars' burrow I sat exposed on a little shelf on the declivity. At first hesitant to approach their nest, the parents gradually became accustomed to me and brought food to their young. They foraged chiefly at the top of the woodland, from high, exposed perches darting out to capture volitant insects, much in the manner of a large flycatcher or a Swallow-wing. Approaching their burrow, they would pause in the treetops above it, drawing my attention by calling *weet weet* several times in a high, thin voice, not unlike that of a Tufted Flycatcher or an Eastern Wood Pewee.

While the parent jacamars delayed on a high perch, I examined their prey through my binoculars. They never brought more than a single item, grasped in the tip of their long bills, but this was usually substantial. About half of the insects brought to the nest were large dragonflies, from which the wings had usually been knocked off, although rarely these insects were delivered to the nestlings with transparent wings still attached. Next in the order of abundance came butterflies of small or medium size, which were always taken into the burrow intact. The stout bodies, short wings, and hooked antennae of many of these butterflies clearly revealed that they were skippers of the family Hesperiidae. Most of the butterflies were dull-colored, but one had bright orange-and-black wings. It was noteworthy that I did not once see a slender-bodied, long-winged heliconian butterfly in the jacamars' bills, although heliconians with striped wings were abundant in the moist ravine below the burrow. Heliconians are often distasteful to birds and other animals. Moreover, those in the ravine did not fly high in the air, where the jacamars foraged. An occasional insect of some other kind, such as a dipterous fly and what appeared to be a small cicada, completed the nestlings' diet.

One morning, while I sat on the ground watching the nest, a big, black Tayra came down the slope above me, almost colliding with me before it turned left and ran toward the burrow. The animal frightened away a parent perching on an exposed root in front, waiting to take in a dragonfly. I, too, was alarmed, fearing that this large, nearly omnivorous member of the weasel family had discovered the burrow and, even if I chased it away now, would return in my absence and dig it out with strong claws. But the

Tayra passed above the nest, apparently unaware of it, and vanished into the woods.

A few days later, while I stood beside the road above the burrow, watching the parent jacamars bring food, a fledgling emerged and flew up into a tree in front of me. Both parents immediately joined it and began to sing a crescendo of sharp *weet's* and twitters, building up into high, thin trills. Again and again they repeated this song, with slight variations, while they turned their bodies from side to side and twitched their tails rapidly up and down, beating time to their notes. At intervals the fledgling accompanied them in a weaker voice, flagging its tail as the parents did. This long-continued performance was not unlike the most animated outbursts of the Rufous-tailed Jacamar, but the voice of these birds was thinner, as befitted their slighter bodies. Obviously, the parents' emotions were strongly stirred by the emergence of their first fledgling; they seemed to be congratulating it, or themselves, on the momentous occasion. I was reminded of a similar outburst of song by a parent Vermilion-crowned Flycatcher whose fledgling had just flown from the nest.

Soon the young jacamar flew off through the treetops and was lost to view. The emergence of another fledgling, later that morning, evoked song from the one parent then in sight. This time the performance was shorter, suggesting that the parent's emotions were less strongly stirred. The first flights of this young jacamar also revealed power and control. As the fledglings rested in the treetops, the sunshine falling upon their dark dorsal plumage picked out more metallic green than I could detect on the parents beside them. Was the slightly brighter juvenal plumage an inheritance from remote ancestors as brilliant as most contemporary jacamars are, or was it only that their fresh feathers were less worn than those of the parents?

After the departure of the fourth young jacamar, I returned to examine the burrow more thoroughly than I had cared to do while it was still occupied. While I twisted the flexible vine that I used as a probe, to make sure that it had reached the tunnel's end, two frightened jacamars flew out, almost bumping into me. Perplexed by this unexpected exit, I looked in with the light and beheld two white-throated juveniles peering down the shaft at me. It was then past the middle of the afternoon. Evidently these young jacamars had returned, long before sunset, to rest, and possibly to sleep through the night, in their natal burrow. I had never known Rufous-tailed Jacamars, young or old, to roost in their burrows, although many birds of other families, including barbets, woodpeckers, ovenbirds, swallows, and wrens, do use their holes or nests for sleeping, and lead their young back to lodge in them.

After this exciting discovery, I sat at a distance to watch. Presently another young jacamar, hearing the voices of its parents off in the woods, flew out to join them. Then, with much calling and trilling, a parent arrived with two young, and all rested on a stout root that passed in front of the tunnel. Soon the parent flew away and the two young entered. Then one flew out. Each of the two juveniles now outside was finally led back by a parent, who entered with it. By a quarter past six the whole family, including both parents and the four young, had retired for the night. So much daylight remained that I continued for the next half hour to watch and make sure that none came out again. Then I looked in with a flashlight but could see only two of the six that, as I was certain, were still inside, some evidently behind the others. Forty minutes after the last jacamar had gone to rest, a Southern House Wren still sang as I walked homeward under a darkening sky.

Nine days after their first flight, I watched the four young jacamars enter the burrow alone, without being escorted by the parents, who did not retire until three-quarters of an hour later. For at least six weeks, the family continued to sleep in the burrow. While I watched on the evening of July 6, the sky suddenly darkened as a strong wind blew up, bringing rain, and sending five or six jacamars into the tunnel in rapid succession. After they were well settled, I peeped in with the flashlight and distinguished five resting side by side, facing me, with their slender bills tilted upward. Probably the sixth was behind. This was the last time I could visit them.

Evidently my question had been answered. The Pale-headed Jacamars nest in a burrow twice as long as that of the Rufous-tailed Jacamars because they will use it as a dormitory for the whole family, as the larger species is not known to do. The greater depth of the burrow in a bank of hard soil doubtless increases the sleepers' safety. It is desirable to check this conclusion at other Pale-headed Jacamars' burrows, but I can find no record of any other nest of this species. With rare exceptions, however, a single bird's nest, carefully studied, reveals the pattern of behavior typical of the species.

The Barren Hills

The rain that fell in April and early May was mostly in the form of brief, light showers, too widely separated to keep the ground moist. Not until mid-May did the long, severe dry season finally end. On the afternoon of the seventeenth, a deluge fell from a black sky, converting the clear little rivulet that flowed below the house into a wildly rushing, muddy torrent. Now at last verdure returned to pastures that had long been parched. Here and there in the open woods and fields a splendid amaryllis with pale red flowers five inches across, each with a greenish center, had sprung up in clusters a few weeks earlier, as though in anticipation of the rains, and it continued to add welcome touches of color to the greening earth. On most days in June, showers that were often hard fell in either the morning or afternoon, but the other half of the day was often sunny. How beautiful now were the rare rainless days when white clouds embellished the clear blue sky and bright sunshine illuminated the fresh verdure of the fields and surrounding lightly wooded hills!

The valley or basin in which La Araguata lies is surrounded by steep, rocky, sparsely wooded hills, rising to loftier mountains in the distance. By July bird song and breeding were waning, and, with fewer nests to watch, I wandered more widely. One morning early in the month I climbed a hill north of the farm. The stony ground, covered with small, loose rock fragments that rolled treacherously underfoot, bore short grass in dense tufts. Amid the herbage stood scattered small trees, with gnarled trunks and branches and thick, rough bark. They no longer flowered and I could not identify them.

The shrubs that grew sparingly between the trees, mostly of the melastome and coffee families, likewise had thick, corky bark, the utility of which was attested by the flourishing state, with bright green leaves and often also flowers, of many whose bark had been charred by recent fires. Most of these shrubs bore thick, stiff leaves. Those of an abundant shrub were often over a foot long, curled and crinkled while still green, and so hard that they sounded like stiff cardboard when shaken together. This shrub, evidently a species of the large rubiaceous genus *Palicourea*, was surmounted by generous panicles of small, tubular, yellow flowers on yellow stems that brightened the greening slopes.[2] These slopes, which once may have supported impressive forests, had evidently been so abused by agriculturists, their domestic animals, and their fires, with resulting erosion, that they now supported only a sparse, xerophytic vegetation.

The higher I climbed, the fewer kinds of birds I saw. Most numerous among the scattered low trees were Fork-tailed Flycatchers, who sometimes made a sharp, clicking sound as they flew airily from tree to tree. They were eating the little black berries of the curious, corky-barked shrub with bright yellow panicles that I took to be a species of *Palicourea*. Most of these flycatchers were in worn plumage, with short outer tail feathers. Fork-tailed Flycatchers nested sparingly in the vicinity, then became so much more abundant in June that I suspected an influx of migrants from southern South America, where winter had begun. Yellow-bellied Elaenias, Lesser Elaenias, an unidentified small flycatcher, a Roadside Hawk, two Crested Bobwhites, and several Black Vultures that soared over the ridge complete the meager list of birds that I saw high on the hill.

I continued to climb until from the crest I enjoyed a wide view. The surrounding ridges were no less barren than that on which I stood; some in the distance were almost wholly grass-covered, with few or no trees. Here and there, in the folds and creases of the hills, were heavier stands of trees, with a closed canopy. From one of these patches of richer woodland rose the deep roaring of Howling Monkeys—the *araguatas* for which the farm was named. Some of the steep but less stony slopes around me were planted with crops, chiefly maize and the bitter cassava, a staple food of the poorer Venezuelans. The thick, starchy roots of this manihot were dug up and grated. The poisonous sap was then squeezed out

---

2. This appears to be the *Palicourea rigida* of which Alexander von Humboldt wrote, "the large and tough leaves . . . rustle like parchment when shaken by the winds" (1852–1853, vol. 1, p. 243).

in crude wooden presses, much less neat than the long, slender woven baskets, which contracted when forcibly elongated, that the Indians used for this purpose. Then, on a wide, flat pan of iron or clay, over an open fire, the white pulp was baked into broad, flat sheets, which I used to see going to market in great stacks on heavily laden donkeys.

Nobody could explain to me the advantage of this bitter cassava, widely used in South America, over the "sweet" variety that alone I have met in Central America and grow on our farm. The sweet cassava contains no harmful substance that must be removed before the roots can be cooked and eaten—and here, where the tortilla of maize is a staple food, the cassava is never, to my knowledge, prepared in the form of thin, dry wafers. Could it be that the bitter cassava is shunned by animals that would eat the sweet variety? This would have been a great advantage when Indians planted it in small clearings amid great forests through which rooting peccaries roamed.

Far below, through my binoculars, I watched men, women, and children planting on still bare hillsides or cultivating their young maize plants with heavy, short-handled hoes. When ripe, the corn would not be made into thin tortillas but ground and patted into *arepas* about three inches in diameter by an inch thick, a most substantial breadstuff. The palm-thatched, clay-walled huts, floorless and windowless, in which these tillers below me dwelt were scattered far and wide over the hills. Often they stood on elevations at a distance from the nearest stream, from which the women would carry water in large, brimful tins, skillfully balanced on their heads, with a leaf floating on the surface to diminish spilling.

For contrast, I looked northward, where in the far distance the growing industrial city of Valencia spread over a level plain, its tall factory chimneys rising above the surrounding trees. Beyond the city the Coastal Range rose steeply, its southern slopes, so barren when we arrived in March, now verdant after six or seven weeks of rain, but still devoid of trees and larger shrubs. Before the month's end we would cross this range to La Guaira and the ship that would carry us to Panama, on the first stage of our homeward journey.

CHAPTER 12

Birds and Ants

Bicolored Antbird (above); Spotted Antbird (below)

In many of the earth's wilder regions, birds are the most conspicuous of terrestrial vertebrates, if not actually the most abundant. Ants are among the most widespread and abundant of insects. In warm lands they swarm in bewildering variety and incredible numbers. They are everywhere, from hollows in the
ground to high treetops. Their nests are of the most varied types,
including labyrinthine subterranean galleries, silken pouches
woven amid foliage, and great stalactitelike structures of gray pa-

pery material hanging below lofty boughs. Their architecture is almost as varied as that of the birds themselves. Inevitably, these two abundant forms of life interact in many ways. On the one hand, perpetually hungry ants frequently harm birds, especially their eggs and helpless young; on the other hand, they are often of service to birds, sometimes in unexpected manners.

Ants as Enemies of Birds

Let us first consider the injuries that ants inflict upon birds. One of the ever-present, perplexing problems of the housekeeper in tropical lands is to keep food out of reach of ants. All sweet confections, food rich in proteins, and fruits not well enclosed in their own thick rinds must be guarded in well-sealed jars or tins or else placed on shelves supported upon legs that rest in vessels of water. Birds lack such arrangements to hold swarming ants aloof from their eggs and nestlings, both of which these insects eagerly devour. How, then, do they escape destruction?

Often they do not escape destruction. In warm tropical lowlands, the number of birds' nests despoiled by ants is great. In certain regions where I have studied birds, ants appeared to rank second only to snakes as destroyers of eggs and nestlings. Keeping their nests clean, as most passerine birds do, makes them less likely to attract these insects. Moreover, the shells of eggs protect developing embryos from them. I doubt whether any but the largest ants can pierce an uncracked eggshell; certainly, this would take minutes, during which the parent birds might remove the assailants. Once I watched army ants (*Eciton*) swarm through a Yellow-faced Grassquit's nest and over her tiny, thin-shelled eggs. Returning later, I found the eggs unharmed. Army ants are constantly on the march; their visit to the nest did not continue long, and doubtless the female grassquit stayed away until they withdrew.

Smaller, less active ants may invade a nest and remain longer, causing the incubating parents to fidget until they crack an egg. Then the insects enlarge the fracture and crawl inside to devour the contents. This seems the most probable explanation of the destruction by ants of eggs that were intact when they arrived.

In the sandy bank of a meandering brook in the Guatemalan lowlands, I found a Green Kingfishers' burrow. From its entrance beneath the roots of an old stump, the tunnel slanted upward until the chamber at its inner end was only two and a half inches below the surface. After I closed the small opening that I had made at the rear of the chamber to examine the eggs, fiercely stinging brown fire ants found their way into it. Evidently they stung the parent kingfishers, who now incubated far less constantly than formerly. After a few days, I noticed that all three of the eggs had been dented, one deeply, apparently by the birds themselves as they squirmed around when tormented by the ants. Then the small insects quickly worked in through the cracks and devoured the embryos. If, while examining or measuring a set of eggs, we chip or crack one even slightly, it should be promptly removed from the nest, lest it attract ants that may eventually cause the loss of the whole set.

Many kinds of birds protect their nests from ants by picking them off, either throwing them away or devouring them. Castle-builders periodically go over the outside of their elaborate edifices, putting the materials in order and removing intruding creatures. Once I watched a Slaty Castlebuilder, whose nest sheltered two newly hatched nestlings, spend twelve minutes picking small ants from his great pile of sticks, the supporting branch, and some vines that touched the nest. The vigorous jerk that the bird gave his head after plucking off each ant suggested that he tossed it aside instead of swallowing it.

On another occasion, I watched a female Gray-capped Flycatcher pluck larger ants from the doorway of her roofed nest, which likewise cradled newly hatched nestlings. First she shook her head vigorously, as though casting them from her, but then she made the movements of swallowing, so that I was uncertain whether she ate the ants or crushed them in her bill and threw them away. Even in the temperate zones, birds must sometimes rid their nests of ants in the same fashion. On the prairie in Wyoming, Frances Welton Mickey (1943) saw a female McCown's Longspur pick ants from her nestlings and out of the nest. In southern Australia, John Warham (1954) watched a pair of Splendid Blue Wrens hastily snapping up small reddish ants that were approaching their nest. They continued this activity for about half an hour, during which they neglected to feed their nestlings. In Ecuador, I watched a pair of tiny Golden-fronted Piculets pluck many termites from the doorway of their nest chamber in a dead trunk, much as other birds remove ants.

A Gray-headed Chachalaca, whose broad, shallow nest low in a bush was made largely of matted grass stems, tried vainly to continue incubation when termites deposited much clay on her three eggs. The thin-walled, open-meshed nests of many tropical birds offer few hiding places to ants and other small intruders and facilitate their removal by the parents. Sometimes small birds cling below their nests and spend many minutes picking at them and the supporting twigs, apparently removing insects.

Even when invading ants fail to pierce the eggshells, they may cause the death of the embryos within them. Some years ago a pair of Baird's Trogons carved a nest cavity in a massive decaying trunk in front of our house. Early each morning the male came to call his mate from her eggs and begin a session of incubation that usually continued until the early afternoon. One morning he left prematurely and flew to the forest, where he evidently met his mate. Returning at an hour when she was usually absent, she entered the nest cavity after some hesitation. A moment later she darted out, shook herself vigorously with half-lifted wings, and pecked at her plumage. After a few minutes of this, she entered again, but promptly emerged and shook herself as before. Then she silently flew back to the forest. Bringing a ladder, mirror, and light, I inspected the cavity where the two white eggs lay and found them swarming with fire ants. I did not know how to remove them from the rotting wood without using poison that would jeopardize the eggs and possibly the parents. However, by the following day the ants had withdrawn and the trogons resumed incubation. They continued to attend the nest for a total of fifty-one days—thrice the normal incubation period of seventeen days—before the unhatchable eggs inexplicably vanished.

After they escape from the protecting shell, young birds become more vulnerable to ants. Indeed, at an early stage of hatching, when, after hours of effort, the birdling has perforated the shell, it opens a breach that sometimes permits the entry of its enemies, the ants. If these are numerous, or if from lack of vigor or some other cause the little bird is slow in escaping from the pierced shell, ants may creep in and kill the hapless creature before it can emerge. One May, I followed the efforts to hatch of a Vermilion-crowned Flycatcher that developed in an inverted position, its head in the narrow end of the egg, where the movements that result in breaking out were evidently greatly impeded. The birdling struggled long and heroically to win its freedom from the shell; but ants, entering the gap it finally made, attacked the tissues about its nostrils with fatal consequences.

Once fire ants established a colony almost beneath two eggs of the Pauraque that lay on fallen leaves beneath a shrub in a pasture. For safety, I moved the eggs a short distance; but every time I did so, the parents stupidly replaced them on the original spot, probably by rolling them over the ground. When at last, after tapping for two days, the occupant of one of the eggs pierced its shell, the ants swarmed in and began to devour it before it could emerge. A larger chick may resist such an invasion of its shell. In Texas, J. J. Ramsey (1968) found ants entering a Roseate Spoonbill's pipped egg and biting the occupant. When he returned to the nest a week later, the chick was alive and showed no ill effects from the attack.

Ants attack nestlings of many kinds and ages. No type of nest known to me is antproof. Tanagers and hummingbirds in open nests, woodpeckers and trogons in holes in trees, jacamars and motmots in burrows in the ground—all are subject to incursions by ants. Very young nestlings are usually killed and devoured in the nest; nestlings nearly or fully feathered may escape their persecutors by jumping out, but such premature exposure is often fatal to them.

In Panama, one afternoon in January, I watched a Rufous-tailed Hummingbird feed her two vigorous, nine-day-old nestlings. By ten o'clock that night, the young hummingbirds were dead and covered with fire ants, which for two days continued to swarm over the corpses, until only a little heap of tiny bones remained in the nest. Later that same year, ants attacked two three-day-old Scarlet-rumped Black Tanagers in a neighboring tree. One vanished between my visits, the other was found in the grass beneath the tree with no external signs of injury. I cleansed the nest of ants by soaking it with alcohol, and, after this had evaporated, I replaced the surviving nestling, whose parents continued to attend it. But, despite my efforts to keep the ants out of the small tree by placing a gummy barrier around the trunk, they returned next day and renewed their attacks upon the survivor, which was later found hanging dead from one of the lower branches, where a wasp was eating its flesh.

In Guatemala, at a later date, fire ants attacked three feathered Golden-fronted Woodpecker nestlings, in a hole ten feet up in a barkless trunk that stood in a pasture on low ground where ants were abundant. Although the young woodpeckers, nearly three weeks old, pecked at the tormentors that crawled over their plumage, they could not defend themselves from the multitude of their small assailants. After removing the ants as best I could, I replaced the young birds in their chamber for the night. Returning next morning with an arsenical preparation for disinfecting the crevices in the wood where the ants lurked, I found two of the woodpeckers lying dead in the bottom of the hole, covered with fire ants. On the ground near the base of the stub lay the third nestling, likewise dead and swarming with the same ants. In vain the hapless bird had climbed out of the hole in an effort to escape them.

From a burrow of the Rufous-tailed Jacamar in a steep hillside in the same region, invading ants of another kind drove four seventeen-day-old nestlings, fairly well feathered but unable to fly. On a morning after a rainy night, I found them all alive, lying on the open ground in front of their burrow. One of the females had a badly swollen eye, doubtless from the sting of an ant. After cleaning out the burrow, I replaced the four; but the following day the two young males were dead, apparently as a result of exposure or the stings of the ants or both. Ants so often infested the boxes that I attached to trees around our house in Costa Rica for Southern House Wrens, sometimes killing the nestlings, that I finally abandoned the attempt to provide nest sites for these birds.

Fire ants thrive in sunny places, such as vegetable gardens, pastures, and lawns, where they swarm up the legs of the person who carelessly stands upon their low mounds and punish him sorely. They avoid closed forests and dense thickets, where the ants most likely to attract attention are the army ants that march in long columns and deploy in spreading swarms. Sometimes these ants leave the heavier vegetation to raid gardens and houses, where they attack cockroaches and pillage all the nests of many types that wasps attach to walls and beams, carrying away the larvae and pupae and leaving the hexagonal brood cells forlornly empty.

From the popular accounts of army ants that credulous editors sometimes admit to their pages, one might infer that no animal, however big, is safe from their legions, and that they destroy every bird's nest that they encounter. On the contrary, I have never known them to harm a bird of any kind, and on several occasions I have seen them pass over or around nests without attacking the occupants. Long ago, sitting in a blind, I watched the larger army ants (probably *Eciton burchelli*) swarm up a bush and over the little open nest where a female Variable Seedeater sat warming her two eggs. To my surprise, she continued calmly to incubate while the ants crawled over the nest's rim all around her, until they withdrew without having inflicted visible injury on either her or her eggs. I have already told how army ants crawled over a grassquit's exposed eggs without harming them. Recently I watched a horde of these ants pass beneath the frail open nest that Streaked-chested Antpittas had built in the crown of a low tree fern beside a forest path. When some of the ants climbed up to the nest where the male antpitta sat brooding a newly hatched nestling, he picked them off, perhaps half a dozen in all, and swallowed them. When, some hours later, the army moved away, the nestling was still safe and sound, although soon afterward it vanished completely, probably having been eaten by a snake or a squirrel.

In the Caribbean lowlands, army ants flowed around and over the mouth of the long burrow in the forest floor where feathered nestlings of the White-fronted Nunbird rested. I could not watch these young puffbirds in the ground, but, after the ants departed, they continued to come to the burrow's mouth to take food from their four attendants. In all of the foregoing episodes, the army ants were of the larger kind, belonging to the genus *Eciton*. When a swarm of the smaller army ants, *Labidus praedator*, passed over a short burrow inhabited by feathered nestlings of another species of puffbird, the White-whiskered Softwing, the result was the same—the young birds were not harmed. It is not likely that some of the army's scouts, which poke into every nook and crevice, failed to reach the nestlings in both burrows, and I would have given much to have seen what happened if and when they did. Although my half-dozen observations on the behavior of army ants at occupied birds' nests are not a sufficiently wide foundation for the generalization that they rarely attack nestlings, army ants certainly are less harmful than some other kinds of ants, especially fire ants.

The preferred victims of army ants are insects of many kinds, spiders, scorpions, centipedes, and the like. Above all, they relish the immature stages of other Hymenoptera, and when they find a nest of wasps or other ants, including the populous subterranean cities of the leaf-cutting ants (as I have repeatedly seen), they carry away all the young brood. They may sting the legs of the person who stands in their midst, though no more painfully than fire ants do, but they are hardly attracted to vertebrates. A reason for this may be that they do not, like certain other ants, consume their prey where it is found, but dismember and carry it back in small pieces to their bivouac, and animals like mammals, birds, and reptiles resist such fragmentation.

I have watched birds that habitually forage with army ants, including antbirds and woodcreepers, perch unconcerned while the ants passed over their scaly feet. A collector in Nicaragua shot a Fasciated Antshrike that fell in the path of a swarm of army ants, where he could not easily retrieve it. When he returned next day, expecting to add a nicely cleaned skeleton to his collection, he found his bird still intact. The ants had not even eaten into the bare skin around its eyes (Huber 1932). When I threw a freshly killed snake into the midst of a hunting swarm of Eciton ants, they finally flowed onward without having bitten into it. Movement incites these blind ants to attack. By remaining perfectly immobile, insects such as certain walking sticks and "a green, leaf-like locust" watched by Thomas Belt (1888) in Nicaragua, survive amid the swarm. Perhaps, for the same reason, lifeless vertebrates that army ants happen to encounter fail to engage their attention.

In *Jungle Peace* (1918), William Beebe told how army ants attacked a small frog and a toad that were trapped in a deep pit dug in sand. He rescued the frog with ants clinging to it, while the toad, despite a few ant bites, saved its life by secreting an acrid substance distasteful to the ants—the first vertebrate, remarked Beebe, that he had ever known to withstand army ants (p. 214 of 1925 reprint edition). Later, he saw the ants carry part of a small frog from the pit. T. C. Schneirla, a leading authority on army ants, saw "snakes, lizards, and nestling birds killed on various occasions," and added that "undoubtedly a larger vertebrate which, because of injury or for some other reason, could not run off, would be killed by stinging or asphyxiation" (Schneirla 1956, p. 389).

Ants as Food of Birds

Just as snakes, which prey so heavily on eggs and nestlings, are eaten by many kinds of birds and are the principal food of some, including the Laughing Falcon, so ants, which pillage many nests, contribute to the diet of numerous kinds of birds. When we speak of birds that eat ants, we think first of woodpeckers, one species of which was formerly called the Ant-eating Woodpecker and still bears the specific name *formicivorus*, although it is now more appropriately known as the Acorn Woodpecker. The tongues of woodpeckers that eat many ants are slender white organs, up to four inches long, that can be pushed far into narrow galleries and crannies in wood or soil, gathering the mature ants, larvae, and pupae that touch their sticky, saliva-coated surfaces and drawing them back into the birds' mouths. The tongue of the Green Woodpecker of Europe has a flattened end, the better to catch ants and their young brood. When a woodpecker's tongue is retracted, its basal branches (hyoids) curve around the back and top of the skull to enter the hollow of the upper mandible, or else they bend around an eye.

Flickers spend much time on the ground, on or near anthills, gathering great quantities of ants. Pileated Woodpeckers dig deep, rectangular pits in dead trunks to remove large carpenter ants. As told in Chapter 10, the Lineated Woodpeckers of tropical America procure their ants in a very different way. The smaller Cinnamon Woodpeckers peck into the swollen gall-like nodes on the twigs of the Laurel tree to devour the little Azteca ants that dwell in them; but, as far as I have seen, they do not so greatly injure the slender tree. The piculets, smallest of the woodpeckers and among the most diminutive of birds, subsist largely upon ants. They seek chiefly kinds that inhabit slender dead branches and twigs, with short bills pecking into the soft decaying wood to extract the white larvae and pupae, meanwhile gathering up the worker ants that scurry over the branches. They nourish their young chiefly with "ant eggs." Although piculets bring food to their young in their bills and mouths, larger woodpeckers that nourish their nestlings with many ants usually regurgitate to them. Woodpeckers with a more varied diet of insects and fruits usually feed their young directly from the bill.

When the Eciton army invades the dooryard, its ranks are decimated by the domestic chickens that eagerly gather the ants—a peppery food! In the forest, I have seen tinamous hovering about the outskirts of a foraging swarm of army ants, but I could not learn whether they ate the ants themselves, the fugitives stirred up by them, or both. Ants enter into the diets of birds of the most varied habits, some of which, from their aerial foraging, we would never expect to eat these creatures of the dust. According to A. C. Bent (1942, p. 450), ants account for about 10 percent of the food of the Barn Swallow, some of whose stomachs were entirely filled with wingless forms. Thirteen percent of the Yellow-bellied Flycatcher's food consisted of ants (Bent 1942, p. 178). Even ducks, such as the Blue-winged Teal, often eat ants. These small, laborious insects, whose very name conveys the thought of swarming multitudes, must in aggregate supply a vast amount of nourishment to the feathered world.

Ants as Purveyors of Food to Birds

In the forests and thickets of tropical America, ants appear to contribute much less food to birds directly, with their own bodies, than indirectly, by driving into the open and making readily available the multitude of insects and other small creatures that lurk in the ground litter, amid green foliage, or on the bark of trees, where they are not readily detected. The hunting ants that swarm over the ground and up shrubs and trees, setting animals of all kinds in motion and thereby nullifying the value of all those refinements of form, color, and behavior on which they rely to elude those that would devour them, are commonly known as army ants.

The species that birds chiefly follow is *Eciton burchelli*, an ant of medium size, brown or dark brown in color, with powerful mandibles and a sting, and rudimentary eyes sensitive to light but useless for vision. A nomad without fixed abode, this ant hunts by day in multitudinous hurrying hordes and gathers at nightfall in cylindrical or ellipsoidal masses, from a foot to a yard in diameter, containing hundreds of thousands of their tightly packed bodies, all hanging together from an overhead support, and enclosing the single queen and young brood. These amazing temporary structures with living walls may develop amid the close-set branches of a low shrub, beneath a fallen log, or in a hollow tree, sometimes high above the ground. For about two weeks the site of the bivouac is shifted nightly, then for about three weeks it remains in the same place, all in regularly alternating intervals, determined by the phases of the reproductive cycle.

Less attractive to birds are the hunting swarms of the smaller, reddish black *Labidus praedator*, which in wet weather emerge from their subterranean abode to flow over the forest floor in seething sheets several yards broad. After a few hours, they vanish into the ground again. Both species of army ants are very widely distributed over tropical America, from northeastern Mexico to northern Argentina.

In their deployed formation, the larger army ants advance over a front usually at least three or four yards wide and rarely as many as twenty. The many thousands of hunting ants scurry about in all directions, over and under the ground litter, through the lower vegetation, and up the trunks of trees, restlessly seeking their prey. When overcome and, if large, cut into pieces of convenient size, the victims, held beneath the carriers' bodies, are transported back to the bivouac in a thin column that may be hundreds of yards long. Other ants in this column hurry forward to join the fray, but the slender formation is maintained by those walking in both directions. The ants do not push out from the sides of this transport column to explore adjacent terrain, and an insect or man may rest close beside it yet remain undisturbed. The birds distinguish between the two formations; they hover about the deployed battle front, alert to capture the fugitives, but are rarely found beside the long, often winding transport column.

In a banana plantation in the Motagua Valley of Guatemala, I watched a battalion of large, blackish army ants forage. Only the preceding day, the weeds had been chopped off close to the ground by laborers with long machetes, leaving it covered with a loose litter of drying plants, mingled with huge leaves freshly cut from the bananas and still green. Although when I have met army ants in the forest the attendant birds have claimed most of my attention, here were none to distract me as I intently watched the mute strife between the hunters and their motley victims.

When I glanced over the weed-littered ground at a distance from the ants, I noticed few living animals. One might hastily conclude that this freshly cleaned plantation contained little food for ants or birds. But the advancing army demonstrated clearly that the reverse was true: invertebrate life abounded. Over and through the dying herbage poured the relentless horde, as mercilessly death-dealing to all the creatures harboring there as a stream of volcanic lava flowing over a town. Slowly but steadily the army pushed forward, over an irregular front four to six feet broad. The passage over dry leaves of such multitudes of hurrying ants and small fleeing creatures made a low rustling sound; as when the first drops of an autumnal shower patter down on the fallen foliage of a northern forest. Columns of ants filed up and down the stems of the banana plants; nothing should escape them. And every mobile creature that lurked beneath the litter instinctively rushed out. Spiders of many kinds were among the most conspicuous; lizards, roaches, ants of other kinds, crickets, grasshoppers, wood lice swelled the crowd of fugitives.

The larger spiders, such as could straddle a silver half dollar, seemed often to escape the horde of ants, but not without some lively encounters. As the ants drove them forth from their refuge beneath the litter, the spiders rushed forward, to pause a short distance ahead of the advance guard, perhaps at the top of the stubble of a cut-off weed, or on some upstanding shred of a severed banana leaf. Here the spider might linger unmolested until surrounded by the main body of the army. Then some adventurous scout would ascend to its point of vantage and with a nip on a leg send it dashing down, to scamper wildly over litter darkened by the destroying throng. With luck, the spider would emerge triumphant upon another little promontory of vegetation, with one or two ants clinging to its legs. A swift movement of the leg with the attached ant to the spider's mouth and a pinch by its mandibles would dislodge the assailant. Then, if fortune favored, the spider might stand alert, with forelegs raised, until the army passed on. But I saw one fairly big spider fall, covered with ants, among the litter. The final struggle took place beneath the leaves, out of sight. Considering the odds, I did not doubt its outcome.

A good-sized grasshopper landed among the ants and was promptly covered by the crowd that rushed up to dismember it. But the most numerous victims, and those that most aroused my sympathy, were some red ants, as long as the army ants but more delicately built, that were driven from beneath fallen weeds, each carrying a white larva or pupa in its mandibles. Hurrying ahead of the army ants, they climbed well up on fallen banana leaves. Finally, one of the dusky army ants that wandered helter-skelter back and forth, apparently guided by neither sight nor scent, but trusting to chance and their great multitudes to contact their prey, would bump into a fleeing red ant. The two would clinch and grapple, perhaps slipping down among the hordes that darkened the ground where the ants were densest, and the issue of the contest was no longer in doubt.

While one dusky warrior went off carrying the precious pupa that the red ant had tried so hard to save, others fastened themselves upon the poor vanquished one and left it dead or dying, or else dragged it away along with much other booty. Nevertheless, after the whole army had passed on, some of the red ants remained, still bearing those promises of future ants that they had succeeded in rescuing; for, more agile than the army ants, they had climbed far up on the upturned edges of freshly cut banana leaves that were still green, and their pursuers had not attempted to scale the slippery, nearly vertical surfaces.

It will readily be seen how such a general shifting about and forward movement of small animals that usually hide can benefit the birds. Instead of searching tediously through foliage and ground litter, they have only to follow the army ants and watch for the creatures that these scare up. The ants help hungry woodland birds as a grazing horse or cow benefits the anis, Cattle

Egrets, or domestic chickens that keep close to its head, alert to seize the grasshoppers and other insects it stirs up; as a dog aids the hunter; or as a prairie fire makes food more available to birds of prey. In the absence of ants, a bird that depends upon them sometimes finds a substitute. At intervals over several years, a Bicolored Antbird followed me through the forest by my house, snatching up the insects, little frogs, and other tiny creatures that rose from the ground as I walked, dragging my feet. He continued to keep me company until I tired of working for him, and came so near that I could almost touch him. Similarly, in dry weather when army ants were hard to find, I have watched Gray-headed Tanagers, also habitual ant-followers, perch low above chickens scratching at the forest's edge, alert to seize any insect that escaped them.

All over tropical America, birds have learned to profit by the activities of the army ants, and a few species have become so dependent that they could hardly survive without them. In this category are several species of antbirds (a small minority of the 231 species in this great, exclusively Neotropical family), of which the best known is the Bicolored Antbird, intensively studied by Edwin O. Willis (1967). The Ocellated Antthrush and several South American species that have been less thoroughly studied appear to be equally dependent. The Spotted Antbird, although a persistent ant-follower, seems better able to forage without them. A number of woodcreepers, especially the short-billed dendrocinclas, although fairly constant attendants of the ant swarms, seem quite competent to gain a living without their help. Another very constant attendant, the shy Gray-headed Tanager, appears to have a hard time finding enough to eat if it cannot attach itself to an ant swarm. In their absence, it may visit a feeding shelf for bananas. The foregoing, which might be called the professional ant-followers, are the birds most frequently seen at ant swarms in Central America and northern South America. With the exception of northern populations of the Red-throated Ant-Tanager, the so-called ant-tanagers of the genus *Habia* only rarely accompany ants.

Many other birds occasionally forage with army ants, probably drawn by the calls of the professionals and the universal hope of finding something desirable where others appear to be having good luck. When a mixed flock of woodland birds that usually forage at greater heights meets a swarm of the ants and their followers, the former may delay a while to mix with the professionals and share the feast, then resume their independent course. Almost any bird of the undergrowth, and some from higher levels, will take advantage of the passage of an ant swarm through its territory or home range. Such occasional ant-followers include tinamous, falcons, cuckoos, motmots, puffbirds, ovenbirds, antshrikes, antwrens, cotingas, flycatchers, wrens, thrushes, wood warblers, tanagers, and finches. When the army ants extend their raids into the open, they may attract an excited crowd of black anis, who find the hunting horde an acceptable substitute for the cattle that they more often use to stir up insects for them. Wintering thrushes and wood warblers from northern lands not infrequently join the crowd assembled around the army ants, usually hovering on its outskirts, leaving the more richly productive center to the residents.

Although in every region where army ants plunder, the motley crowd of birds that follows them is of different specific composition, its general characteristics are nearly everywhere the same. The tropical forest, for all its wealth of bird life, seems much of the time to be silent and deserted. Its feathered citizens are resting amid massed foliage a hundred feet overhead, skulking invisibly in the undergrowth, or hunting through tangles of vines and creepers where they escape the eye. But, of a sudden, the silence is broken. Before he is aware of what he has done, the lone wanderer has burst into the midst of a crowd that seems to have drawn all the feathered life of the surrounding forest. The birds melt away through the underwood, voicing their annoyance at this inconsiderate intrusion in a medley of squeaks and chirps, churrs and trills, in a dozen different keys. Glancing at the ground where he stands, the unintentional trespasser finds it swarming with small brown or blackish ants, which do not hesitate to crawl over his shoes or even higher, and, if they reach bare skin, to give an admonitory nip or sting. If prudent, the wanderer hurries beyond the edge of the battle formation, stamps and brushes the Ecitons from shoes and legs, and stands quietly to watch a show that is certainly one of the most animated that the tropical forest offers.

Soon the birds, reassured by the intruder's immobility, come flitting and hopping back to their interrupted feast. Most are not excessively shy, and the watcher quickly learns that each has its characteristic way of foraging. Antbirds cling a foot or two above the ground to slender stems, preferring those that are upright, and look searchingly about them. A roach or spider rushing out from beneath fallen leaves causes the antbird to hop down into the midst of the ants, seize the fugitive, and rise in a trice to some low perch, where it may mandibulate its victim before swallowing it. Tanagers usually watch from higher perches. Slender brown woodcreepers cling upright to tree trunks, often between ascending columns of ants, a few feet or yards above the ground, to which they descend momentarily when some fleeing creature tempts them, then carry it back to the trunk, against which they may beat their victim before they swallow it. Or else they catch flying insects in the air, or steal prey from the ants that hunt over the bark and through its fissures. Small forest flycatchers snap up in the air insects trying to escape by flight. Tiny manakins likewise catch insects on the wing, or capture those that crawl up the stems of saplings vainly seeking safety; while wood wrens lurk about the outskirts of the crowd, without much doubt intercepting the poor refugees that slip beyond the outposts of the army.

All these birds are interested in the fugitives—insects, spiders, centipedes, scorpions, small frogs and lizards—rather than in the ants themselves. Although many of them from time to time drop down into the midst of the voracious ants, they remain only a moment and seem rarely to be attacked or bitten. I have watched the ants turn back or detour when they collided with the feet of a Bicolored Antbird perching on a vine along which they filed. Others marched in a long column between the feet of a Tawny-winged Dendrocincla clinging to a trunk. In neither instance did the ants attack the bird. Sometimes, however, they attach themselves to the feet of a bird who has descended among them to seize a victim, causing the bird to pick them off and toss them away. It appears that the ants are incited to attack by movement, as when a bird alights in their midst in pursuit of a roach, but they tend to ignore the birds when they rest motionless or lie dead.

The birds' immunity from more than a casual attack by the army ants raises an interesting evolutionary problem. These birds are important competitors who must substantially decrease the booty of a formidable army which, one might suppose, would try to get rid of them, even if they prefer invertebrate to vertebrate flesh. Have the ants learned, over their generations, that if they attacked active birds they would only be nipped or mangled for their trouble? Or can it be that, since their atrophied eyes cannot distinguish their competitors, they are not even aware of how much potential prey they are losing?

The enumeration of all the species involved in these mael-stroms of hungry and of fugitive life that center about the hunt-ing ants; the description of all the stratagems that the fugitives employ to effect their escape; the devices of the hunters to over-come them; the efforts of parasitic flies to lay eggs on the ants' victims—the history of so much strife and carnage might fill as many books as have been written about the Napoleonic wars. The gifted pens that have described the expeditions of the army ants have treated only certain aspects. The complete story of this most complex natural phenomenon remains to be written.

One of the largest aggregations of birds, as to both individuals and species, that I have seen with army ants was found in the Costa Rican mountains at an altitude of about 3,500 feet. At least twelve species of birds had gathered about an immense swarm of ants that over an area several yards broad darkened the fallen dead leaves, beneath lofty forest. The most conspicuous, if not the most numerous, of the birds that fell upon the creatures trying to escape the devouring regiments were the Bicolored Antbirds, easi-ly recognized by their rich brown upper plumage and white cen-tral under parts and by their incessantly repeated, rather derisive song and peculiar whining call. With them were two male Im-maculate Antbirds—the first I ever saw—everywhere black in plumage, except a small white patch at the bend of the wing, dif-ficult to detect unless the birds flew. Their almost uniformly somber hue was relieved by the bare blue skin around each eye and at the base of the bill and a triangle of palest blue behind each eye. Like the Bicolored Antbirds, these long-legged, long-tailed birds perched near the ground, to which from time to time they dropped to seize some tempting morsel, then promptly rose to eat it while clinging to a low sapling. More retiring and less easy to watch was a male Bare-crowned Antbird, likewise nearly every-where black, but with three narrow white bars on each wing. The whole top of his head was bald and bright blue.

The woodcreeper family was represented by the Ruddy Dendro-cincla and the browner Tawny-winged Dendrocincla. A pair of nervous Gray-headed Tanagers, olive green above, yellow on breast and abdomen, were a conspicuous part of the company. Of the flycatchers, a brisk Sulphur-rumped Myiobius and a tiny Golden-crowned Spadebill were present, catching small flying in-sects set in motion by the ants on the ground below them. The plump little manakins were represented by greenish females and young males only; the brighter adult males were at this season too closely attached to their courtship assemblies to attend dis-tant gatherings. Both the Yellow-thighed and the Blue-crowned manakins perched low amid the underwood, above the swarming ants, and captured fugitives by short, swift dashes. One of the female Yellow-thighed Manakins dropped down amid the ants to capture a lizard, then carried it up to a low perch, against which she proceeded to beat it. Although a very small lizard, it was too big and heavy for her short bill, and it soon slipped from her grasp. She followed it to the ground, but was unable to recover it.

A Lowland Wood-Wren hopped about amid the undergrowth at the edge of the swarm, keeping himself well hidden from me, but revealing his presence by a bright, cheery song, repeated over and over. The most unexpected member of this heterogeneous avian assemblage was a wintering Olive-backed Thrush, possibly a na-tive of British Columbia or even Alaska. It stood on a fallen log around which the ants were swarming, looking well fed and too indolent to move when I came near. Although not so expert as the antbirds and woodcreepers at this business of snatching prey from the army ants, doubtless it gathered up more than one crumb that fell from their table—why otherwise would it have continued to move along with the ants and their followers? Elsewhere I have seen others of its kind hanging about the outskirts of foraging ants.

In the Costa Rican mountains, army ants are not uncommon even as high as six thousand feet. On these cool, rainy heights, few of the heat-loving antbirds attend them. The black Immaculate Antbird is the only member of the family that I have seen with ants at this elevation. But even a mile above sea level, army ants attract a varied throng of birds that forage chiefly in other ways, but, like birds everywhere, are too alert and economical of effort to neglect rich supplies of easily gathered food. Collared Redstarts, Slate-throated Redstarts, and Tufted Flycatchers dart about near the ground, snatching up small flying creatures. Three-striped Warblers pluck off insects that the ants have driven up on low vegetation. The Slaty-backed Nightingale-Thrush, whose bright orange bill, orbital rings, and feet contrast handsomely with its dark plumage, is another rather constant follower of the army ants in humid mountain forests with dense undergrowth. As it rests low, keeping its eyes open for small creatures that try to escape the ants, it gives its wings a little nervous flit several times each minute. The Wren-Thrush, Sooty-faced Finch, Chestnut-capped Brush-Finch, and Ochraceous Wren occasionally forage with army ants in the Costa Rican highlands.

One might suppose that the noisy crowd of birds with the army ants would attract every predator, terrestrial or winged, in the vicinity and expose the ant-followers to great danger. Nevertheless, they appear to be fairly safe. The many watchful eyes, the many voices quick to sound the alarm, all amid vegetation that offers convenient safe refuges, more than compensate for the conspicuousness of the gathering. The same seems to be true of the mixed flocks that wander through tropical and temperate-zone woodlands, not following ants. In the midst of companions as watchful as themselves, birds evidently feel, and are, more secure than when alone.

I recall no published record of a predator catching a bird that was following army ants. R. A. Johnson (1954), who studied army ants and their attendants on Barro Colorado Island in the Panama Canal Zone for eight weeks in 1948, once saw a small hawk strike at a Bicolored Antbird, who fled, screeching, from the raptor and managed to escape. Far from trying to catch an ant-follower, the single predator that I have seen at an ant swarm behaved as the other birds did. One morning in July, as I stood watching a most interesting group of ant-followers in the forest near my house, an immature Collared Forest-Falcon suddenly dropped down into their midst, making them scatter with a medley of alarm calls.

Since this falcon preys upon birds, including domestic chickens, my first assumption was that it had tried to seize one of the party, but continued watching cast doubt upon this. The falcon rose from the ground to perch two or three yards above the ants and rested there while the smaller birds, recovering confidence, resumed their previous activities, sometimes catching insects eight or ten yards from the raptor.

Soon it was evident that the falcon himself (I assume the sex) was watching for insects stirred up by the ants. His first attempt to seize one by dropping from his perch to the ground was unsuccessful. After hopping around in search of it, once vanishing under a log, he rose to a perch with empty bill and feet. On his second descent, the big bird caught a long-legged creature that might have been a spider, carried it to a perch, and started to dismember it. But the young raptor was clumsy, permitted his victim to drop, followed it to the ground, and rummaged through the dead leaves until he recovered it. Then he took it up to a log and swallowed it, long legs and all.

During the two hours that I watched, the falcon seized and ate at least four large insects. At intervals he hopped over the ground, evidently hunting something he had seen, slightly shifting the litter with his feet but not effectively scratching, as a gallinaceous bird does. Sometimes he pushed beneath fallen branches and into brush in a manner unexpected in a bird of prey. Returning to a perch, frequently with nothing to show for his effort, he often gave attention to his feet, as though ants were clinging to them. Sometimes he stood on one foot, the other drawn up and almost buried in the white plumage of his abdomen. I heard not a sound from him. In central Brazil, Willis (1972b) watched Lined Forest-Falcons accompanying ant swarms for hours, often returning repeatedly to the same area, and capturing only large insects, never a bird, as far as he saw.

Each longer flight of the Collared Forest-Falcon to keep up with the advancing ants made some of the smaller birds scurry about and cry out in alarm. But soon they returned to their insect catching all around him, now even closer than at first. He was almost fearless of me. The Gray-headed Tanagers seemed less afraid of the falcon than of me, but the Bicolored Antbirds ventured much closer to me than to him. An attendant at this ant swarm as unexpected as the falcon was a noisy Bright-rumped Attila, which consistently stayed higher than the others and caught insects with a style all of its own, often with a dash that carried it far beyond the flying creature that it seized. It also swooped upon insects trying to save themselves by crawling up the tree trunks. Here the attila faced competition, for a Barred Woodcreeper, a Ruddy Dendrocincla, and a Tawny-winged Dendrocincla clung to these trunks to pick off refugees.

Ants as Providers of Nest Sites

A very different way in which ants may be of service to birds is by providing them with nest sites. Because of the failure of some naturalists to distinguish between ants and termites, reports of birds laying their eggs in "ants' nests" must be read with caution. Some of these reports refer, not to the nests of true ants, but to the big edifices of hard black, brown, or gray material, arranged in irregular plates, that termites or "white ants" construct. Termites are not even closely related to ants but resemble them in their social habits and countless multitudes. I have rarely known these soft-bodied, slow-moving creatures to injure birds in any way. Their homes, known as termitaries, furnish nest sites for a number of kingfishers, parrots, trogons, woodpeckers, jacamars, and puff-birds, all of which carve chambers in the bulky structures. The winged sexual termites that issue from the termitaries in swarms that fill the air, often after the termination of one of the first light afternoon showers that start off the wet season, provide abundant food for every bird not too clumsy to catch such slow-flying, fragile creatures. The acrid-scented worker and soldier termites are less often eaten by birds, but chickens devour them greedily.

The best-authenticated example of a bird that lays its eggs in a true ants' nest is the Rufous Woodpecker of India and Ceylon. The nests occupied by this bird are built by a species of *Crematogaster* among the branches of trees, from ten to fifty feet up. Composed of a sort of tough, grayish-brown papier-mâché made of wood fibers, fragments of bark, and filaments of a green alga that grows over rocks and tree trunks in damp places, these nests have roughly the form of a football from eight inches to two feet in diameter. Into the side of one of these structures the wood-peckers carve a round entrance, about two inches in diameter, which leads to a nearly spherical chamber five or six inches wide and high. Here the female lays three white eggs with unusually thin, fragile shells.

Rufous Woodpeckers eat large quantities of this same kind of ant. Whether they consume any of the ants whose nest they inhabit is a disputed question. However, they do not regularly destroy the whole population, for they are often found rearing their families amid the ants, whose galleries leading into the woodpeckers' chamber appear not to be sealed off. The insects run over the birds' eggs and nestlings without harming them, although they ferociously attack other intruders. Perhaps the secret of the woodpeckers' immunity is the persistent peculiar odor they acquire from eating so many ants of the same kind, perhaps including some from the nest into which they dig their chamber. It is well known that many insect commensals in the nests of social insects are immune from the attacks of their hosts, probably because they have the distinctive odor by which each of these insects recognizes its own nest mates. To the ants, their uninvited avian guests may be just unusually large members of their society.

Sometimes the Rufous Woodpecker carves its nest cavity into a termitary or the wood of a tree instead of an ants' nest. Likewise, the Buff-spotted Woodpecker of Africa may lay its eggs in either an arboreal ants' nest or a termitary. Another African bird, the Red-headed Lovebird, has also been reported to occupy ants' nests as well as termitaries, but possibly these "ants' nests" belonged to "white ants" or termites (Hindwood 1959).

Ants as Protectors of Birds' Nests

Birds not infrequently build nests in ant-infested trees, or close beside ants' nests, apparently because the ants protect them from nest-plundering animals. A bird that lightly comes and goes may build and rear its family among fiercely stinging, noncarnivorous ants without arousing their fury; they appear to become habituated to the regular gentle shaking of the branches. Most of the birds that rely upon ants or wasps for protection lay their eggs in roofed nests or deep pouches that shield the occupants from the stinging or biting insects. A flightless animal trying to reach such a nest is likely to be driven from the tree with stings or bites.

The dozen species of bull's-horn acacias, or *cornizuelos*, that grow in the drier regions of Mexico and Central America have open foliage and, moreover, are rarely laden with creepers because their ants destroy competing vegetation. Despite the poor concealment that they offer, these small trees and shrubs are chosen as nest sites by many kinds of birds in addition to the three species of wrens that I found nesting in them in Mexico, as told in Chapter 1. Several species of orioles and flycatchers attach pensile nests to exposed twigs; other flycatchers build domed structures in crotches; while wrens, as we have seen in Chapter 1, guard their eggs and young in well-enclosed, often elbow-shaped, nests. Such structures give their occupants a measure of isolation from the stinging *Pseudomyrmex* ants that constantly patrol the acacias, for these ants rarely enter the doorways. Nevertheless, all these birds appear to avoid acacias with the densest population of ants, possibly because the insects would too often attack them in the early stages of nest construction, when they are most exposed and vulnerable.

Sometimes the birds situate their nests beside one that stinging wasps have built in the acacia tree, thereby availing themselves of a double guard. When Janzen (1969) gently placed arboreal snakes and lizards in acacias, the ants promptly drove them out with stings and bites. He also gathered evidence that nests in ant-infested acacias are more successful in producing fledged young than those in surrounding plants of other kinds, which doubtless explains why the acacias contain many more birds' nests than one would expect if nests were randomly distributed through the vegetation. More statistics on the relative success of nests in acacias and in surrounding trees are desirable, but the ornithologist who peeps into covered nests built amid *Pseudomyrmex* colonies often pays so dearly for his temerity that he is reluctant to examine many of them. Although the acacia trees and their ants have developed a mutually beneficial symbiosis, the birds do not appear to benefit either the host tree or the resident ants.

The most widespread and conspicuous myrmecophytes or "ant plants" in tropical America are a number of species of Cecropias, with hollow trunks and branches that are inhabited by small ants of the genus *Azteca*, as described in Chapter 10. These slender, rapidly growing, coarsely branching trees with very open crowns provide poor concealment and few good nest sites for birds; their ants, which lack stings and bite only weakly, offer inadequate protection. Accordingly, the Cecropias rarely attract nesting birds. The ant-infested Laurel likewise offers few nest sites and weak protection, but once I discovered a Scarlet-rumped Cacique, a White-winged Becard, and a Gray-capped Flycatcher building on the same high, exposed branch, which also bore a small wasps' nest. Only the cacique finished her structure.

In Africa, birds of several kinds, including large raptors, have been found breeding in trees inhabited by ants that stung the people who tried to climb to the nests, sometimes so severely that they abandoned the attempt. In Nigeria, P. I. R. Maclaren (1950) demonstrated the Bronze-headed Mannikins' strong preference for placing their covered nests with a side entrance in trees where the large and vicious red weaver ants, *Oecophylla smaragdina*, have built nests by binding living leaves together with silk secreted by their larvae.[1] In a certain parkland containing ninety-four trees suitable for nesting by both the birds and the ants, nineteen held ants' nests, and seven of these also sheltered twelve mannikins' nests. The remaining seventy-five trees that lacked ants' nests contained only five mannikins' nests in as many trees, three of which were infested with ants from neighboring trees. Only two out of seventeen nests were in trees where the birds received no protection from the ants, although such trees were by far the most abundant in the grove.

The Mystery of Anting

Hitherto we have considered interactions of ants and birds that either harm or benefit the latter in definite, readily understood

1. This mannikin belongs to the Old World waxbill or grass-finch family (Estrildidae) and is not related to the New World manakins of the family Pipridae.

ways: ants injure birds by destroying their eggs and young; they serve birds as food, as purveyors of food, by providing nest sites, and by protecting nests that birds build in ant-infested trees. Now we turn to an interaction between these two kinds of organisms, initiated and indeed often eagerly sought by the birds themselves, for advantages which, despite much observation and discussion, continue to puzzle us. This perplexing avian activity is known as "anting," because the bird deliberately applies ants to its plumage, or invites them to crawl through it. By extension, the same term is commonly applied to the act of anointing the feathers in a similar fashion with pungent or odorous materials other than ants.

It is difficult to follow the movements of free birds while they ant and to see exactly what they do with the small object in the tip of the bill. Indeed, it is not easy to watch free birds ant at all, for they usually do so at unpredictable times and places. In nearly half a century of bird watching in tropical America, I have seen only eleven species of birds ant, a few of them on several widely separated occasions, making about twenty brief incidents in all. Naturalists in the north have watched free birds continue to ant for much longer intervals, in circumstances that permitted closer scrutiny of their behavior. But, for an intimate view of the activity, let us turn to the systematic experiments that H. R. Ivor (1943), a Canadian aviculturist, made in his aviary with seventy-three birds of thirty-one species, of which twenty, representing seven families of passerines, actually anted. When Ivor scattered a shovelful of ant-infested soil on the floor, dozens of birds would promptly settle upon it. Sitting or reclining among his fearless birds, he was able to watch them at reading distance. Even in such exceptionally favorable conditions, he found it hard to follow the rapid movements of the anting birds. Nevertheless, by repeating his observations many times, he formed a clear picture of what they did. He described his experiences as follows:

> The moment an ant was sighted by any bird which anted, there seemed to be an instantaneous and instinctive reaction. The ant was picked up and held in the tip of the bill; the eyes were partly closed; the wing was held out from the body

but only partly spread; the wrist was drawn forward and raised, thus bringing the tips of the primaries far forward and touching the ground; the tail was always brought forward and under to some extent, on the same side as the extended wing, and often so far that the feet were placed upon it. Stepping on the tail at times caused the bird to fall on its side or even on its back. The ant, which may or may not have been crushed, *was swiftly rubbed on the ventral surface of the outer primary or primaries, beginning, so far as could be seen, just below the wrist and extending to the tip.* I could not determine whether or not the ant was rubbed on more than one primary; whether it was rubbed on the shaft, the margin or the inner web; certainly it was never rubbed on the dorsal surface. (Ivor 1943, p. 52)

Ivor never saw one of his birds rub an ant on any other part of the plumage, or on the legs, or deposit an ant amid the feathers. After its application to the wing feathers, the ant was sometimes eaten and sometimes discarded. It is noteworthy that of the thirty-one species tested, ten failed to ant but ate the insects. Only one, the Pine Siskin, neither anted nor ate ants.

During the height of the anting season, from mid-April to near the end of July, "the act of anting seemed to engender a state of ecstasy so overwhelming that even domination and enmity were forgotten." Others have also noticed that birds become so intensely absorbed in anting that they lose their habitual wariness, often becoming oblivious to danger to a degree that is rare even while they eat. To some watchers, anting birds, tumbling over or turning a backward somersault, have appeared intoxicated or delirious. We may wonder how rubbing an ant along a feather, as devoid of nerves as a mammalian hair, can yield pleasant sensations. Yet it may be helpful to remember that grooming and being groomed appears to give great satisfaction to monkeys, apes, certain rodents, and other mammals, hairy and not so hairy.

Most observers agree that the under surface of the wings, especially the tips of the primary feathers, is the chief target of the anting bird; certainly all that I have watched ant in the tropics were placing their heads beneath their partly extended wings. The base of the forwardly directed tail, against which the wing tips are often pressed, is sometimes also treated. Lovie M. Whitaker[2] who made an exceptionally thorough study of anting and its extensive, widely scattered literature, was impressed by how often her hand-raised female Orchard Oriole applied the ants, singly or in clusters grasped in the bill's tip, to the under tail coverts and base of the tail. Her bird dabbed with rapidly quivering head instead of stroking the feathers with the ants. Although occasionally the oriole touched them to her sides and flanks, this appeared to be unintended. Only rarely have birds been reported to apply ants to the back or rump, or even the outer surfaces of the wing quills, whose inner sides receive so much attention. Common Grackles, which anoint practically all accessible parts of their plumage, ant with various aromatic materials, such as walnut hulls and orange skin, perhaps more frequently than with insects.

In addition to the active anting that has so far engaged our attention, some birds ant "passively": they sit or sprawl on an ant-hill or ant-infested ground, spread their feathers, and permit the ants to run all over them, doubtless often reaching, and biting, their skins. Sometimes they lie as though sunbathing; or else they sit with body almost erect, tail extended over the ground, and wings spread widely in front of the breast, their tips touching the ground so that the ants can run up them—an attitude assumed by passively anting European Jays. Passive anting is practiced chiefly by birds at least as big as one of the larger jays or thrushes, including certain crows, quails, and grouse. Occasionally the passively anting bird takes an ant in its bill and applies it to its plumage, thereby combining the two methods of anting, or it makes the movements of active anting with empty bill. Apparently, passive anting has not been recorded in tropical America.

K. E. L. Simmons, who treated anting in an article on "Feather Maintenance" that he wrote for the *New Dictionary of Birds* (1964), knew of over 200 species in over thirty passerine families for which anting had been recorded. In the years that have elapsed since that was written, other species have been added. Simmons was not convinced that any of the recorded instances of anting by nonpasserines should be so designated. But in her list (antedating

2. Whitaker (1957) gives a comprehensive bibliography of anting. More recent literature is cited by Potter and Hauser (1974).

the article by Simmons) of 148 anting species, Whitaker included sixteen nonpasserines: seven members of the pheasant family, four kinds of woodpeckers, three of parrots, the Wild Turkey, and the Great Horned Owl.

Although widespread, especially among passerines, anting is certainly very sporadic—a conclusion that does not rest wholly on the obviously fragmentary observations of the activity in free birds. A Painted Bunting that for thirty-one months was the constant companion of Whitaker's persistently anting Orchard Oriole never indulged in this activity, nor did a House Sparrow, Loggerhead Shrike, or Black-billed Magpie that were repeatedly given an opportunity to do so. Yet several other people have watched House Sparrows and magpies ant, as likewise Indigo and Lazuli buntings, close relatives of the Painted Bunting. Similarly, at least half of the ten species that always remained aloof from the anting parties in Ivor's aviary have been seen anting elsewhere. In 1,496 hours of watching at ant swarms where two to eight Bicolored Antbirds were present, Edwin O. Willis (1967, p. 32) noticed anting only twenty-six times. This spotty distribution of anting among species and individuals must be given full weight when we try to fathom its significance. An essential activity, such as preening, is commonly practiced by every individual of a species, if not by all birds everywhere.

As the name implies, anting is most often done with ants, usually with species in which the sting is vestigial or absent, although Willis's Bicolored Antbirds sometimes used stinging army ants (*Eciton burchelli*) and another stinging species, *Ectatomma ruidum*. Most often, especially in temperate North America and in Europe, birds have been seen anting with species of the subfamily Formicinae, which do not sting but spray their enemies with formic acid, sometimes ejecting it as far as twenty inches. Even when such ants are not applied directly to the bird's skin, they might moisten it with acid if the feathers are erected to expose it. Whitaker's oriole anted with stingless species which from anal glands exude a repugnant liquid, smelling of rancid butter, that is evidently butyric acid. Bravely testing with her tongue the ants that her oriole used, Whitaker found that all produced a burning sensation, especially when crushed. The stronger the ant's heating effect, the more intensely the oriole anted with it.

In most of the anting episodes that I have witnessed, the species used was *Camponotus senex textor,* a small, wholly harmless ant that, by means of its larvae, weaves silken nests amid clustered leaves.

In lieu of ants, birds have anted with at least forty other items, living or lifeless and mostly odorous or pungent. Wasps, beetles, earwigs, grasshoppers, bugs, and centipedes are among the arthropods employed. Inanimate materials with which birds have anted include moth balls, limes, pieces of orange peel, hulls of English walnuts, downy leaves, table mustard, vinegar, hot chocolate, soapsuds, and hair tonic. A Blue Jay anted with burning cigarette stubs; a Rook, with lighted cigarettes, extinguished but still hot cigarettes and matches, and small live embers. With empty bill, this same bird went through the motions of anting when it could expose its body to smoke.

In the North Temperate Zone, the great majority of recorded anting episodes occurred on the ground, often on a lawn or golf course, where anthills are not uncommon. Not infrequently, birds have anted on pavements or graveled roadways. Among the much less numerous instances of birds anting in trees was that of the Blue Jays that Eloise F. Potter (1970, p. 700) watched perform in the top of a mature pine.

The anthills that I have most often noticed in tropical America are the small, loose heaps of soil that fire ants raise on lawns and pastures; but, as far as I can learn, birds of all kinds leave this peppery ant strictly alone. They also ignore the spiny Atta ants, which march over the ground, bearing small pieces of green leaves, in long columns that pour into deep subterranean chambers. Birds very rarely ant with the army ants that they follow for other ends. This leaves the many kinds of arboreal nests as the kinds most readily available for anting. All the anting episodes that I have witnessed in the tropics took place in trees or shrubs, never on the ground. Even the terrestrial Buff-rumped Warbler anted low in a tree. The other birds involved were the Tawny-winged Dendrocincla, Streaked-headed Woodcreeper, Barred Woodcreeper, Plain Xenops, Oleaginous Pipromorpha or Ochre-bellied Flycatcher, Green Honeycreeper, Blue Tanager, Speckled Tanager, Buff-throated Saltator, and Variable Seedeater. I saw the xenops ant on three or four widely separated occasions, the dendrocincla and the honeycreeper thrice, the Blue Tanager twice, the Speckled Tanager twice (mated birds simultaneously), and each of the others only once. While anting in a tree, the bird often brings its tail forward, under the body, as far as its perch permits. Sometimes it rubs the inside of the wing and the underside of the tail in one sweeping movement. My Variable Seedeater hung upside down while anting, as Whitaker's oriole sometimes did when she anted clinging to the wire mesh of her cage wall.

It was amusing to watch a Barred Woodcreeper ant. I met the big brown creeper just within the edge of tall second-growth woods, beside a pasture. It picked from the bark of a tree a large, dark-colored insect that might have been an ant, and, holding it between the tips of its strong mandibles, rubbed it beneath a wing, then swallowed it, as I clearly saw. Next, the bird clung beside a large silken nest of *Camponotus* ants that it found nearby, apparently plucked off an ant, and, extending a wing forward, rubbed it beneath the partly spread primary feathers. Again it clung beside the ants' nest, and again it passed its bill beneath a wing. It did this repeatedly, while it perched on, or rather clung from, slender branches near the silken nest, in a posture I had never before seen a woodcreeper take—a posture that would have been more appropriate for a bird that perches. That this was not a natural or secure position for the big woodcreeper was attested by the fact that several times it lost its balance and seemed on the verge of falling. Except in the first instance, I could not see whether it swallowed the ants that apparently it rubbed beneath its wings. Later, I watched a dendrocincla ant while clinging in a similarly awkward attitude.

One of the oldest observations on anting (in the broad sense) was published in 1847 in *The Birds of Jamaica* by Philip Henry Gosse. A friend told him how the Tinkling Grackle, now known as the Greater Antillean Grackle, would pick up a fallen lime in its bill and carry it up to a perch. Here, holding it in a foot, it gently rubbed the aromatic fruit over its side, beneath a wing, then transferred the lime to the other foot and rubbed the other side in the same way. The grackles would continue this procedure by the hour. This is the only record I know of a bird anting with an object held in a foot, but it is not incredible in an icterid, others of which, including the Baltimore Oriole, hold plucked flowers beneath a foot while extracting the nectar.

Records of anting by tropical American birds are not numerous. In Mexico, Miguel Alvarez del Toro (quoted in Whitaker 1957) noticed anting by the Golden-fronted Woodpecker, Gray's Thrush, Black-throated Oriole, Streaked-backed Oriole, and Red-throated Ant-Tanager. In Brazil, Helmut Sick (1957) watched two small tanagers, the Blue-necked and the Gilt-edged, performing so high in trees, and so briefly, that he was not sure that they held ants when they pased their bills beneath their wings. While studying the attendants of army ants, Edwin O. Willis (1967; 1968; 1969; 1972*a*; 1972*b*) noticed anting by the Plain Brown Dendrocincla and four species of antbirds—Bicolored, Spotted, Lunulated, and White-breasted. Mostly they used insects other than army ants. In captivity, far from their native homes in tropical America, the Purplish-backed Jay, Slate-colored Solitaire, Blue or Turquoise Dacnis, Troupial, Seven-colored Tanager, and Yellow-billed Cardinal have anted.

Anting is contagious behavior. The sight of one bird anting often attracts another, of the same or a different kind, which joins the first or else supplants it among the ants. Although the anting episodes that I have seen lasted at most a few minutes, some birds persist surprisingly long. Horace Groskin (1943) watched a Scarlet Tanager continue, with short interruptions, for more than an hour; and G. H. Parks (1945) saw an equally protracted anting session by a Common Grackle using green magnolia fruits. Whitaker's female Orchard Oriole commonly continued to apply ants to her plumage for twenty-five minutes, but sometimes the bird persisted until the ants were removed after three-quarters of an hour. She might ant on as many as ten consecutive days. In one month, she performed on at least nineteen of the twenty-four days when she had an opportunity to do so, and on some of these days in both morning and afternoon. Evidently anting was a favorite or a compulsive occupation of this well-fed captive bird. After a long, strenuous anting session, she appeared weary and often slept.

Why do birds ant? Most of the things that we see birds do are obviously useful to them, but what can they gain by applying ants or some substitute to their plumage? The explanations of this strange procedure are almost as diverse as the objects, living and lifeless, that birds have been seen using instead of ants. An old explanation was that birds stick ants among their feathers as rations on their long migratory journeys, much as a human traveler carries food in his knapsack. But none of the previously mentioned tropical American birds that anted is known to be migratory. Others have watched anting by captives unable to travel, or by free migratory species settled in their summer homes, months away from their fall migration. Moreover, after anting, the ants are either eaten or discarded, not left in the plumage. Birds have better ways of storing fuel for long migratory flights; they lay up fat beneath the skin, where it does not distort their streamlined forms, as a substantial quantity of insects attached to their plumage might do.

Another suggestion is that the formic acid sprayed by certain kinds of ants when roughly handled acts as an insect repellent and is applied by birds to remove parasites. This explanation could at best be valid in a minority of cases. Many of the ants used do not excrete formic acid, and some anting birds have been carefully examined without detecting any external parasites. Most anting birds apply the insects only to the larger wing feathers, and perhaps also the tail feathers, while, if parasites were present, they would probably be most numerous, and certainly most irritating, in the body plumage. The same consideration weakens the view that the secretions of ants, formic acid or otherwise, somehow help to keep the plumage in good condition. If these secretions are so beneficial, why do so many birds apply them so extremely locally instead of giving as much as possible of their plumage the benefit of the treatment? The notion that the formic acid in the ants which the birds often swallow after anting combats internal parasites is worthy of investigation.

The old idea that anting is a method of preparing insects for eating has been newly supported by Willis (1972b), who noticed that, at the army ant swarms, it was practiced chiefly by low-ranking birds excluded from the best positions for foraging and, presumably, taking less desirable insects, whose distasteful secretions they rubbed off on their plumage. Plain Brown Dendrocinclas, whom he saw ant sixty-seven times, alternately chewed various items in the tips of their bills, shook them, and brushed them through their wing quills or under tail coverts. After this treatment, they usually ate the prey but sometimes dropped it, then repeatedly wiped their bills, as though to remove an unpleasant taste. Although perhaps applicable to certain special cases, this can hardly be a generally valid explanation of anting, for the correlation between anting and eating the object so used is low. Of birds given the same kind of ants, some eat the insects without applying them to their plumage, others may either swallow or toss aside those they use for anting. Moreover, one might suppose that birds would prefer to wipe the unpleasant secretion upon a twig or trunk instead of carrying it around on their plumage, as though a person were to clean his food on his clothes.

A more subtle notion is that ants' secretions, spread over the plumage, produce vitamin D in sunlight, as oil from the preen gland does. Ingested during preening, this would supplement the anting bird's usual supply—a possibility that appears not to have been tested. Others have speculated that formic acid, which has been used to give tone to human muscles and alleviate their fatigue, may be similarly comforting to birds.

The notion that anting soothes the skin or yields pleasant sensations has been widely held. Examining all available dated records of anting by free birds in temperate North America, and collating them with long-continued observations of her own, Potter (1970) found that the activity had been recorded for more individuals of more species in August than in any other month. August is also the time when nearly all North American passerines molt. From this, she concluded that birds ant to soothe skin irritated by new feather growth. Heavy or prolonged rainfall during the molting season induces unusually intense anting, an activity that is most often seen between dawn and ten o'clock in the morning, when all avian activity tends to be greatest. Potter and Hauser (1974) regarded anting and sunbathing as alternative methods of soothing skin irritated by molting.

Whitaker suspected that her Orchard Oriole so often applied ants to the base of the tail feathers and the under tail coverts because the thermogenic ants that the bird preferred produced a pleasantly warm sensation, perhaps stimulating her sexually. However, Whitaker considered the possibility that the ants were used to relieve irritation caused by undetected minute parasites in the oriole's anal region. Other observers have been impressed by the ecstatic or beatific attitude of the anting bird, its indifference to threats or approaches that ordinarily cause flight or withdrawal, as though it would permit nothing to interrupt its intense enjoyment.

If the anting episodes that I have watched gave pleasure, it was certainly not prolonged. Sometimes, indeed, the anting bird appears far from happy. The whole plumage of Derek Goodwin's anting European Jay soon became a seething mass of ants, which swarmed up its legs, wings, and tail. "How the bird can stand it is astonishing," wrote Goodwin, "and indeed its whole demeanour suggests a scarcely bearable irritation. When an ant (presumably) chances to squirt formic acid into the Jay's eye the bird at once closes it, hops away and stands as if dazed with pain for a second or two, but soon returns to the ants. Invariably as soon as it has finished anting the Jay takes a most vigorous and thorough water bath, followed by equally thorough preening" (Goodwin 1951, p. 622). The Jay's session with the ants appears to be a compulsive activity rather than a source of pleasure.

The rule that the number of explanations of a phenomenon is inversely proportional to our understanding holds with full force in the case of anting. Some of the benefits attributed to the activity may indeed be real yet far from being generally associated with it, and they may be incidental rather than the reason for its origin. Accordingly, they provide no adequate explanation of the behavior in its whole breadth and depth. Since anting is practiced by hand-reared birds that have had no opportunity to watch others perform, it is evidently an innate rather than a learned activity, although it may be modified by experience. The typical movements of active anting, so widespread and similar among passerine birds of many families, point to the inheritance of this habit from a common ancestor. Probably we would need to know under what conditions, in response to what needs, this hypothetical ancestor acquired the habit, in order to understand it.

Possibly anting was originally performed with some particular species of ant, or group of related species, that benefitted the birds in a certain way, perhaps by secreting formic acid. The descendants of the ancestral anters, scattered widely over the Earth in diverse ecological situations with different ant faunas, innately recognize ants and associate them with the activity of anting, but they appear not at first to discriminate between species, although from experience they may acquire certain preferences, selecting some kinds for anting but ignoring others. They may even fail to distinguish ants from other small insects. Their failure to discriminate between species may lead to anting with kinds of ants that do not yield the benefits for which anting originally developed.

Whereas some birds are incited to ant by seeing the insects, others appear to be stimulated to do so by tastes or scents, especially by such as are strong or pungent. Here, again, we notice an amazing absence of selectivity. It is most unlikely that all the substances which birds may use for anting, especially in the neighborhood of man, can benefit their plumage, and some may injure it. However, if anting often proved harmful, it would have been eliminated by natural selection. Probably, even if it frequently fails to serve its original purpose, it does so often enough, or has acquired enough secondary uses (which may vary from bird to bird) to have ensured its perpetuation in many individuals of a substantial number of passerine families. Can it often be no more than a pleasure that leaves no ill effects?

Not only is anting one of the most perplexing of avian activities; in the light of our imperfect understanding, it frequently appears to be one of the most useless or irrational. If, for a moment, we may forget evolutionary theory and avian psychology to indulge in a flight of fancy, we might imagine that anting birds, who often leave the ground strewn with mangled, dying or dead ants, are wreaking vengeance on the insects that so often destroy their nestlings.

CHAPTER 13

The Dawn Songs of Tropical Birds

Boat-billed Flycatcher

Of the special ways that birds sing, one of the most curious and arresting is the dawn song. Many birds are most vocal at daybreak; but some deliver in the dim early light songs that they rarely repeat during the remainder of the day unless they are highly excited. A few exceptional species resume their twilight singing after sunset. Dawn songs are largely the contributions of less gifted musicians, chiefly among the American flycatchers and related families, and a few of the less musical songbirds. Although the flood of liquid melody that thrushes pour over the earth at daybreak is often called a dawn chorus, these superb songsters sing much at all hours of the day, with the same notes, if not the same long-sustained effort, as at dawn; so that, to avoid confusion, we might reserve the term "dawn song" for a twilight performance that differs substantially from the phrases that the same bird commonly delivers in full daylight.

North Americans whose zeal takes them from their beds early on summer mornings have heard the dawn song of the Eastern Wood Pewee, which has received high praise for its musical quality. Resting upon a high, exposed perch in the gray early light, the small gray bird repeats his simple phrases with variations that diminish monotony. The two phrases most frequently uttered sound like *peeé-we* and *pe wé*, both delivered with rising inflection, but with the emphasis alternately on the long-drawn first syllable and the shorter second syllable. At unpredictable intervals, the little flycatcher varies this regular alternation with a phrase in falling inflection that often passes unnoticed by the human listener. While singing, he twists from side to side on his high perch and often executes an about-face. For many minutes, he continues with hardly a pause; but before the moon has paled he ceases; and one rarely hears this song again until, in the dim light of late evening, he resumes it for a shorter interval. This twilight song appears to be a musical elaboration of the pewee's familiar, plaintive call note, which may be heard at almost any hour of the day.

Happily, at low latitudes the bird watcher need not so drastically curtail his sleep in order to hear the dawn songs of flycatchers. These auroral recitals by members of the largest avian family in the Americas are so numerous and varied that they add substantially to the total volume of natural sounds in the New World. Some are rarely beautiful and pure in tone; others so quaint that one might imagine them to be the accompaniment of a fantastic elfin dance; yet others seem to express forlorn dejection; a few amaze us by their insistent harshness; and some display no noteworthy quality, unless it be their tireless persistence.

First for sweetness of tone among all the flycatchers' dawn songs I place those of the big, yellow-breasted species of *Myiodynastes*. Their appealing softness is the more surprising because the usual notes of these hole-nesting flycatchers incline toward unpleasant sharpness or harshness. The dawn song of the migratory Sulphur-bellied Flycatcher is an utterance of rare beauty. Perching in the dim gray light of early dawn upon an exposed leafless twig at the very top of a lofty tree, he repeats tirelessly, over and over, in a soft, liquid voice, *tre-le-re-re, tre-le-re-re.* I have timed him while he continued this attractive refrain for more than a quarter of an hour, without intermission. What a contrast between this soft, cool, pellucid dawn song and the high pitched, strained, excited notes that he voices later in the day, when he seems to call *Weel-yum, Weel-yum,* like an old dame screaming in a cracked voice for her distant grandson!

The big Streaked Flycatcher, which closely resembles the Sulphur-bellied in plumage, likewise seeks a high, conspicuous station to deliver his soft, sweet, clear-toned *kawé teedly wink,* which he may repeat with scarcely a pause for nearly half an hour. Like the Eastern Wood-Pewee, he often sings after sunset in the same pleasant strain, and at times more briefly, in a more subdued voice, in full daylight. One March, a partial eclipse of the sun caused a Streaked Flycatcher to begin his crepuscular song soon after four o'clock in the afternoon. The Golden-bellied Flycatcher of the epiphyte-burdened forests of the Costa Rican highlands has an equally attractive dawn song, a soft, musical *tree-le-loo,* which sometimes he may be heard repeating later in the morning, close by the mossy nest that his mate has built in a cranny among the matted roots of epiphytes, high in a moss-draped tree, or on a verdant cliff beside a waterfall. By contrast, the call notes of this rare, little-known flycatcher are high and sharp.

For loud, stirring notes, none of the other flycatchers quite equals the Boat-billed, one of the largest members of this multitudinous family. Resting in the gray dawn high in a tree, sometimes that in which his mate will soon build her open nest, he tirelessly repeats a clear, spirited, ringing note that sounds like *cheer.* At irregular intervals, he punctuates this loud call with a very different slurred note, *bo-oy.* He may continue this for over half an hour. I have never heard him sing in the evening twilight. His usual daytime call is a whining *churr.*

Although nearly as big as the Boat-billed Flycatcher, the Tropical Kingbird delivers a much weaker, softer dawn song, which seems to issue from the throat of a smaller bird. Over vast areas in the warmer parts of the Americas, the high-pitched twitter of this widespread flycatcher is one of the first bird notes to greet the newborn day. The clear, pleasing notes rise as though by steps, in two or three series, each consisting of a few rapidly trilled syllables. Usually each ascending sequence is preceded by an indefinite number of short, distinct (not trilled), clear notes, sounding like *pit*. The whole song may be represented so:

where short dashes represent the note *pit*, the zigzag lines the trilled notes. Early in the nesting season, this performance continues, with brief intermissions, for about half an hour. The high-pitched twitter that the kingbird utters later in the day is readily distinguished from his dawn song.

Another noteworthy twilight song is that of the yellow-breasted Vermilion-crowned or Chipsacheery Flycatcher, who announces his name quite distinctly, a hundred times over, before sunrise on April and May mornings. His voice is pleasant and earnest rather than musical, and he interposes simple monosyllables and disyllables among the repetitions of his characteristic polysyllable, thus: *chipsacheery pe-ah chip chup chipsacheery, pe-ah . . .* , and so on, endlessly. This is the song of the race *Myiozetetes similis columbianus*, as I have heard it in the Térraba Valley of Costa Rica. The northern race of this same species, *M. similis texensis*, has a quite distinct dawn song—one of the most striking examples that I know of geographical variation in the voice of a single species. The song of the latter consists of a clear monosyllable, *cheee*, repeated a variable number of times, followed by a garbled version of the distinctly enunciated *chipsacheery* of the southern race. These flycatchers begin later than many of the dawn-singing members of their family, and they sometimes continue into the broad daylight, after the others have become silent.

Although the related Gray-capped Flycatcher differs only slightly from the Vermilion-crowned in appearance, he has a very different dawn song. In the dim early light, when all the bird world raises its paean to the newborn day, he shouts out, over and over, *hic, bit of a cold; hic, bit of a cold.* At least, this is what I seem to hear him crying; and his hoarse, strained voice makes it easy to believe that he is telling the truth about himself. Gray-caps do not perform as long or as continuously as many other flycatchers. Later in the day, they are among the noisiest members of their family, frequently shouting in thick, quaint voices; but they deliver their harsh dawn song only at daybreak in the nesting season, more rarely in the evening twilight, and under the stress of unusual excitement while the sun is high.

For quaintness, no other dawn songs that I know surpass those of the little, high-crested Tufted Flycatchers of the Central American mountains. In Guatemala they sang for many minutes in the morning twilight, in high, thin voices: *de bee, de bee, de bic a de bee, de bic bee, de bee* . . . Equally amusing is the dawn song of the southern race of the Tufted Flycatcher in the Costa Rican highlands. The odd little ditty is sung in the highest and thinnest of voices, so rapidly that I tried vainly to distinguish every syllable. Although the following paraphrase cannot claim accuracy, it may at least suggest the song's character: *bip-bip-bip didididup-bip-bip-bibibiseer* . . . This should be read as fast as human lips can move, and then allowance made for the more rapid utterance of the bird. The final syllable, *seer*, is abruptly ascending. Continued breathlessly for fifteen or twenty minutes, this singular refrain might set the tempo of an elfin dance.

Quaint, too, is the dawn song of the Lesser or Bellicose Elaenia. In a dry, lackluster voice, this small flycatcher repeats rapidly a phrase that sounds like *a we d' de de.* Often in the evening twilight, and far more rarely at dawn, this dweller in low thickets and weedy fields mounts high into the sky to sing his odd refrain. The rather similar dawn song of the Mountain Elaenia consists in the monotonous repetition of a dry *d'weet.* Sometimes the performance is slightly varied: *d'weet, d'weet, d'weet a d'weet,* or *cheet a cheet, cheet a cheet, cheet a cheet* . . . From time to time, the gray bird diversifies his modest ditty with a low, soft, plaintive trill that seems to emanate from a melancholy spirit. (The Lesser Elaenia never utters notes in keeping with such a mood.) I have heard Mountain Elaenias, perching in the tops of low trees scattered through a mountain pasture, sing continuously for many minutes around eight o'clock in the morning, while a dense enveloping cloud cast a twilight dimness over the landscape.

Another odd dawn song is the *Fred-rick fear*, clearly enunciated over and over, of the Dark Pewee, a neighbor of the Mountain Elaenia and the Tufted Flycatcher in the Costa Rican highlands. The related Greater Pewee of the Guatemalan mountains also quite unmistakably warns Frederick to fear, but neither bird re veals what he is to be afraid of.

The Dusky-capped Flycatcher, an inhabitant of light woodlands and shady clearings, more widespread than any other of these quaint minstrels, sings a more varied song, containing a short, sharp *whit*, a long-drawn, plaintive *wheeeu*, an emphatic whistle cut off short, *whee-do*, and a long, harsh trill. These diverse notes, mixed in varying proportions, are dispensed with scarcely a pause from the first promise of the new day until that promise has been fulfilled. This bird sometimes sings an evensong, too; and on cloudy afternoons its harsh, long-drawn whistles and plaintive trills float down from the tops of trees at the forest's edge, but rarely in a long-continued song, as in the twilight.

For persistent asseveration, in tones that sound angry rather than good-humored, no other flycatcher that I know can match the little, gray, loose-crested Yellow-bellied Elaenia. While the stars still twinkle brightly overhead, and only the paleness above the eastern horizon announces the approach of a new day, he awakes in the thicket where he slept and sounds a long-drawn, harsh *weeer*, in a questioning voice, as though he demanded an-grily to know who had dared to arouse him so unreasonably early. The interrogation may be repeated after a brief interval, and soon it is followed by a harsh *we do*, vehemently assertive. Now for perhaps half an hour the assertion is endlessly reiterated. Al-though the elaenia has a varied vocabulary, his other notes are re-served for later in the day; while performing in the twilight, he limits himself strictly to these two notes, *we do*. The only lati-tude he allows himself is to pronounce them from time to time in a tone even more fiercely insistent.

We do, we do, we do, WE DO, we do, we do . . . he declaims interminably, until the hearer, however incredulous at first, is constrained to admit that they do—whatever it might be that the importunate bird claims that they do. Although many flycatchers mount high in the trees for their dawn singing, the elaenia is content to declaim from a lower perch, possibly that upon which he roosted. In keeping with his seemingly belligerent mood, he lays his crest flat while he performs, like a horse with ears laid back, ready to fight. During the remainder of the day, he voices the notes of his dawn song even more rarely than other flycatchers. I have seldom heard him sing in the evening twilight.

In the mournful, plaintive quality of his dawn song, no other flycatcher quite equals the Paltry Tyranniscus. His is the most self-effacingly melancholy outpouring that I have heard from any bird. *Yer-de-dee, yer-de-dee* the wee gray bird whispers, then voices a faint, quavering, forlorn *pe-pe-pe*. Some individuals add a slight, clear trill at dawn, but most greet the new day as though dismayed by the prospect of living through it. Plaintive, too, but not so ineffably dejected, is the dawn song of the Black Phoebe: *fé-be, fe-bé, fé-be, fe-bé*, monotonously continued. Phoebe delivers his dawn song in full daylight more often than most flycatchers. Sometimes he sings while flying around with the axis of his body nearly vertical.

The dawn songs of certain flycatchers are perhaps most noteworthy for their monotony. Among these is the song of the Olive-chested Flycatcher, which in September and October I heard in the eastern foothills of the Ecuadorian Andes and have described in Chapter 4. This bird has sometimes been classified as a race of the widespread Bran-colored Flycatcher and sometimes as a separate species. Although I have seen much of the Bran-colored Flycatcher in Costa Rica, I never heard it sing a dawn song there. Possibly these two closely similar forms differ in this respect.

At Esmeraldas in western Ecuador, I heard the Vermilion Flycatcher perform in an equally monotonous way at dawn, when he tirelessly repeated a simple phrase of two syllables. While I visited a coffee plantation in eastern Costa Rica, a Tropical Pewee sang at great length every morning, in a tree just beyond my bedroom window. *Weet weet weet*, he proclaimed, in a high, sharp voice. At times he interrupted the monotonous reiteration of this monosyllable with a low, musical disyllable, *we-ye*, which sometimes he prolonged into a short, low warble.

While male flycatchers sing long and tirelessly at daybreak, the

females, more than those of any other avian family that I know
intimately, sing in their nests, with little trills and warbles, soft
churring notes, and low-voiced murmurings—utterances that
suggest contentment and perhaps also maternal devotion. Could
Lowell have been thinking of a flycatcher when he wrote:

> He sings to the wide world, and she to her nest,—
> In the nice ear of Nature which song is the best?[1]

In the cotinga family, I have heard only one species give a dawn
song, although doubtless certain others do so. This is the White-
winged Becard, a sparrow-sized bird that wanders through clearings with scattered trees and along the forest edges, usually staying high. Few birds have softer, sweeter notes than this member
of a family renowned for the loudness rather than the melody of
its utterances. At daybreak the largely black male perches amid
dense foliage while he repeats a verse of about eight dulcet notes
that follow each other so swiftly that they are difficult to count.
Each song begins with an accented note, then falls slightly in
pitch to the final note, which receives a minor emphasis. Sometimes continuing this charming recital for nearly an hour, the becard may deliver three or four hundred songs before he is silenced
by the growing daylight. Individuals in the flycatcherlike olive
and yellowish plumage of the females, possibly young males, sing
like the adults. Sometimes I have found two of these female-
plumaged birds singing competitively late in the day, and even
late in the year, after nesting has ceased.

Although the best avian songsters may sing profusely in the
twilight, they as a rule repeat the same songs freely at other
times; they lack special dawn songs. As we would expect from
this, such songs are exceptional among the true songbirds, the
Oscines; yet we do find them in a few species with poorly developed voices. It is as though at the magic hour of daybreak, when
every tuneful bird raises its voice to celebrate its escape from the
perils of night, when it can hardly see, into the joy and freedom
and fleet-winged security of day, even those little gifted with melody are impelled to swell the blithesome chorus, and they try to

---

1. James Russell Lowell, ''The Vision of Sir Launfal,'' Prelude.

compensate with tireless persistence for what they lack in sweetness and volume of voice.

Many finches are songsters too accomplished to restrict their recitals to the dim light of dawn. Nevertheless, this vast family contains species that are poorly endowed vocally, and some of them sing chiefly, if not exclusively, in the twilight. Among these is the Yellow-thighed Finch of the Costa Rican highlands, a small, dark gray and black bird with lemon-colored thighs, that haunts the edges of the moss-draped, dripping forests of these humid heights. At daybreak the male delivers a short, rapid, breezy ditty, in a peculiar high, dry tone. One seemed to sing *tee tiddy dee dee wink wink*. Another had a shorter refrain, which fitted the words *pity me sweet*; after he had repeated this many times, he added another syllable and sang *pity me sweet sweet*. Still another Yellow-thighed Finch sang *diddidchercherup* very rapidly in a thin, rather sharp voice that increased in volume toward the end of each phrase. These high-pitched, bizarre utterances, repeated tirelessly before sunrise but rarely later in the day, resemble the songs of flycatchers more than those of the more tuneful finches and sparrows. After sunrise, I heard Yellow-thighed Finches sing only their longer, tinkling greeting song. This chiming utterance is given by both members of a pair as they come together after a separation; but, as far as I could learn, the dawn song belongs exclusively to the male.

The Yellow-throated Brush-Finch is another finch with a weak voice, which sings long and continuously in the dim morning twilight but sparingly later in the day. It is widespread in the Central American highlands. In the mountains of Guatemala, one bird seemed to lament:

> O see me! O see!
> I'm weary, pity me,

in a voice quite in keeping with the burden of his dirge.

The honeycreepers are a family of very small songbirds often clad in the most brilliant plumage, but poorly endowed with song. None that I have heard is a good songster; but the widespread, yellow-breasted Bananaquit is a persistent vocalist, who repeats his animated, squeaky trills through much of the day and much of the year. The exquisite Blue or Red-legged Honeycreeper has a true dawn song. Of the utmost simplicity, it consists of the monotonous repetition of a single note, a clear but weak and somewhat plaintive *tsip*, repeated at intervals of a second or two, with the interjection, after every two or three of these notes, of the honeycreeper's usual, rather nasal, mewing call: *tsip tsip chaa tsip tsip chaa tsip tsip tsip chaa* . . . and so on, interminably, until his weak voice is silenced by the growing light, as though unworthy of a bird so splendidly enameled. Although I have studied with some care the nest life of the Blue Honeycreeper, I never heard him sing except in the morning twilight, in the manner of the flycatchers.

The brilliant tanagers are mostly poor songsters, so that we might expect to find a number of dawn singers in this family. Nevertheless, as far as I know, true dawn songs are given only by the Red-crowned Ant-Tanager, which, paradoxically, is one of the family's better songsters. One July, I watched birds on a beautiful coffee plantation in the department of Quezaltenango on the Pacific slope of Guatemala. Here deep, narrow valleys were separated by long, steep-sided ridges. On the ridges grew the coffee bushes, shaded by high trees of many kinds, some of which had been spared for this purpose when the original forest was felled. The ravines were filled with dense, tangled vegetation, which sheltered many retiring birds who found the plantations too open and exposed. Among them were ant-tanagers of two species, the Red-crowned and the Red-throated.

At dawn, the Red-crowned Ant-Tanagers would leave the thickets where they lurked all day and mount to high, exposed branches of the shade trees in the plantations on the ridges, sometimes choosing the topmost twig of a lofty tree. Here they sang for half an hour or more before sunrise, with clear, far-carrying notes answering each other from neighboring ridges and filling all the air with melody. At this late season, no other birds sang so long and continuously at dawn. I noticed considerable individual variation in the verses of the tanagers, which consisted of seven to nine loud, sweet notes that suggested plaintive earnestness rather than overflowing, light-hearted joy. One tanager repeated his pretty verse, at the rate of eight times per minute, for thirty-three minutes with hardly a pause. His was no exceptional performance, for some of his neighbors sang for nearly an hour.

The ant-tanagers began their dawn songs later than the Gray's Thrushes and most of their other bird neighbors, possibly because they snatched a bite of breakfast before embarking upon their long course of song; possibly, also, because in the dense, tangled thickets deep in the ravines where they slept, daylight came later to awaken them. When all were singing, they made such a volume of sound that songsters of other species were hardly audible. Although each tanager seemed too absorbed in his own performance to pay much attention to the others, the general effect was that of responsive singing rather than a chorus. While an ant-tanager sang, he sometimes, possibly always, spread and exposed the usually concealed scarlet feathers in the center of his crown; but only by stationing myself on some neighboring, higher hilltop could I enjoy a satisfactory, if distant, view of the singing birds. After remaining for half an hour or more on the same lofty perch, each tanager glided abruptly, sometimes seeming almost to fall, from the treetop down a steep slope to the thicket where he dwelt. Through the remainder of the day, I heard these tanagers give only rare, brief snatches of song, never from the elevated stations that they favored at daybreak.

In the forests on the Pacific slope of southern Costa Rica, the dawn-songs of Red-crowned Ant-Tanagers of another race claim attention from late January or February until May or June. Instead of rising to high, exposed perches as their northern cousins do, these birds prefer to sing from concealment, usually while resting low amid the exceedingly dense tangle of bushes and vines at the forest's edge, where, shy and wary, they are extremely difficult to glimpse in the dim light before sunrise.

The song of this race also differs from that of the Guatemalan race, and to me is less pleasing; it lacks varied phrasing and sweet fluidity of tone and is too mechanical in character to express much feeling. *Peter-bird Peter-bird Peter-bird*, the tanager seems to sing, or at times *intervene, intervene, intervene*, all in a voice loud, bright, and crisp but hardly liquid. He repeats this trisyllable six to fifteen times in a uniform, unbroken flow of sound, then pauses for eight or ten seconds, then resumes his refrain,

continuing so for half an hour or more, until the growing light
has filtered into the dense foliage that conceals his ruddy form.
Later in the day, he delivers this song only sparingly, and then
usually when excited by a rival, just as flycatchers do. But this
loquacious bird, whose loud, rather harsh notes in sharply contrasting tones call attention to himself and his mate in the forest,
has other songs more pleasing than his dawn song. One is a low,
sweet warbling, which at times he has the bad taste to interrupt
by loud, harsh call notes. Less intent upon singing than at dawn,
he breaks this melody short just when one wishes that he would
continue. I have not heard this warble at dawn, and far too seldom
later in the day.

I have dealt imaginatively with these dawn songs, as the most
effective way to give the reader an idea of their character and
charm. However revealing sonagrams may be to the experts who
work with them, to the uninitiated they fail to convey any con-
ception of the quality of a bird's utterance. Although I have dwelt
upon the impression that each dawn song made upon me as I
stood listening to it in the dim light, I never supposed that the
songster felt as I did. The Paltry Tyranniscus that sounded so forlorn may have been no less cheerful than the Tufted Flycatcher
who seemed so merry; the angry-sounding Yellow-bellied Elaenia
may have been in as serene a mood as the sweetly singing
Streaked Flycatcher. Much as we would like to know how each
bird feels as he sings, we must confess our ignorance of his psy-
chic state.

Even the biological function of these twilight songs is not
wholly clear. Most of the dawn singers that I have watched have
stayed too constantly in one spot to demarcate their territory by
their singing stations. Only exceptionally did I find the songster
performing in the nest tree, and sometimes no dawn song was
audible near a nest attended by a male of a species that gives such
songs. Nevertheless, the fact that a territorial dispute evokes
dawn songs at hours when they are not ordinarily heard, suggests
that they are not unrelated to territory. If this is correct, why do
not these flycatchers and other dawn singers proclaim their territories more continuously through the day, as numerous birds do?
Since many of the birds that have claimed our attention in this

chapter live in pairs through much or all of the year and already have mates, they can hardly be singing to attract partners. Probably, if the dawn singing is more than an outlet for brimming exuberance after a restful night, while waiting for the day to grow bright enough for effective foraging, its chief function is to apprise the birds of the location of neighbors, so that they may avoid nesting too close together. Often, while listening to one bird sing his dawn song, I have heard no other of the same species.

The Appreciative Mind

How often, in our moments of supreme delight, when life is at its fullest and best and petty cares forgotten, do we pause to examine the sources of our joy? Certainly not often, for analysis of our situation seems to be more characteristic of intervals when life stagnates, when we are beset by difficulties and sorrows, than when we live most joyously and intensely. Or the pious man may simply thank God for his blessings, without stopping to consider the manifold means by which God works; while those emancipated from traditional modes of thought may thank their enormous good luck to be alive and in such a rewarding situation; or they may accept it all without thought and gratitude. Yet the effort to discover and acknowledge all that contributes to the fulfillment of our lives, however alien to our habits it may be, is a fruitful practice, able to deepen our understanding of ourselves and our world. It may be the foundation of natural piety.

According to our temperament and circumstances, our moments of fulfillment may be frequent or rare, and they may come in the most varied situations: in the midst of a happily united family; in a social gathering; in some exhilarating activity that unites sense and nerve and muscle in harmonious interaction, as in a strenuous and perhaps dangerous sport; in popular acclaim of a political victory or artistic triumph; in a garden; or in the midst of wild nature. Perhaps in this last situation the elements that contribute to our delight are most varied and apparent; moreover, we can contemplate them in uninterrupted solitude.

On a sparkling morning in April, I stood in the tropical rain forest on a ridge near my home. The earliest showers, precursors of the long rainy season, had broken the drought of March, cleared the smoky atmosphere, soaked the parched earth, and refreshed withering vegetation, which seemed to rejoice in renewed life. The sun rose brilliantly into the bluest of skies. All around me amid the verdure, Olive-backed Thrushes, pausing here on their long migration from South America to distant coniferous forests, repeated liquid spirals of song, introducing a boreal note into this tropical woodland. Beside me the clean, slender gray trunk of a palm soared far upward, to spread the long, thin fingers of its fronds in a symmetrical rosette against the sky. The sun's slanting rays, falling obliquely upon the foliage masses of the great trees, set them aglow in diverse shades of green that emphasized the height and cool depths of the umbrageous crowns.

At this season the treetops were full of migrating birds, traveling northward or preparing to depart. Baltimore Orioles, resplendent in orange and black, whistled brightly as they searched for insects amid the high foliage. Now and then a Scarlet Tanager, far overhead, permitted a fleeting glimpse of his brilliance. Chestnut-sided Warblers, including males in bright new nuptial plumage, flitted restlessly through the treetops, where a Yellow-throated Vireo proclaimed his unseen presence with snatches of slow song. From around me in the underwood came the clear trills and harsh little calls of Blue-crowned Manakins, diminutive birds dressed in velvety black, who on this wooded ridge had established a courtship assembly to advertise their availability to the demure green females of their kind. Off in the clearing where the house stood, brown thrushes and black tanagers with vivid scarlet rumps were singing blithely, as though to celebrate the return of the refreshing rains.

As I stood enjoying the incomparable spectacle of tropical nature in its blithest mood, my spirit, soaring upward toward the high treetops and the birds that flitted through them, lived and felt with rare intensity. In this exalted state, I began to reflect upon the immensity, in space and in time, of the forces and processes to which I owed my presence here, the multiplicity of circumstances that contributed to my enjoyment. A star that could contain a million earths was sending its rays through 93 million miles of space to illuminate the woodland for me. This radiant energy had to be filtered and tempered by passage through a blanket of atmosphere many miles thick to remove or mitigate rays that might fall with harmful effects upon the surrounding vegetation, or upon me. Thousands of millions of years of slow evolutionary change were needed to produce the noble and beautiful vegetable forms that delighted me, the colorful and tuneful birds that gladdened my spirit. Without prompting or aid by me, the trees that soared above me had been slowly growing for hundreds of years before I took them under my protection. Some of the birds around me had made long and perilous journeys in order, I could almost believe, to grace my woodland by their presence.

More than this, sunshine, trees, birds—the whole great spectacle of nature—would have meant no more to me than to a stone or a clod of earth had I not been prepared by a long evolution to perceive and respond to them. Sprung from the same vertebrate stock that gave rise to the birds, and perhaps, going much farther back, from the same primitive ancestors that, evolving in a different direction, became the progenitors of trees, I was the product of as many years of evolutionary change as any of the organisms around me. What long ages it took to develop vision like mine, capable of clearly distinguishing small details and of clothing its objects in delightful colors! Countless models must have been tried and discarded, innumerable slight variations tested and rejected or retained, before the human eye was perfected. Similarly with ears that not only respond to a wide range of aerial vibrations but make many of them sources of delight; with noses sensitive to the most delicate fragrance. And, above all, the mind that perceives the surrounding world, greets it joyously, cherishes it in memory, strives to understand it, and perhaps passes a moral judgment upon it—what an immense span of time it took to develop such a mind!

Then I reflected how rare, in the life of an individual and even in that of a community, are moments such as I then experienced, when one responds somewhat adequately, with joyous gratitude, to what nature has been so long preparing for our enjoyment, and preparing us to enjoy. Throughout the valley, men were bending over their machetes, preparing land for sowing, backs rather than eyes turned toward this delightfully blue sky; women were patting out tortillas in smoky kitchens. How many spared a moment to contemplate earth's beauty this fair morning? Farther off, millions of people were toiling in noisy factories, selling things in stuffy shops, feverishly hurrying hither and thither in quest of wealth, lying in pain in hospital beds, drilling for war. Among thousands of people, it seems that only a few, here and there, are at any time so situated, and so endowed by nature, that they can respond to the beauty and wonder of the cosmos with the keen appreciation that it merits.

How much of one's own life, too, is spent in preparation for the short intervals of fruition such as I then enjoyed! I recalled how, earlier in the year, I had been sick, then passed depressing days of convalescence. Later came weeks when the dry-season sky was murky with smoke from fires set to clear fields for planting, when afternoons were oppressively hot and hard to live through. I remembered, too, how difficult it had been for me to establish myself here where I could study and enjoy tropical nature, the long years of effort to pay for my land.

Not only do these privileged moments of fullest realization require a vast preparation, whether on the cosmic or the human side, but their occurrence is precarious. So many contingencies, and some so slight, might prevent them. For miles around, forest as beautiful as that in which I stood had been felled and burnt to make farms. Only because a naturalist from far away had admired and bought this small tract did it still stand. And even with ownership, he could not give it adequate protection; about me on the ground lay rotting trunks of stately palms—ancient growths that thieves had felled for the pound or two of edible tissue at the tender growing point of each one. A mishap on the farm, a strayed horse or cow, an upset in the household, might have kept me from the forest this sparkling morning. A restless night, a toothache, a worrying message, any one of a hundred common accidents might have diminished or all but destroyed my capacity to respond feelingly to earth's beauty on so rare a day.

And even when, after vast preparation, after overcoming countless obstacles and avoiding a thousand possible impediments, one responds to earth's majesty and beauty by fullest living, the interval of exaltation is all too brief. The morning's freshness yields to midday heat; the body's buoyancy at daybreak vanishes with fatigue. Even the mind at length grows weary of that which most delights it.

Despite their fragility, the rare moments when we respond with fullest feeling to nature's glory, when we are glad to be alive and grateful for the privilege of living on so favored a planet, are infinitely precious. They may be the end and justification of the whole immense, inconceivably long process which created the world that we know and placed us in its midst. In them, things the most diverse collaborate to produce a unitary effect; things as great as the sun and as small as a butterfly; as ancient as earth and as young as the morning; as solid as the mighty soaring trunk and as fragile as a flower; as enduring as the mossy gray rock and as fleeting as a bird's song—all are, so to speak, brought to a focus in the appreciative mind.

Doubtless all animals enjoy their existence; certainly we should wish it so. But perhaps only to man, on this planet, is it given to enjoy with gratitude and understanding of the sources of his delight. The two poles between which the universe evolves appear to be the immensity of space and the plasticity of matter, on the one hand, and appreciative, grateful minds on the other. Perhaps the latter, whatever the form of the body that supports them, are the goal or fulfillment of the whole stupendous process, with all the strife and pain that seem inseparable from the movement that gives birth to beauty and joy. At least, since that morning, years ago, when I had this vision, the conviction has grown upon me that this is the most fruitful interpretation of the significance of our presence here.

Whatever most delights us and makes us glad to live on so fair a planet; whatever enhances our existence by its grace and beauty; whatever intensifies our appreciation of nature's vastness and bounty; whatever stirs our imagination and stimulates us to exercise all our powers, mental and physical, in the effort to learn and understand; whatever stiffens our determination to protect the natural world from devastating exploitation—whatever does this for us has a special claim to our love and gratitude. Things the most diverse can exercise this beneficent influence: trees, wildflowers, butterflies, the teeming life of the seas, the immense diversity of glittering crystalline forms, or simply the infinitely varied face of the earth, with its mountains and valleys and plains, its sky adorned with gleaming clouds by day and sparkling stars at night, its sunrises and sunsets—the list of things that bind our spirits to our planet could be made long. For a large and growing number of people, birds are the strongest bond with the living world of nature. They charm us with lovely plumage and melodious songs; our quest of them takes us to the fairest places; to find them and uncover some of their well-guarded secrets we exert ourselves greatly and live intensely. In the measure that we appreciate and understand them and are grateful for our coexistence with them, we help to bring to fruition the agelong travail that made them and us. This, I am convinced, is the highest significance of our relationship with birds.

Bibliography

Arp, W. 1965. *Avifauna venezolana*. Caracas: Banco Central de Venezuela.

Beebe, W. 1918. *Jungle peace*. New York: Henry Holt and Co. (Modern Library reprint, 1925.)

Beebe, W., G. I. Hartley, and P. G. Howes. 1917. *Tropical wild life in British Guiana*, vol. 1. New York: N.Y. Zool. Soc.

Belt, T. 1888. *The naturalist in Nicaragua*. 2d ed. London: Edward Bumpus.

Bent, A. C. 1942. Life histories of North American flycatchers, larks, swallows, and their allies. *U. S. Natl. Mus. Bull.* 179: i–xi, 1–555.

Bond, J. 1936 (and later eds.). *Birds of the West Indies*. London: Collins.

Catalogue of the birds in the British Museum (Natural History), vols. 1–27. 1874–1895. Various authors.

Chapman, F. M. 1929. *My tropical air castle*. New York and London: D. Appleton and Co.

Cherrie, G. K. 1916. A contribution to the ornithology of the Orinoco region. *Mus. Brooklyn Inst. Arts and Sci., Sci. Bull.* 2:133a–374.

Fiebrig, K. 1909. *Biol. Cent.* 29:1ff.

Goeldi, E. A. 1900–1906. *Album de aves amazonicas*. 48 col. pls. Supplement to *Aves do Brasil*, 1894. (Artist, E. Lohse.) Pará: Goeldi Museum.

Goodwin, D. 1951. Some aspects of the behaviour of the jay *Garrulus glandarius*. *Ibis* 93:414–442, 602–625.

Gosse, P. H. 1847. *The birds of Jamaica*. London: John Van Voorst.

Groskin, H. 1943. Scarlet Tanagers "anting." *Auk* 60:55–59.

Hindwood, K. A. 1959. The nesting of birds in the nests of social insects. *Emu* 59:1–36.

Huber, W. 1932. Birds collected in northeastern Nicaragua in 1922. *Proc. Acad. Nat. Sci. Phila.* 84:205–249.

Hudson, W. H. 1920. *The birds of La Plata*. 2 vols. London: J. M. Dent and Sons.

Humboldt, A. von. 1852–1853. *Personal narrative of travels to the equinoctial regions of America during the years 1799–1804 by Alexander von Humboldt and Aimé Bonpland*. Translated and edited by T. Ross. 3 vols. London: Henry G. Bohn.

Ivor, H. R. 1943. Further studies of anting by birds. *Auk* 60:51–55.

Janzen, D. H. 1969. Birds and the ant x acacia interaction in Central America, with notes on birds and other myrmecophytes. *Condor* 71:240–256.

Johnson, R. A. 1954. The behavior of birds attending army ant raids on Barro Colorado Island, Panama Canal Zone. *Proc. Linn. Soc. N.Y.* 63–65:41–70.

Maclaren, P. I. R. 1950. Bird-ant nesting associations. *Ibis* 92:564–566.

Mickey, F. W. 1943. Breeding habits of McCown's Longspur. *Auk* 60:181–209.

Parks, G. H. 1945. Strange behavior of a Bronzed Grackle. *Bird-Banding* 16:144.

Potter, E. F. 1970. Anting in wild birds, its frequency and probable purpose. *Auk* 87:692–713.

Potter, E. F., and Hauser, D. C. 1974. Relationship of anting and sunbathing to molting in wild birds. *Auk* 91:537–563.

Ramsey, J. J. 1968. Roseate Spoonbill chick attacked by ants. *Auk* 85:325.

Ridgway, R. 1901–1919. The birds of North and Middle America. *Bull. U.S. Natl. Mus.*, 50, parts I–VIII.

Schaefer, E. 1953. Contribution to the life history of the Swallow-Tanager. *Auk* 70:403–460.

Schauensee, R. M. de. 1970. *A guide to the birds of South America*. Wynnewood, Pa.: Livingston Publishing Co.

Schimper, A. F. W., ed. 1888–1901. *Botanische Mittheilungen aus den Tropen*. 9 vols.

Schneirla, T. C. 1956. The army ants. *Smithsonian Report for 1955*, pp. 379–406.

Sibley, C. G., and J. E. Ahlquist. 1973. The relationships of the Hoatzin. *Auk* 90:1–13.

Sick, H. 1957. Anting by two tanagers in Brazil. *Wilson Bull.* 69: 187–188.

———. 1967. "Bico de Ferro"—overlooked seedeater from Rio de Janeiro (*Sporophila*, Fringillidae, Aves). *An. da Acad. Brasileira de Ciências* 39:307–314.

Simmons, K. E. L. 1964. Feather maintenance. In *A new dictionary of birds*, ed. A. L. Thomson. London: Nelson.

Skutch, A. F. 1954–1969. *Life histories of Central American Birds.* 3 vols. *Pacific Coast Avif.*, nos. 31, 34, and 35. Berkeley: Cooper Ornithological Society.

———. 1968. The nesting of some Venezuelan birds. *Condor* 70: 66–82.

———. 1969. A study of the Rufous-fronted Thornbird and associated birds. *Wilson Bull.* 81:5–43, 123–139.

———. 1971. *A naturalist in Costa Rica.* Gainesville: University of Florida Press.

———. Forthcoming. *The imperative call.* Gainesville: University of Florida Press.

Snow, B. K. 1961. Notes on the behavior of three Cotingidae. *Auk* 78:150–161.

———. 1972. A field study of the Calfbird *Perissocephalus tricolor. Ibis* 114:139–162.

Sturgis, B. B. 1928. *Field book of birds of the Panama Canal Zone.* New York and London: G. P. Putnam's Sons.

Warham, J. 1954. The behaviour of the Splendid Blue Wren. *Emu* 54:135–140.

Whitaker, L. M. 1957. A résumé of anting, with particular reference to a captive Orchard Oriole. *Wilson Bull.* 69:195–262.

Willis, E. O. 1967. The behavior of Bicolored Antbirds. *Univ. Calif. Publ. Zool.* 79:1–127.

———. 1968. Studies of the behavior of Lunulated and Salvin's antbirds. *Condor* 70:128–148.

———. 1969. On the behavior of five species of *Rhegmatorhina*, ant-following antbirds of the Amazon basin. *Wilson Bull.* 81: 363–395.

———. 1972a. The behavior of Spotted Antbirds. *Amer. Ornith. Union, Ornith. Monogr.*, no. 10.

———. 1972b. The behavior of Plain-brown Woodcreepers, *Dendrocincla fuliginosa. Wilson Bull.* 84:377–420.

Index

Illustrations are indicated by boldface numbers.